INTRODUCTION TO AGRICULTURAL ENGINEERING

(A Problem-Solving Approach)

Second Edition

Lawrence O. Roth, PE
and
Harry L. Field

CBS

CBS Publishers & Distributors Pvt. Ltd.

New Delhi • Bengaluru • Chennai • Kochi • Kolkata • Mumbai
Hyderabad • Nagpur • Patna • Pune • Vijayawada

CBS Pubs ISBN: 81-239-0471-1
Chapman ISBN: 0-412-06991-1

First Indian Edition: 1996

This edition has been published in India by arrangement with Chapman & Hall, Inc., New York

Published by:
Satish Kumar Jain for CBS Publishers & Distributors Pvt. Ltd.,
4819/XI Prahlad Street, 24 Ansari Road, Daryaganj, New Delhi - 110002
delhi@cbspd.com, cbspubs@airtelmail.in • www.cbspd.com
Ph.: 23289259, 23266861, 23266867 • Fax: 011-23243014

Corporate Office: 204 FIE, Industrial Area, Patparganj, Delhi - 110 092
Ph: 49344934 • Fax: 011-49344935
E-mail: publishing@cbspd.com • publicity@cbspd.com

Branches:

- ***Bengaluru:*** 2975, 17th Cross, K.R. Road, Bansankari 2nd Stage, Bengaluru - 70 • Ph: +91-80-26771678/79 • Fax: +91-80-26771680 E-mail: cbsbng@gmail.com, bangalore@cbspd.com
- ***Chennai:*** No. 7, Subbaraya Street, Shenoy Nagar, Chennai - 600030 Ph: +91-44-26681266, 26680620 • Fax: +91-44-42032115 E-mail: chennai@cbspd.com
- ***Kochi:*** Ashana House, 39/1904, A.M. Thomas Road, Valanjambalam, Ernakulum, Kochi • Ph: +91-484-4059061-65 Fax: +91-484-4059065 • E-mail: cochin@cbspd.com
- ***Kolkata:*** 6-B, Ground Floor, Rameshwar Shaw Road, Kolkata - 700014 Ph: +91-33-22891126/7/8 • E-mail: kolkata@cbspd.com
- ***Mumbai:*** 83-C, Dr. E. Moses Road, Worli, Mumbai - 400018 Ph: +91-9833017933, 022-24902340/41 • E-mail: mumbai@cbspd.com

Representatives:

- Hyderabad: 0-9885175004
- Nagpur: 0-9021734563
- Patna: 0-9334159340
- Pune: 0-9623451994
- Vijayawada: 0-9000660880

Printed at:
J.S. Offset Printers, Delhi

CONTENTS

Preface

This book is for use in introductory courses in colleges of agriculture and in other applications requiring a problematical approach to agriculture. It is intended as a replacement for An Introduction to Agricultural Engineering by Roth, Crow, and Mahoney. Parts of the previous book have been revised and included, but some sections have been removed and new ones added. Problem solving has been expanded to include a chapter on techniques, and suggestions are incorporated throughout the example problems.

The topics and treatment were selected for three reasons: (1) to acquaint students with a wide range of applications of engineering principles to agriculture, (2) to present a selection of independent but related, topics, and (3) to develop and enhance the problem solving ability of the students.

Each chapter contains educational objectives, introductory material, example problems (where appropriate), and sample problems, with answers, that can be used for self-assessment. Most chapters are self-contained and can be used independently of the others. Those that are sequential are organized in a logical order to ensure that the knowledge and skills needed are presented in a previous chapter.

As principal author I wish to express my gratitude to Dr. Lawrence O. Roth for his contributions of subject matter and guidance. I also wish to thank Professor Earl E. Baugher for his expertise as technical editor, and my wife Marsha for her help and patience.

HARRY FIELD

1
Problem Solving

OBJECTIVES

1. Be able to define problem solving.
2. Be able to describe the common problem-solving methods.
3. Be able to select the appropriate method for solving a problem.

INTRODUCTION

We are faced with a host of problems on a daily basis. Some problems involve people and human relations, whereas others require a mathematical solution. In this chapter, we will deal with problems involving mathematical solutions and several ways in which these problems can be approached.

MATHEMATICAL PROBLEM SOLVING

Mathematical problem solving is the process by which an individual uses previously acquired knowledge, skills, and understanding to satisfy the demands of an unfamiliar situation. The essence of the process is the ability to use information and facts to arrive at a solution.

Problems can be solved in different ways. One of the objectives of this chapter is to increase the reader's knowledge of problem solving methods. Six different approaches to solving mathematical problems will be discussed: diagrams and sketches, patterns, equations, units cancellation, use of formulas, and intuitive reasoning.

DIAGRAMS AND SKETCHES

Some problems involve the determination of a quantity of items, such as the number of nails per sheet of plywood or the number of studs in a wall. In solving these types of problems, it usually is helpful to draw a sketch or a diagram.

Problem: How many posts are needed to build a fence 100 feet long with posts 10 feet apart?

Solution: For many people the first response would be 10:

$$\text{Posts} = \frac{100 \text{ ft}}{10 \frac{\text{ft}}{\text{post}}}$$

$$= 10 \text{ posts}$$

but a diagram (Figure 1.1) shows that the correct number of posts is 11.

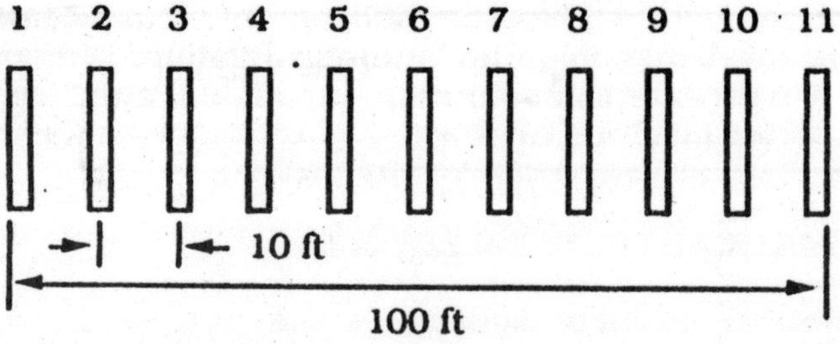

Figure 1.1. Number of posts.

This is an example of a situation where a wrong answer is possible if you do not interpret the problem correctly. In this example, 10 represents the number of spaces, not the number of posts.

PATTERNS

The solution to some problems may depend upon one's being able to discover a pattern in an array of numbers or values. Frequently it is convenient to examine the patterns in a sample rather than the entire population. Once a pattern is discovered and shown to be consistent for the sample, it can be used to predict the solution for the entire population.

Problem: A dairy farmer has five children. Each child is responsible for one part of the daily ration for the family's 100 dairy cows. The oldest is responsible for the grain, the second for the minerals, the third for the hay, the fourth for the silage, and the fifth for water. Instead of feeding each cow, the first child decides she will not feed the cows at all that day. The second child decides just to feed every other cow, the third child feeds every third cow, and so on. Dad soon discovers how the cows were fed, and needs to know which cows did not receive any feed or water.

Solution: When one is faced with this type of problem, it is usually helpful to set up a table. In this case it would be very time-consuming to set up a table for all 100 cows. Instead, select a sample of the cows. If a pattern is true for the sample, there is a high probability that the pattern will be true for a large group. Determining the size of a sample is not always easy. Pick one, and if a clear pattern does not appear, increase the size until a pattern develops. We will start with the first 10 cows (Table 1-1)

Table 1-1. Patterns in numbers, first sample.

		Cow Number									
Ration	Child	1	2	3	4	5	6	7	8	9	10
Grain	1	N	N	N	N	N	N	N	N	N	N
Mineral	2		Y		Y		Y		Y		Y
Hay	3			Y			Y			Y	
Silage	4				Y				Y		
Water	5					Y					Y

In this sample, cows #1 and #7 did not receive any grain, mineral, hay, silage, or water. Is this enough information to establish a pattern? We will predict that the next cow that did not receive any feed or water is #11. Why? To test this prediction, the sample size must be extended to include a larger number of cows.

Table 1-2. Patterns in numbers, second sample.

		Cow Number									
Ration	Child	11	12	13	14	15	16	17	18	19	20
Grain	1	N	N	N	N	N	N	N	N	N	N
Mineral	2		Y		Y		Y		Y		Y
Hay	3		Y			Y			Y		
Silage	4		Y				Y				Y
Water	5					Y					Y

Table 1-2 shows that the prediction was right; cow #11, along with #13, #17, and #19, did not receive any grain, minerals, hay, silage, or water. It is now safe to consider that the prediction could be used to identify all of the animals within the herd that did not receive any grain, minerals, hay, silage, or water (those animals represented by prime numbers, that is, a number divisible only by itself and one).

EQUATIONS

The solution to some problems requires the development of a mathematical equation based on a pattern or another type of relationship between the numbers. Many equations already have been developed and have been adopted for everyday use. For example, the area of a circle is:

$$A = \pi r^2 \qquad (1\text{-}1)$$

Occasionally it is necessary to develop an equation before the problem can be solved.

Problem: How much wire is needed to build a single wire fence around a rectangular field measuring 450 feet long and 350 feet wide?

Solution: In this example there are three quantities: length, width, and perimeter. It should be obvious that the perimeter is a function of the other two. Begin by assigning the variables L to represent the length, W to represent the width, and Pr to represent the perimeter. Then, because a rectangle has two lengths and two widths, the perimeter can be found as follows:

$$Pr = (2 \times L) + (2 \times W) \qquad (1\text{-}2)$$

$$= (2 \times 450 \text{ ft}) + (2 \times 350 \text{ ft})$$

$$= 900 + 700$$

$$= 1600 \text{ ft}$$

UNITS CANCELLATION

Some problems are more complex than the examples we have used, and many do not have patterns or previously developed equations. Equations can be developed for some of these problems, but an alternative approach is units cancellation. Problems of this type will usually involve several quantities. All of these quantities, except π, will have a unit such as feet, pounds, gallons, and so on. Units cancellation follows two mathematical principles: (1) the units of measure associated with the numbers (feet, gallons, minutes, etc.) follow the same mathematical rules as the numbers; (2) the units of the numbers behave according to the rules of fractions. For example:

$$2 \times 2 = 4 \text{ (or } 2^2\text{)}$$

With units of feet the same equation is:

$$2 \text{ ft} \times 2 \text{ ft} = 4 \text{ ft}^2$$

To review the rules of fractions study the following example:

$$\frac{3}{4} \times \frac{4}{5} = \frac{3 \times 4}{4 \times 5} = \frac{3}{5}$$

In this example the 4's in the numerator and denominator cancel out (4/4 = 1). If units of measure are included, they behave in the same way:

$$\frac{3 \text{ ton}}{4 \text{ hr}} \times \frac{4 \text{ hr}}{5 \text{ day}} = \frac{3 \text{ ton}}{5 \text{ day}} = 0.6 \frac{\text{ton}}{\text{day}}$$

In this example the 4's and the units associated with them cancel out. The uncancelled units become the units for the answer. The following example shows another variation of this principle (where gal = gallon and hr = hour):

$$5 \frac{\text{gal}}{\text{hr}} \times 3 \text{ hr} = 15 \text{ gal} \qquad (1\text{-}3)$$

In this example the units for hours cancel each other, leaving the units of the answer in gallons. Now we will examine a problem where units cancellation is used to find the correct answer.

Problem: What is the weight (lb) of one pint of water?

Solution: If a scale and a one pint measure were available, it would be a simple task to weigh one pint of water. An alternative is to use the conversion factors found in a table of weights and measures (Appendix I) and units cancellation.

Note that in this example two types of measure are used, volume and weight. The real nature of the problem is to find the conversion value(s) that will convert from volume (pints) to weight (pounds). To begin, refer to Appendix I and identify conversion factors that use both volume and weight. You should find that 1 cubic foot contains 7.48 gallons, and 1 gallon contains 8 pints. This is a start, but you need something more. If you also know that water weighs 62.4 pounds per cubic foot, the problem can be solved with (lb = pounds, gal = gallons, pt = pints, and ft^3 = cubic feet):

$$\frac{\text{lb}}{\text{pt}} = \frac{62.4\ \text{lb}}{1\text{ft}^3} \times \frac{1\ \text{ft}^3}{7.48\ \text{gal}} \times \frac{1\ \text{gal}}{8\ \text{pt}} \quad (1\text{-}4)$$

$$= 1.04\ \frac{\text{lb}}{\text{pt}}$$

The units of pints, gallons, and cubic feet are arranged so they cancel each other, leaving in the answer the desired units of pounds and pints.

This example illustrates several principles of units cancellation. First, it is very important to begin by writing down the correct units for the answer. Second, write down the equals sign (=), and then begin entering the values and their units. The first value entered should have one of the desired units in the correct position, even if it is a units conversion value from the table. Starting with one of the units of measure in the correct position will eliminate the possibility of having the problem inverted. Next enter a value that will cancel out the unwanted units, if any, in the first value entered. Continue to add variables and cancel units until the units of the answer are all that remain. If all of the units cancel except those that are desired for the answer, and the units are in the correct position, then the only possible mistake is a math error.

The process of units cancellation is also useful for problems requiring the development of a new unit. For example, a very common quantity in agriculture is power. Power can have different units, depending on whether it is electrical or mechanical. The units of mechanical power are foot-pounds per minute. The solution to a problem in which a 24-ounce weight was moved 15 feet in 5 seconds would look like this (with oz = ounces, sec = seconds, lb = pounds, ft = feet):

$$\text{Power}\left(\frac{\text{ft-lb}}{\text{min}}\right) = \frac{15\text{ ft}}{5\text{ sec}} \times \frac{60\text{ sec}}{1\text{ min}} \times \frac{1\text{ lb}}{16\text{ oz}} \times \frac{24\text{ oz}}{1} \tag{1-5}$$

$$= \frac{21{,}600\text{ ft-lb}}{80\text{ min}}$$

$$= 270\ \frac{\text{ft-lb}}{\text{min}}$$

(Note that ft-lb is a hyphenated word, not foot minus pound.) This same process will work just as well for problems with more complex units and more variables.

FORMULAS

For some problems a previously developed equation may be used. There are at least two important considerations in using these equations.

1. You must enter the numbers with the correct units of measure. All formulas are designed with specific units for the numbers. If the units are incorrect, the answer will be incorrect. An example is the equation used to determine the application rate of a boom type sprayer:

$$\text{Application rate}\left(\frac{\text{gal}}{\text{ac}}\right) = \frac{5940 \times \text{Flow rate}\left(\frac{\text{gal}}{\text{min}}\right)}{\text{Speed}\left(\frac{\text{mi}}{\text{hr}}\right) \times \text{Nozzle spacing (in)}} \tag{1-6}$$

It should be obvious that the units in Equation (1-6) do not work. This equation is an example of a situation in which conversion values that are always used are combined into a units conversion constant (5940). If any one of the values is entered in different units, the answer will be incorrect. If we solve for the application rate using units cancellation and conversion values, the source of the constant becomes apparent.

$$\frac{gal}{ac} = \frac{gal}{min} \times \frac{60\ min}{hr} \times \frac{1\ hr}{1\ mi} \times \frac{1\ mi}{5{,}280\ ft} \times \frac{43{,}560\ ft^2}{ac} \times \frac{12\ in}{ft} \times \frac{1}{in}$$

$$= \frac{60 \times 43{,}560 \times 12}{5{,}280}$$

$$= 5940$$

2. You must be able to rearrange the formula to solve for the unknown value. For example, Equation (1-6) could be rearranged to solve for nozzle spacing in inches (nsi):

$$\text{Nozzle Spacing (nsi)} = \frac{5940 \times \text{Flow rate}\left(\frac{gal}{min}\right)}{\text{Speed}\left(\frac{mi}{hr}\right) \times \text{Application rate}\left(\frac{gal}{ac}\right)} \qquad (1\text{-}7)$$

INTUITIVE REASONING

Intuitive reasoning is a process by which an individual arrives at a correct answer through insight or a hunch, usually without being able to explain the process used. The actual process depends on the individual and cannot bc defined in progressive steps.

Problem: You ask your employees to determine how many vehicle seats in the parking lot need their covers replaced. They return with an answer of 150. Then you realize you need to know the numbers of pickups (single seat) and of cars (two seats). Your employees remember that there were the same number of cars in the lot needing seat covers as pickups; so how many car and how many pickup seat covers do you need?

Solution: Some people would solve this problem algebraically, but intuitive reasoning can be used to reason out a series of approximations. If there were 20 cars and 20 pickups, you would need 60 seat covers [(20 x 1) + (20 x 2) = 60], if 40 then 120, if 60 then 180. The answer must be less than 60 and more than 40. The correct number of vehicles is 50. Which means you would need 50 pickup seat covers and 100 car seat covers.

PRACTICE PROBLEMS

1. How many nails are needed to attach a 4 ft x 8 ft sheet of plywood if the recommendation is to use one in each corner and at 6 inch intervals around the edge. (Hint: Draw a diagram)
   Answer: 48 nails
2. Complete the following:

A. $25 \dfrac{\text{gal}}{\text{hr}} \times 5 \text{ hr} =$

B. $\dfrac{45.0 \text{ hp}}{5.5 \dfrac{\text{gal}}{\text{hr}}} =$

C. $\dfrac{0.035 \dfrac{\text{gal}}{\text{rev}}}{0.003 \dfrac{\text{ac}}{\text{rev}}} =$

D. $\dfrac{0.025 \dfrac{\text{lb}}{\text{rev}} \times \dfrac{1{,}000{,}000 \text{ seed}}{1 \text{ lb}}}{0.034 \dfrac{\text{ac}}{\text{rev}}} =$

Answers:

A. 125 gal; B. $8.2 \dfrac{\text{hp-hr}}{\text{gal}}$; C. $11.7 \dfrac{\text{gal}}{\text{ac}}$; D. $735{,}000 \dfrac{\text{seed}}{\text{ac}}$

2
Significant Figures and Standard Form

OBJECTIVES

1. Be able to define precision, accuracy, and uncertainty when working with numbers.
2. Understand the difference between exact and approximate numbers.
3. Be able to determine the number of significant figures.
4. Understand a technique for rounding numbers.
5. Understand the uses of standard form.

INTRODUCTION

There is no substitute for a good understanding of numbers and mathematical processes in solving modern agricultural problems. In this unit we will discuss several features of numbers and techniques to use with numbers.

PRECISION, ACCURACY, AND UNCERTAINTY

It is important to understand three characteristics of numbers in solving agricultural problems: precision, accuracy, and uncertainty. Precision refers to the size of the unit of measure used to obtain the number. For example, if a sack of feed is weighed on a scale measuring to the nearest 0.1 pound, the weight is not as precise as it would be if the smallest unit of measure where 0.01 pound.

The accuracy of a number refers to the number of decimal places obtained in the answer. The greater the number of decimal places, the greater the accuracy. A measurement of 12.15 feet is more accurate than a measurement of 14.4 feet.

The uncertainty of a number is the amount it is expected to vary. If the uncertainty is not stated after the number, say, 14.5 ft ± 0.01, then you may assume it is ± half of the smallest unit. (See Table 2-1.)

Table 2-1. Levels of uncertainty.

Number	Uncertainty
25	± 0.5
15.7	± 0.05
2.567	± 0.0005

Source: Theory and Problems of Technical Mathematics, Schaum's Outline Series, McGraw-Hill Book Company, New York, 1979.

EXACT AND APPROXIMATE NUMBERS

Jobs in agriculture use two different types of numbers, exact and approximate. The two common examples of exact numbers are those obtained by counting and ratios. For example, if you count the number of horses in a pen and arrive at 10, you have exactly 10 horses, not 10 and 1/2 or 9 and 3/4. Ratios are exact numbers because 3/4 of a circle is exactly 3/4 of a circle. One note of caution about ratios. Ratios expressed as a decimal, say, 2/3 = 0.6666666..., are approximate numbers because some ratios expressed as a decimal contain repeating digits.

Any number obtained by a measurement is an approximate number. The actual value of an approximate number is uncertain because all measuring devices have a limit to their precision. If you have a ruler that is graduated in 1/16 of an inch, then the ruler is only accurate to the nearest 1/16 of an inch. The following example illustrates this point.

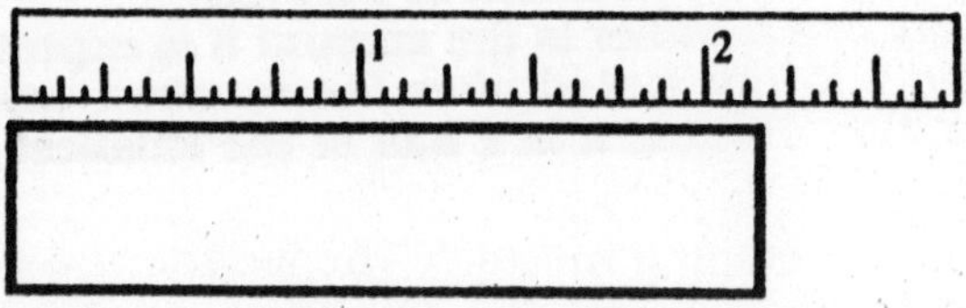

Figure 2.1. Example of an approximate number.

In Figure 2.1, the length of the rectangle is not aligned with any of the marks on the scale (ruler). You must record the length of the box as either 2 and 1/8 inch or 2 and 3/16 inch. Regardless of the value you choose, the answer you record is only close to the actual length, and thus is an approximate number.

When approximate numbers are used, digits can be introduced into the problem that are not accurate (significant). If these digits are included, the accuracy of the answer may decrease with every computation. The potential for error is especially great if a calculator is used because most calculators show eight or nine numbers, regardless of their significance to the problem. The task of the calculator operator is to determine how many digits are significant and to round accordingly.

SIGNIFICANT FIGURES

The principle of significant figures is used to determine the number of digits that should be kept in a number after mathematical computations. The rules for determining significant digits are different for exact and for approximate numbers.

Because there is no uncertainty with exact numbers, all of the digits are considered to be significant. When rounding answers produced with exact numbers, assume that they have the same number of significant figures as the largest approximate number.

The number of significant digits for an approximate number depends on the precision of the measuring instrument. If the precision of the unit of measure is unknown, assume it is ± half of the smallest unit in the number. If you are given the weight of a steer as 550 pounds and are not given the precision of measure, (0.5 lb, 0.1 lb, 0.01 lb, etc.) the actual weight of the steer could be 550 ± 0.5 pounds. Because of the uncertainty, the weight of the steer has three significant digits.

Zeros are considered to be significant unless they are being used to hold the numbers in the correct column. For example, if a measurement made with a ruler of 0.1 foot precision is exactly 2 feet long, it would be written as 2.0 feet. In this case the zero is considered significant. A measurement of 0.0625 inch has three significant figures because the zero is holding the numbers 625 in the correct place.

Problem: You are helping measure the weight of a calf on scales that measure to the nearest 0.5 pound. You are told the calf weighs 102 pounds. How many significant figures does the weight have?

Solution: The number of significant figures is three. Because the actual weight of the calf could be between 101.6 and 102.4 pounds, any weight within that range would have been read as 102 pounds. If the weight is exactly 102 pounds, the weight of the calf should be recorded as 102.0 pounds. Then the weight has four significant digits.

Consider the following situation:

Problem: What is the area (ft^2) of a room if the width is 12 ft 3 in and the length is 22 ft 3/16 in?

Solution: The first step is to convert the dimensions to decimal form, 12 ft 3 in = 12.25 ft, and 22 ft 3/16 in = 22.1875 ft. Completing the multiplication gives a value of 271.79687 ft^2. How many digits are significant?

Two rules have been developed to help determine the number of significant digits during mathematical computations.

1. Adding or subtracting: the answer should be rounded to the number of decimal places in the least precise number.
2. Multiplication and division: the answer should be rounded to the number of significant figures in the least accurate number.

For this problem, rule number two applies. The product, 271.79687, should be reduced to four significant figures. The correct area for the room is 271.8 ft^2.

ROUNDING NUMBERS

Rounding is used to eliminate figures that are not significant. If the digits to be rounded are to the left of the decimal point, the digits are replaced by zeros. For example, if you need to reduce the area of an acre, 43,560 ft^2, to two significant digits, round to 44,000 ft^2. If the digit being dropped is greater than 5, add one to the next digit remaining. If the digit being dropped is less than 5, the first remaining digit is unchanged. If the digit being dropped is exactly 5, leave the remaining digit even. If the remaining digit is odd, add one, if it is even, leave it as is. For example, if the number 43,560 is rounded to one significant digit, the answer is 40,000; rounded to two it is 44,000; and rounded to three it is 43,600.

STANDARD FORM

Standard form, or scientific notation as it is sometimes called, is used to express large or small numbers in a more convenient form. Standard form uses powers of ten to replace the nonsignificant digits of a large or small number. Standard form uses a whole digit, then a decimal point, and then the rest of the significant figures. For example, if the number 1,000,000 has one significant figure, it is expressed as 1.0×10^6. This number is read as "one point zero times ten to the sixth power." To use standard form effectively you must understand the powers of numbers and how they can be manipulated during mathematical computations.

First a review of the powers of ten:

$10^0 = 1$

$10^1 = 10$ $\qquad 10^{-1} = 0.1 = \frac{1}{10}$

$10^2 = 100$ $\qquad 10^{-2} = 0.01 = \frac{1}{100}$

$10^3 = 1000$ $\qquad 10^{-3} = 0.001 = \frac{1}{1000}$

$10^5 = 100000$ $\qquad 10^{-5} = 0.00001 = \frac{1}{100000}$

There are several helpful rules to use when working with powers of 10:

Rule 1: When a number 10 and its exponent are moved from the denominator of a fraction to the numerator, or from the numerator to the denominator, the sign of the exponent is changed. Thus:

$$\frac{1}{10^3} = \frac{10^{-3}}{1} \text{ and } \frac{10^{-4}}{1} = \frac{1}{10^4}$$

Rule 2: When two or more numbers in standard form are multiplied together, the powers of 10 can be added. Thus:

$$10^3 \times 10^5 = 10^{(3+5)} = 10^8$$

$$10^5 \times 10^{-2} = 10^{(5+(-2))} = 10^3$$

$$10^{-4} \times 10^{-3} \times 10^4 = 10^{(-4+-3+4)} = 10^{-3}$$

and[1]:

$$4 X 10^3 \times 5 X 10^5 = 20 X 10^{(3+5)} \text{ or } 20 X 10^8$$

Rule 3: **When two or more numbers in standard form are divided, the powers of 10 are subtracted. Thus:**

$$\frac{10^4}{10^3} = 10^1 \quad \text{and} \quad \frac{10^{-4}}{10^2} = 10^{-6}$$

and:

$$\frac{4 X 10^4}{5 X 10^3} = 0.8 X 10^1 \text{ or } 8.0 X 10^0$$

Rule 4: **When two or more numbers in standard form are added or subtracted, the numbers must be converted to the same power of 10, and the power of 10 is not affected during the addition or subtraction. Thus:**

$$4 X 10^4 - 3 X 10^3 \quad \text{becomes} \quad \begin{array}{r} 40 X 10^3 \\ - 3 X 10^3 \\ \hline 37 X 10^3 \end{array} \quad \text{or } 3.7 X 10^4$$

and:

$$4 X 10^4 + 3 X 10^3 \quad \text{becomes} \quad \begin{array}{r} 40 X 10^3 \\ + 3 X 10^3 \\ \hline 43 X 10^3 \end{array} \quad \text{or } 4.3 X 10^4$$

PRACTICE PROBLEMS

1. **If a truck weighs 20,045.04 pounds, what is the accuracy of the weight?**
   Answer: 0.01 or one hundredth of a pound
2. **Round the following numbers to the indicated number of significant figures (sf):**
   A. 34,674.89 (2 sf)
   B. 45,653 (3 sf)

---

[1] **Throughout the text, when standard form is used, the upper case X will be used to denote the multiplication of the whole numbers times the powers of 10.**

C. 87.250 (3 sf)
D. 565,875 (5 sf)

Answers:
A. 35,000; B. 45,600; C. 87.2; D. 565,880

3. **Find the product of 4.567×10^2 and 2.30×10^4.**

   Answer: 1.05×10^7

4. **Find the sum of 4.3×10^5 and 7.89×10^6.**

   Answer: 8.3×10^6

3
Simple Machines

OBJECTIVES

1. Be able to describe simple machines.
2. Be able to describe where simple machines are used.
3. Be able to use the principles of simple machines to solve problems.

INTRODUCTION

A machine is any device that either increases or regulates the effect of a force or produces motion. All agricultural machines are composed of combinations and modifications of two basic machines, the lever and the inclined plane. We will study the basic principles surrounding these two machines and illustrate some of their common modifications and uses. (*Note*: In the following discussion of simple machines two assumptions are made: losses due to friction are ignored, and the strength of the materials is not considered.)

LEVER

A lever is a rigid bar, straight or curved, capable of being rotated around a fixed point (fulcrum). When a fulcrum and a bar are used, two different forces exist, the *applied* force (F_a) and the *resultant* force (F_r). The forces, bar, and fulcrum can be used in three ways, called classes (Figure 3.1).

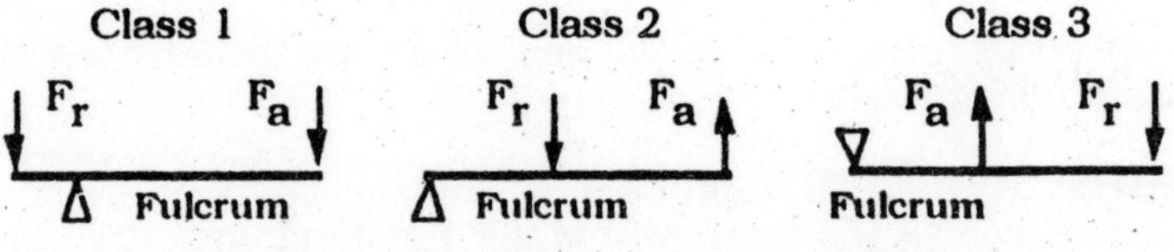

Figure 3.1. Three classes of levers.

The principle of levers can be expressed mathematically as:

$$\text{Applied force} \times \text{Force arm length} = \text{Resultant force} \times \text{Resultant arm length} \qquad (3\text{-}1)$$

$$F_a \times A_f = F_r \times A_r$$

CLASS ONE LEVER

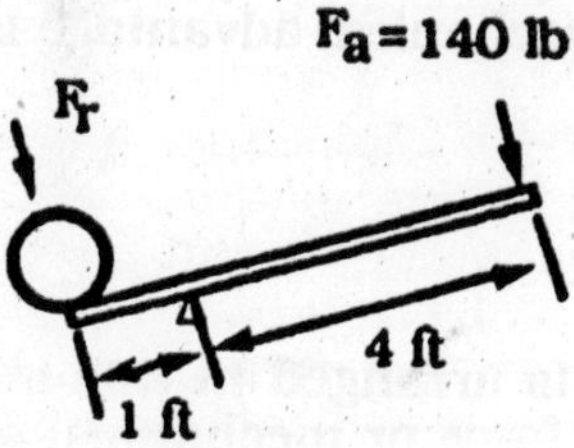

Figure 3.2. Example of a class one lever.

Class one levers are used primarily for their mechanical advantage. The mechanical advantage for the first-class lever is the ratio of the lengths of the two arms. In our discussion of simple machines, mechanical advantage will be defined as the increase of force that occurs through the use of a lever. Expressed mathematically:

$$\text{Mechanical advantage} = \frac{\text{Force arm length}}{\text{Resultant arm length}} \qquad (3\text{-}2)$$

The principles of a class one lever are illustrated by the following problem.

Problem: How much weight can a 140.0-pound person lift with a class one lever if the force arm is 4.0 feet long, and the resultant arm is 1.0 foot long?

Solution: In this problem three of the variables in Equation (3-1) are known: F_a = 140 pounds, A_f = 4 feet, and A_r = 1 foot. To solve the problem, we must use one of the techniques of problem solving--rearranging an equation. In this example we need to rearrange Equation (3-1) to solve for F_r. This gives us:

$$F_r = \frac{F_a \times A_f}{A_r} \qquad (3\text{-}3)$$

Substituting the values produces:

$$F_r = \frac{140 \text{ lb} \times 4 \text{ ft}}{1 \text{ ft}}$$

$$= 560 \text{ lb}$$

With this lever, 140 pounds of applied force is capable of lifting 560 pounds. The mechanical advantage is clearer if the equation is written as:

$$Fr = 140 \text{ lb} \times \frac{4 \text{ ft}}{1 \text{ ft}}$$

When the equation is arranged in this manner, it is easy to see that the increase in force or mechanical advantage is the ratio of the lengths of the two arms. In this example, the amount of force the person could produce (mechanical advantage) was increased 4/1 or 4 times.

In addition to the mechanical advantage, the distance moved and the speed of movement for the two ends of the bar also can be determined. Calculations will show that the distance moved is proportional to the ratio of the length of the resultant arm to the length of the force arm. The speed of movement is proportional to the ratio of the length of the force arm to the length of the resultant arm.

CLASS TWO LEVER

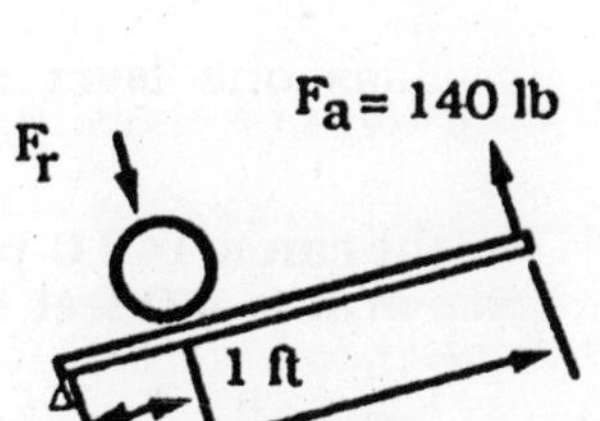

Figure 3.3. Example of a class two lever.

The second class of lever also is used for its mechanical advantage. In this class the mechanical advantage is the ratio of the distance between the fulcrum and the applied force and the distance from the fulcrum to the resultant force. (See Figure 3.3.) The same applied force will be used to illustrate this lever.

The resultant force for an applied force can be determined by using Equation (3-3):

$$F_r = \frac{F_a \times A_f}{A_r}$$

Substituting values:

$$F_r = \frac{140 \text{ lb} \times 5 \text{ ft}}{1 \text{ ft}}$$

$$= 700 \text{ lb}$$

In this class, the mechanical advantage always will be greater than one. In this case the mechanical advantage is 5. This is why a 700 pound load can be moved with a force of 140 pounds.

In this class of lever the distance moved and speed of movement also are proportional to the ratio of the lengths of the two arms.

CLASS THREE LEVER

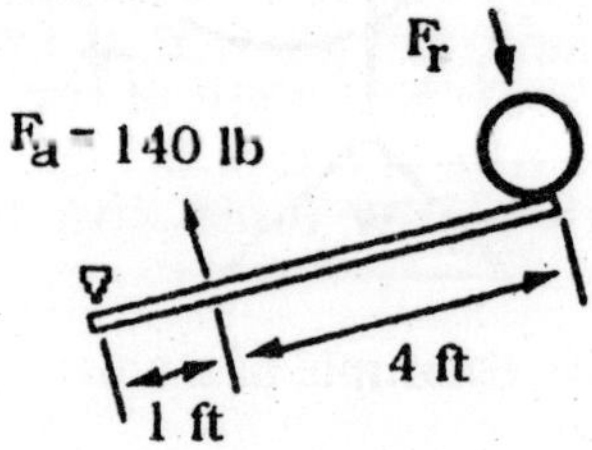

Figure 3.4. Example of a class three lever.

This class of lever is used primarily to increase speed and movement because it reduces the mechanical advantage. The same applied force will be used to illustrate the class three lever.

The resultant force for a class three lever can be determined by using Equation (3-3):

$$F_r = \frac{F_a \times A_f}{A_r}$$

$$= \frac{140 \text{ lb} \times 1 \text{ ft}}{5 \text{ ft}}$$

$$= 28 \text{ lb}$$

As this example illustrates, the mechanical advantage for the third-class lever always will be less than one. Here 140 pounds of applied force only can lift a weight of 28 pounds. The distance moved and the speed of movement are increased proportionally.

WHEEL AND AXLE

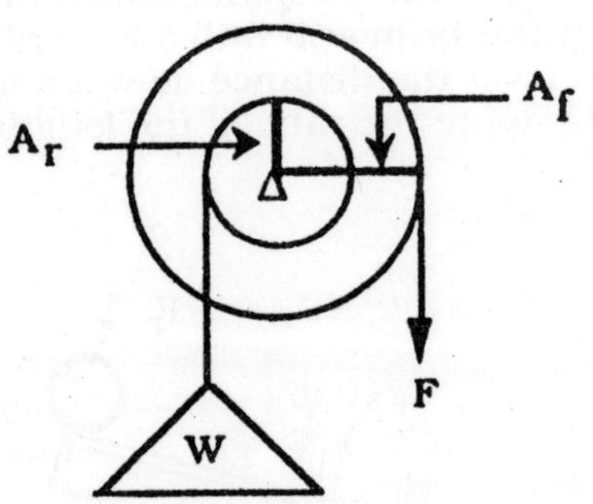

Figure 3.5. Example of a wheel and axle.

The wheel and axle behaves as a continuous lever. The center of the axle corresponds to the fulcrum, the radius of the axle to the resultant arm, and the radius of the wheel to the force arm. The equation for determining the mechanical advantage is very similar to the equation for the three classes of levers:

$$F \times A_f = A_r \times W \quad (3\text{-}4)$$

where:

- F = Applied force
- A_f = Length of applied force arm (radius of pulley)
- A_r = Length of resultant force arm (radius of axle)
- W = Weight being moved

Problem: How much force will it take to lift a 10.0-pound weight with a wheel and axle if the axle is 2.0 inches in diameter, and the wheel is 10.0 inches in diameter?

Solution: The first step is to rearrange Equation (3-4) to solve for the force. Note that the length of the force arm is the radius of the wheel. This gives us:

$$F = \frac{A_r \times W}{A_f}$$

$$= \frac{1.0 \text{ in} \times 10.0 \text{ lb}}{5.0 \text{ in}}$$

$$= 2.0 \text{ lb}$$

This problem clearly shows the mechanical advantage of a wheel and axle: 2 pounds of force will lift a 10-pound weight.

PULLEY

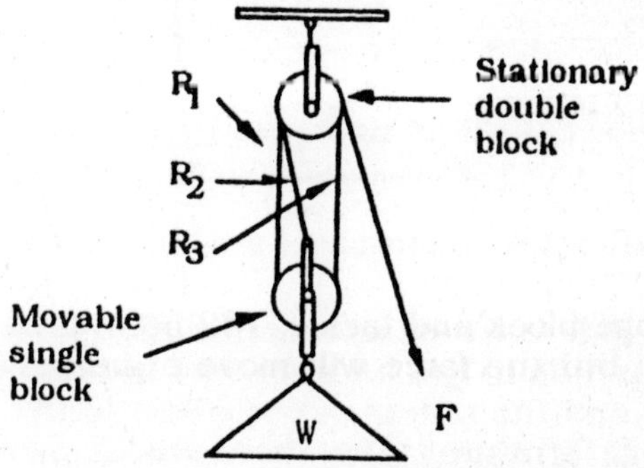

Figure 3.6. Block and tackle.

A pulley is a modification of a first- or second-class lever. Pulleys can be used in several configurations. A single pulley does not produce any mechanical advantage, just a change of direction. When pulleys are combined in pairs, a mechanical advantage is produced.

When pulleys are arranged in combination (Figure 3.6), they are called a block and tackle. The amount of mechanical advantage produced by a block and tackle is proportional to the number of ropes that support the weight. The block and tackle in Figure 3.6 has three ropes, R_1, R_2, and R_3 supporting the weight. In this arrangement the amount of weight that can be lifted is three times the amount of force being applied. Expressed mathematically:

$$R_n = \frac{W}{F} \tag{3-5}$$

where:

W = Amount of weight to be lifted
F = Amount of force applied to the block and tackle
R_n = Number of ropes

Problem: How much pull (F) would it take on the block and tackle rope in Figure 3.6 to lift a 545-pound engine?

Solution: From Figure 3.6, the number of ropes supporting the load is three. The pull can be found by rearranging Equation (3-5) to solve for F:

$$F = \frac{W}{R_n}$$

$$= \frac{545 \text{ lb}}{3}$$

$$= 182 \text{ lb}$$

With a three rope-block and tackle, 182 pounds of force will lift a 545-pound load, but the force will move a greater distance than the load.

INCLINED PLANE

An inclined plane is an even surface sloping at any angle between vertical and horizontal. The mechanical advantage is that the force applied is increased as many times as the length of the inclined plane is greater than the elevation. Instead of lifting the entire weight vertically, part of the weight is supported by the inclined plane.

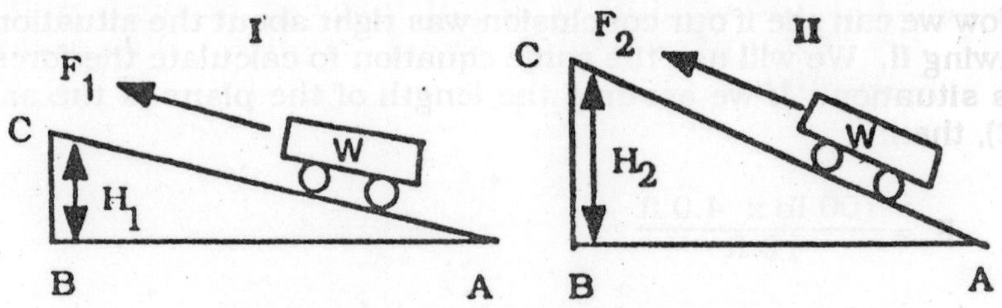

Figure 3.7. Two inclined planes

Compare drawings I and II in Figure 3.7. Intuitive reasoning suggests that if the weight and the distance AC are the same in both cases, less force (ignoring friction) will be required to move the wagon up the inclined plane in the situation represented by drawing I because the change in height is less in I than it is in II for the same length of inclined plane. If we need to know the pounds of force required to pull the wagon, then we must use an equation based on the principles of an inclined plane. Expressed mathematically:

$$F \times AC = W \times BC \tag{3-6}$$

where:

F = Amount of force to pull the wagon (ignoring friction)
AC = Length of the inclined plane
W = Weight of the wagon
BC = Height of the inclined plane

If we analyze drawing I first and assume that the total weight is 100 pounds, the height (BC) is 2.0 feet, and the length of the inclined plane (AC) is 12 feet, then the amount of force that would be required to pull the wagon up the inclined plane is:

$$F = \frac{W \times BC}{AC}$$

Substituting the values gives:

$$F = \frac{100\ \text{lb} \times 2.0\ \text{ft}}{12\ \text{ft}}$$

$$= 17\ \text{lb}$$

Now we can see if our conclusion was right about the situation in drawing II. We will use the same equation to calculate the force in this situation. If we assume the length of the plane is the same (AC), then:

$$F = \frac{100 \text{ lb} \times 4.0 \text{ ft}}{12 \text{ ft}}$$

$$= 33 \text{ lb}$$

It thus is obvious that the steeper the angle of an inclined plane, the greater the force is that will be required to pull a weight up the plane.

SCREW

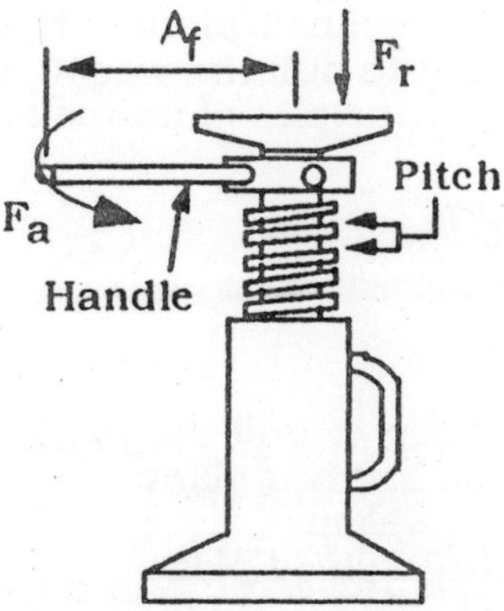

Figure 3.8. Screw.

The screw is a modification of the inclined plane combined with a lever. The threads of a screw or a bolt are an inclined plane that has been rolled into the shape of a cylinder. A lever is used to turn the threads, which causes the load to move along the cylinder. Figure 3.8 illustrates this principle as it is used in a jack, where the jack handle is the force arm. The same principle applies to a bolt and nut. In this case the lever arm is the wrench, and the resultant force is the clamping pressure.

The amount of movement per revolution is determined by the distance between any two threads, called pitch. The mechanical advantage is determined by the ratio of the radius of the lever that is turning the threads and the pitch distance. Equation (3-1) can be used to express this relationship mathematically:

$$F_a \times A_f = F_r \times A_r$$

where:

F_a = Forced applied at the end of the lever arm
F_r = Amount of weight the jack will lift
A_f = Length of the lever arm
A_r = Pitch of the threads

Problem: If the lever arm in Figure 3.8 is 18 inches long and the pitch of the threads is 0.125 inch, how much weight will the jack lift if 50 pounds of force is applied at the end of the lever arm (ignoring friction)?

Solution: Rearranging the equation to solve for F_r gives:

$$F_r = \frac{F_a \times A_f}{A_r}$$

$$= \frac{50 \text{ lb} \times 18.0 \text{ in}}{0.125 \text{ in}}$$

$$= 7200 \text{ lb}$$

This problem illustrates that a small amount of force will lift a large load. You should note that the lever arm will move through a relatively large distance compared to the distance the load is moved. In this example the lever arm moves a distance of $2\pi r$ during the time that the load moves 1/8 inch.

Friction will affect the performance of this machine more than the others. With the proper lubrication it can be kept to a manageable level.

PRACTICE PROBLEMS

1. How much weight will a class one lever lift if the force is 50.0 pounds, the force arm is 3.25 feet, and the resultant arm is 1.50 feet?
   Answer: 108 lb
2. What length of rod is needed to lift a 1500.0-pound weight with a class one lever if the resultant arm is limited to 6.0 inches, and the applied force is limited to 125.0 pounds?
   Answer: 6.0 ft

3. What length of resultant arm is required for a class one lever to lift a 500.0-pound weight if the applied force is limited to 50.25 pounds, and the force arm length is 10 feet?
   Answer: 1.00 ft
4. How many pounds of force would it take for a class three lever to develop 230.0 pounds of resultant force if the applied force arm is 18 and 1/4 inches, and the resultant force arm is 36 and 7/8 inches?
   Answer: 465 lb
5. How many pounds of force will it take for a wheel and axle to lift 1225.5 pounds if the axle diameter is 1.50 inches, and the wheel diameter is 11.50 inches?
   Answer: 160 lb
6. What is the maximum amount of weight that can be lifted by a four-rope block and tackle if the applied force is 75.25 pounds?
   Answer: 300 lb
7. What is the maximum amount of weight that could be pulled up an inclined plane if the force is limited to 50.75 pounds, the inclined plane is 12.25 feet long, and the height is 54.0 inches?
   Answer: 138 lb
8. How much weight can a screw type jack lift if the lever arm is 6.0 feet, the applied force is 68.50 pounds, and the pitch of the threads is 3/8 inch?
   Answer: 13,000 lb

4
Work, Power, Torque, and Horsepower

OBJECTIVES

1. Be able to define work, power, horsepower, and torque.
2. Be able to use the units associated with each term.
3. Be able to identify the appropriate formula for each.
4. Be able to rearrange each formula to solve for a different unknown.
5. Be able to calculate horsepower using force, distance, and time.

INTRODUCTION

In the previous chapter we learned that mechanical devices are constructed from one or more simple machines. The simple machines, and the complex mechanisms constructed from them, use three basic units of measure--force, distance, and time. These three units in various combinations and arrangements are the basis of the principles of work, power, and horsepower.

FORCE (F)

Force is that action which causes or tends to cause motion or a change of motion of an object. To describe a force completely, its direction of action, magnitude, and point of application must be known. What is commonly referred to as a "force" is really two forces, as forces are never present singly, but always in pairs. The two parts are called action and reaction. They are always of equal magnitude, but in opposite directions. In this text, the weight of an object will be considered a force. Forces are commonly measured in units of ounces (oz), pounds (lb), and tons (ton).

DISTANCE (D)

The dimension of distance has two common meanings, displacement and length. Displacement is the movement from one point to another. If you walk one mile, you have displaced a distance of 5280 feet. Length refers to the physical size of an object. For example, the lengths of a standard piece of paper are 8.5 x 11 inches. The common units for distance are inches (in), feet (ft), yards (yd), and miles (mi).

TIME (T)

The concept of time has its root in the natural cycles of the earth. One very visible cycle is the ocean tides. The words time and tide both come from the same root but end differently. The current idea of time is as a measure of an interval of duration. Time may be better described as an accounting technique for relating events. The common units for measuring time are seconds (sec), minutes (min), and hours (hr).

WORK (W)

Work is the result of a force acting (or moving) through a distance. Written as an equation:

$$\text{Work (W)} = \text{Distance (D)} \times \text{Force (F)} \tag{4-1}$$

A numerical value for work may be obtained by multiplying the value of a force by the displacement.

Problem: If a force of 100 pounds displaces 12 feet, how much work has been performed?

Solution: Using Equation (4-1):

$$W = D \times F$$

$$= 12 \text{ ft} \times 100 \text{ lb}$$

$$= 1200 \text{ ft-lb}$$

In this situation 1200 foot-pounds of work was completed. Notice that unless *both* distance and force are present, no work is being accomplished.

Problem: A loaded wagon weighing 10,000 pounds requires 400 pounds of force to pull it along a horizontal surface. If the wagon is pulled for 100 feet, calculate the amount of work done. (In this example we assume that rolling resistance equals zero.)

Solution: Using Equation (4-1):

$$W = D \times F$$

$$= 100 \text{ ft} \times 400 \text{ lb}$$

$$= 40{,}000 \text{ ft-lb}$$

In this problem, the 40,000 pounds of force is not related to the weight of the wagon. It is the force required to pull it.

POWER (P)

Power is the *rate* of doing work. Written as an equation:

$$\text{Power} = \frac{\text{Work}}{\text{Time}} \qquad (4\text{-}2)$$

because work equals distance times force. Then:

$$\text{Power} = \frac{\text{Distance} \times \text{Force}}{\text{Time}}$$

or:

$$P = \frac{W}{T}$$

which also means:

$$P = F \times \frac{D}{T}$$

Because D/T equals velocity (speed), power is the force times the velocity. Thus one can obtain a numerical value for power by combining the appropriate values for distance, force, and time.

Problem: If a force of 100 pounds moves through a distance of 12 feet in 2 minutes, how much power is developed?

Solution: Using Equation (4-2):

$$P = \frac{D \times F}{T}$$

$$= \frac{12 \text{ ft} \times 100 \text{ lb}}{2 \text{ min}}$$

$$= \frac{1200 \text{ ft-lb}}{2 \text{ min}}$$

$$= 600 \frac{\text{ft-lb}}{\text{min}}$$

Notice that the unit associated with power is a combination of the individual units for the variables. In this case the answer is read as "600 foot-pounds per minute." This is the "time-rate" at which work is being done. Remember, *always* write down the units that are associated with a number.

Problem: A person loads a 60-pound bale onto a truck platform 4 feet high in 0.50 minute. How much power is being developed?

Solution: Using Equation (4-2):

$$P = \frac{D \times F}{T}$$

$$= \frac{4 \text{ ft} \times 60 \text{ lb}}{0.50 \text{ min}}$$

$$= \frac{240 \text{ ft-lb}}{0.50 \text{ min}}$$

$$= 480 \frac{\text{ft-lb}}{\text{min}}$$

Up to this point we have used easy-to-understand values with units of feet for distance, pounds for force, and minutes for time. Suppose that in the previous problem the individual could load three 60-pound bales in 0.50 minute. In this example it is easy to make a mistake in determining a value for the force. The solution to this problem is:

$$P = \frac{4 \text{ ft} \times \frac{3 \text{ bales}}{1} \times \frac{60 \text{ lb}}{1 \text{ bale}}}{0.50 \text{ min}}$$

$$= \frac{720 \text{ ft-lb}}{0.50 \text{ min}}$$

$$= 1400 \frac{\text{ft-lb}}{\text{min}}$$

Here the power produced is 1400 ft-lb/min because the weight moved in 0.50 minute is the weight of all three bales (3 x 60 lb).

This problem illustrates a principle of power. If three times the amount of work is done in the same amount of time, the power will be increased three times. What is the impact on the power produced if the distance changes, or if the time changes?

Problem: If a person could load three 60-pound bales onto the 4-foot platform in 10 seconds instead of 0.50 minute, how would this change the power produced?

Solution: Using Equation (4-2):

$$P = \frac{D \times F}{T}$$

$$= \frac{4 \text{ ft} \times 180 \text{ lb}}{10 \text{ sec}}$$

$$= \frac{720 \text{ ft-lb}}{10 \text{ sec}}$$

$$= 72 \frac{\text{ft-lb}}{\text{sec}}$$

The amount of power changed, but this answer cannot be compared to the previous one because the units are different. You might ask, is foot-pounds per second an acceptable unit of measure for power? Yes, but to compare this value for power to the previous one the units must be converted. This can be accomplished in more than one way. If the desired units are ft-lb/min, then a conversion value can be added to the equation. To change the unit of time from seconds to minutes:

$$P = \frac{4.0 \text{ ft} \times 180.0 \text{ lb}}{10.0 \text{ sec} \times \frac{1 \text{ min}}{60.0 \text{ sec}}}$$

$$= \frac{720 \text{ ft-lb}}{0.167 \text{ min}}$$

$$= 4300 \frac{\text{ft-lb}}{\text{min}}$$

Now we can compare this value to the value of 1400 ft-lb/min in the first example. It should be obvious that it takes a greater amount of power to complete the same amount of work in less time. A similar relationship is true for the distance moved. The power requirement will change as the distance moved changes, assuming that the force and the time remain the same.

In summary, power is directly proportional to distance and force, and is inversely proportional to time.

In working with agricultural machinery, speed usually is measured in miles per hour (mph). If this is the case, the units must be changed. Otherwise the answer will be incorrect if Equation (4-2) is used to determine power. Study the following statements:

If Power is equal to work divided by time, then:

$$P = \frac{F \times D}{T}$$

This can be changed to:

$$P = F \times \frac{D}{T}$$

and because D/T (distance/time) is speed, if D/T is in miles/hour, it must be converted to feet/minute. The common conversion factor for speed is: 1 mph = 88 ft/min. This factor is obtained as follows:

$$88\,\frac{\text{ft}}{\text{min}} = \frac{1\text{ mi}}{1\text{ hr}} \times \frac{5280\text{ ft}}{1\text{ mi}} \times \frac{1\text{ hr}}{60\text{ min}}$$

TORQUE (To)

Torque is the application of a force through a lever arm. It is a force that causes or tends to cause a twisting or rotary movement. In equation form:

$$\text{Torque} = \text{Force} \times \text{Lever arm length} \qquad (4\text{-}3)$$

or:

$$\text{To} = \text{F} \times \text{LA}$$

where:

To = Torque (lb-ft or lb-in)
F = Force (lb)
LA = Lever arm length (ft or in)

Because force is measured in pounds and length in feet or inches, the common units of torque are pound-feet (lb-ft) or pound-inches (lb-in).

Problem: If a 50.0-pound force is applied at the end of a wrench that is 1.0 foot long, how much torque is developed?

Solution: Using Equation (4-3)

$$\begin{aligned} To &= F \times LA \\ &= 50.0 \text{ lb} \times 1.0 \text{ ft} \\ &= 50 \text{ lb-ft} \end{aligned}$$

Notice that the answer has been written as "50 pound-feet." To distinguish torque from work we *always* write the torque units with the force unit first, "pound-feet," and we *always* write the units for work with the distance unit first, "foot-pounds."

There is one additional difference between torque and work. We stated that unless there is movement, there is no work. Because torque is a force working through a lever arm, a torque can exist without movement.

Problem: Which of the following will cause a greater torque to be exerted on a shaft: (1) 50.0 pounds of force applied at the end of a 6.0-inch (1/2-foot) wrench, or (2) 15.0 pounds of force applied at the end of a 24.0-inch (2-foot) wrench?

Solution:

(1) $To_1 = 50.0 \text{ lb} \times 0.5 \text{ ft} = 25 \text{ lb-ft}$
(2) $To_2 = 15.0 \text{ lb} \times 2.0 \text{ ft} = 30 \text{ lb-ft}$

Situation (2) will cause greater torque (twisting effect) on the shaft.

HORSEPOWER (hp)

Although power is a basic unit, in agriculture the more common unit is horsepower. Several different measures of horsepower are used. For example, when discussing tractors, you may use engine horsepower, brake horsepower, drawbar horsepower, or power take-off (pto) horsepower. In the following section we will investigate the principles of horsepower. The different measures of horsepower will be discussed in later chapters.

Horsepower is an arbitrary unit that was developed by James Watt to promote his early steam engines. He watched horses pulling loads out of mine shafts and established that one horsepower is equal to performing work at the rate of 33,000 foot-pounds per minute. Expressed algebraically:

$$1\ \text{hp} = \frac{\text{Power}\left(\frac{\text{ft-lb}}{\text{min}}\right)}{33{,}000\left(\frac{\text{ft-lb}}{\text{min}}\right)}$$

or using the units cancellation method:

$$1\ \text{hp} = \frac{\text{P}\left(\frac{\text{ft-lb}}{\text{min}}\right)}{1} \times \frac{1\ \text{hp}}{33{,}000\left(\frac{\text{ft-lb}}{\text{min}}\right)}$$

Note that unless power is in the units of ft-lb/min, the use of the conversion factor 1 hp = 33,000 ft-lb/min will not produce correct results.

Horsepower is commonly shown mathematically as:

$$\text{hp} = \frac{\text{F} \times \text{D}}{\text{T} \times 33{,}000} \qquad (4\text{-}4)$$

This equation requires distance (D) expressed in feet, force (F) in pounds, and time (T) in minutes.

Problem: How many horsepower are developed if a person loads six 60-pound bales onto a truck platform 4 feet high in 1.5 minutes?

Solution: Using Equation (4-4) and the appropriate units conversion:

$$hp = \frac{D \times F}{T \times 33{,}000}$$

$$= \frac{4 \text{ ft} \times \left(6 \text{ bales} \times 60 \frac{\text{lb}}{\text{bale}}\right)}{1.5 \text{ min} \times 33{,}000}$$

$$= \frac{1400}{49{,}500}$$

$$= 0.028 \text{ hp}$$

Now assume that the time required to load the hay is measured as 90 seconds instead of 1.5 minutes. It becomes necessary to convert seconds to minutes or to use a different conversion factor from power to horsepower. A conversion for time can be added to the equation:

$$hp = \frac{D \times F}{T \times 33{,}000}$$

$$= \frac{4.0 \text{ ft} \times \left(6 \text{ bales} \times \frac{60.0 \text{ lb}}{1 \text{ bale}}\right)}{\left(90.0 \text{ sec} \times \frac{1 \text{ min}}{60.0 \text{ sec}}\right) \times 33{,}000}$$

$$= \frac{1400 \text{ ft-lb}}{1.5 \text{ min} \times 33{,}000}$$

$$= 0.028 \text{ hp}$$

PRACTICE PROBLEMS

1. How much work is done when a 60.0-pound bale is moved vertically 5.0 feet?
   Answer: 300 ft-lb
2. In the first situation a 2000-pound weight is raised vertically through a distance of 20 feet. In the second situation a 3000-pound force moves horizontally through a distance of 10 feet. Which situation results in the greater amount of work being done? How much work is accomplished in each case?
   Answer: The first. The 2000-pound weight moving vertically requires more work (40,000 ft-lb). The 3000-

pound force moving horizontally requires 30,000 ft-lb of work.

3. You exert a force (push) of 100 pounds against a thick bric wall. How much work is done?
Answer: None
4. If a plow requires 500.0 pounds of force to pull it through a distance of 300.0 feet in 2.0 minutes, how much power is required?
Answer: 75,000 ft-lb/min
5. A person weighing 150.0 pounds runs up a flight of stairs from one floor to the next, a vertical distance of 10.0 feet, in 5.0 seconds. How much power is developed?
Answer: 18,000 ft-lb/min
6. How much horsepower is required to pull a plow 300.0 feet in 2.0 minutes if the plow requires a force of 500.0 pounds?
Answer: 2.3 hp
7. How many *pound-feet* of torque will be exerted on a shaft by a force of 30.0 pounds being applied at the end of a lever that is 18.0 inches long?
Answer: 45.0 lb-ft
8. Which will cause a greater twisting (torque) effect, 40 pounds applied at the end of a 12-inch lever *or* 12 pounds applied at the end of a 40-inch lever?
Answer: Both cause the same torque, 40 lb-ft.
9. A rope is wrapped around the outside of an 18.0-inch pulley. If a pull of 60.0 pounds is applied to one end of the rope, and assuming that no slipping of the rope on the pulley occurs, how much torque is being exerted on the pulley? *Hint*: The lever arm here would be the radius of the pulley or one-half of the diameter.
Answer: 540 lb-in

5
Internal Combustion Engines

OBJECTIVES

1. Be able to list and describe the events that occur in an internal combustion engine.
2. Be able to describe how a spark ignition (Otto-cycle) engine differs in operation from a compression ignition (Diesel-cycle) engine.
3. Be able to diagram and describe the events that occur in sequence during each stroke of a four-stroke cycle engine.
4. Be able to diagram and describe the events that occur in a two-stroke cycle engine.
5. Given the bore, stroke, number of cylinders, and clearance volume, be able to calculate the:
   (a) Piston displacement
   (b) Engine displacement
   (e) Compression ratio

INTRODUCTION

There are six primary sources of power in agriculture: human labor, domestic animals, wind, flowing water, electricity, and heat engines. In relatively recent times, the source of power for agricultural production has shifted from humans to animals, to external combustion heat engines (steam engines), to internal combustion heat engines (gasoline and diesel). Some day the primary source of power may change to fuel cells, solar energy, or atomic energy, but in the immediate future the primary sources of power for agriculture will continue to be internal combustion heat engines and electric motors.

Internal combustion engines used for agricultural applications range from those used for one-horsepower garden tools to the hundreds of horsepower required for very large tractors. Because engines are very common and necessary in agricultural production, knowledge of how and why they work is essential to a successful agricultural manager. In this chapter the basic engine types and functions are discussed, as are some basic calculations concerning engine size (displacement) and compression ratio.

THEORY OF OPERATION

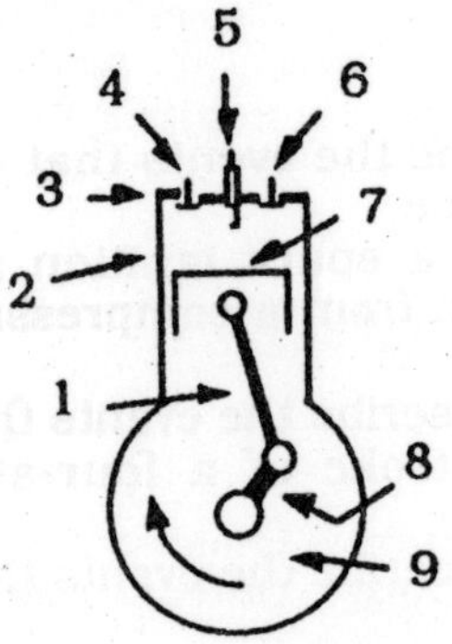

1. Connecting rod
2. Cylinder
3. Cylinder head
4. Intake valve
5. Spark plug
6. Exhaust valve
7. Piston
8. Crankshaft
9. Crankcase

Figure 5.1. Parts of an internal combustion engine.

The function of all internal combustion engines is to convert fuel (chemical energy) to power. This is accomplished by burning a fuel in a closed chamber and using the expansion of the gas to force one wall of the chamber (piston) to move. The linear movement of the piston then is converted to rotary motion (at the crankshaft), which is more useful than linear movement.

All types of internal combustion engines have these eight requirements for operation:

1. Air (oxygen) is drawn into the engine (cylinder).
2. A quantity of fuel is introduced into the engine.
3. The air and the fuel are mixed.
4. The fuel--air mixture is compressed.
5. The fuel--air mixture is ignited.
6. The burning of the fuel--air mixture causes a rapid pressure increase in the cylinder, which acts against the piston, forcing it to move.
7. The use of a connecting rod and a crankshaft converts the linear movement of the piston to rotary motion. The force on the piston is converted to torque on the crankshaft.
8. The products of combustion are expelled from the engine.

Study this sequence to gain a basic understanding of how all internal combustion engines function. The next sections illustrate two ways in which those events are arranged in functional engines.

FOUR-STROKE CYCLE

The four-stroke cycle engine, commonly called 4 cycle, is one of the two types of engine cycles used for both spark and compression ignition engines. In 4 cycle engines the eight events occur during these four strokes of the piston or two revolutions of the crankshaft:

1. Intake
2. Compression
3. Power
4. Exhaust

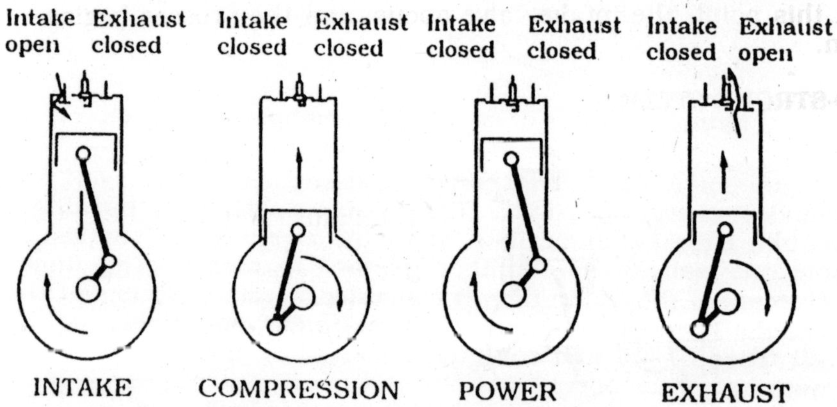

Figure 5.2. Four-stroke cycle.

Study Figure 5.2 and the following description of the events. An engine can be studied at any point in the cycle, but traditionally we start with the intake stroke. During the *intake stroke*, the intake valve opens, and the piston travels from the top of the cylinder (TDC) to the bottom (BDC). In both the spark and the compression ignition engines, the movement of the piston reduces the pressure inside the cylinder, causing air to flow through the intake system and into the cylinder. In the carbureted engine fuel is introduced into the air stream as it flows through the carburetor. Shortly after the piston reaches the bottom of the intake stroke, the intake valve closes, thus trapping the air--fuel mixture inside the cylinder.

The *compression stroke* follows. Because the air--fuel mixture is trapped in the cylinder, as the piston returns to the top of the cylinder during this stroke, the air is compressed, and as it is compressed, the temperature rises. As the piston nears the top of the compression stroke, ignition occurs.

compressed, the temperature rises. As the piston nears the top of the compression stroke, ignition occurs.

The rapid expansion of the burning mixture causes the pressure to rise very quickly, with the rise in pressure forcing the piston away from the cylinder head. This is called the *power stroke.* It is during this stroke that the chemical energy of the fuel is converted to torque.

Before the piston reaches the bottom of the cylinder on the power stroke, the exhaust valve opens, and as the piston returns toward the top of the cylinder, the products of combustion are expelled from the cylinder through the open exhaust valve. This is called the *exhaust stroke.*

At this point, the intake valve opens, and the process begins again.

TWO-STROKE CYCLE

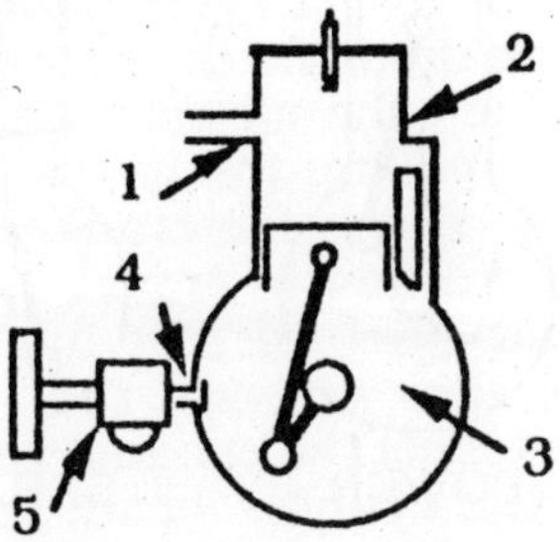

1. Exhaust port
2. Intake port
3. Crankcase
4. Reed valve
5. Carburetor

Figure 5.3. Parts of a two-cycle engine.

The eight required events occur in two strokes of the piston in a two-stroke cycle (2 cycle) engine, or one revolution of the crankshaft. Some variability exists in the ways 2 cycle engines are constructed, but Figure 5.3 will be used to illustrate the primary functions of the common designs. Two very noticeable differences exist between a 2 and a 4 cycle engine. In the 2 cycle, the carburetor is attached to the crankcase, and there are no intake and exhaust valves. Instead, ports in the cylinder wall are exposed and covered by the movement of the piston.

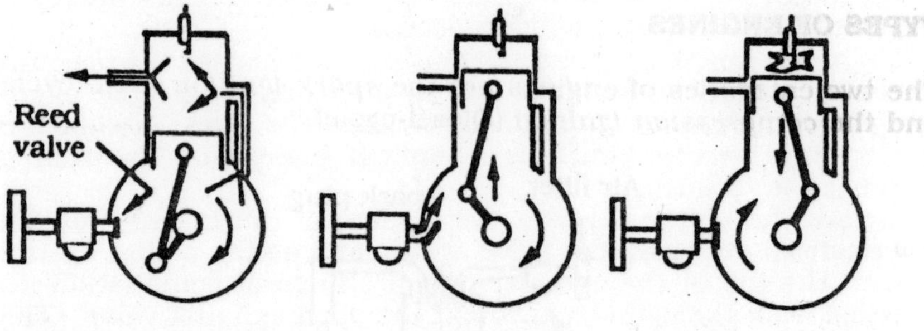

Figure 5.4. Two stroke cycle.

Study Figure 5.4 and the following description of events to understand the 2 cycle engine. In the 2 cycle engine *intake* and *exhaust* occur at almost the same time. As the piston moves away from the head, it first exposes the exhaust port, and combustion pressure starts the process of expelling the gases. At the same time, the reed valve closes. This causes the crankcase to become pressurized. As the piston continues to travel, it exposes the intake port. The pressurized air--fuel mixture in the crankcase flows into the cylinder. This flow delivers the next fuel--air charge for combustion and helps expel the exhaust gases.

As the piston moves toward the cylinder head, first the intake port and then the exhaust port is closed, and *compression* begins. As soon as the intake port is covered, the continuing movement of the piston lowers the pressure in the crankcase, and the air--fuel mixture flows from the carburetor, through the reed valve, and into the crankcase.

As the piston continues toward the cylinder head, the spark plug fires, the piston reaches top dead center (TDC), burning occurs, and pressure builds rapidly in the cylinder. This is called the *ignition* and *power* event. As soon as the piston moves away from the head far enough to expose the exhaust port, the cycle begins again.

If you count the movements of the piston, you will find that it has traveled two strokes for one revolution of the crankshaft. Because both the exhaust and the intake processes are not as efficient as in the 4 cycle engine, the 2 cycle engine will produce less power per stroke. However, because it has a power event each crankshaft revolution, the total power produced by the engine is comparable to that of a 4 cycle engine.

TYPES OF ENGINES

The two categories of engines are the *spark ignition* (Otto-cycle) and the *compression ignition* (Diesel-cycle).

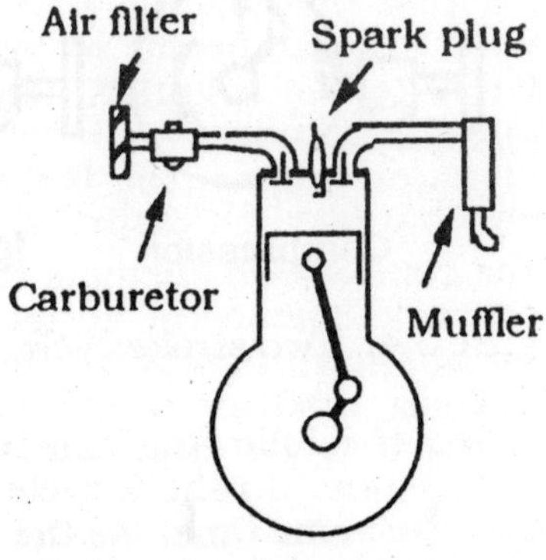

Figure 5.5. Carbureted spark ignition engine.

In the spark ignition engine, the fuel is metered and introduced into the engine by either a carburetor or an injection system. If a carburetor is used, the fuel is metered and added to the air as it flows through the venturi of the carburetor. Mixing occurs as the fuel--air mixture moves through the intake system and into the cylinder. A spark plug ignites the fuel--air mixture at the proper time.

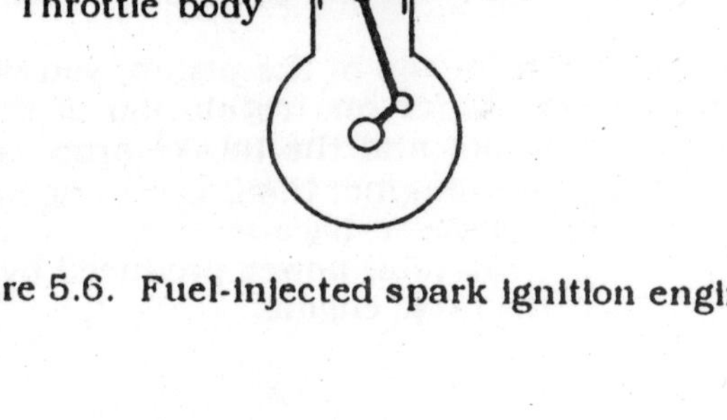

Figure 5.6. Fuel-injected spark ignition engine.

If an engine uses an injection system, it does not have a carburetor. The fuel may be injected into the air at one of two places. In some engines a single injector is located at the throttle body (throttle body injection). This single injector meters the fuel for all of the cylinders. In the second type of injection system, an injector is positioned just outside the port leading into each cylinder (port injection). Each injector meters and delivers the required amount of fuel to the cylinder. The fuel and air are mixed as they flow into the cylinder.

In a compression ignition engine, the fuel is injected directly into the combustion chamber. Compression causes the air temperature within the combustion chamber to rise up to 1000°F and above. At the proper moment, the correct amount of fuel is injected into the combustion chamber. Because of the high temperature, the fuel--air mixture is ignited by spontaneous combustion. Thus, there is no need for a spark plug or a carburetor.

DISPLACEMENT

Displacement is the cylindrical volume that a piston displaces as it moves through one stroke. It is equal to the area of the piston multiplied by the length of the stroke. Displacement is one of the factors that determine the amount of horsepower an engine will produce. Expressed mathematically, piston displacement is:

$$PD = \frac{\pi \times B^2}{4} \times S \qquad (5\text{-}1)$$

where:

PD = Piston displacement in cubic inches (in^3)
B = Bore of cylinder (diameter), in inches (in)
S = Stroke of piston in inches (in)
$\frac{\pi \times B^2}{4}$ = Area of the cylinder (in^2)

The bore and the stroke of an engine has been traditionally expressed as B x S with the dimensions in inches. Thus, if B x S = 3.50 x 4.00, the piston displacement is:

$$PD = \frac{\pi B^2}{4} x S$$

$$= \frac{\pi x (3.50 \text{ in})^2}{4} x 4.00 \text{ in}$$

$$= 38.5 \text{ in}^3$$

Larger engines are constructed with more than one cylinder. For multicylinder engines, the term engine displacement (ED) is used. Engine displacement is the product of the cylinder displacement times the number of cylinders. Expressed in equation form:

$$ED = PD x n \quad (5\text{-}2)$$

where:

ED = Engine displacement (in^3)
PD = Piston displacement (in^3)
n = Number of cylinders

If the engine in the previous example is a four-cylinder engine, then the engine displacement is:

$$ED = PD x n$$

$$= 38.46 x 4$$

$$= 153.8 \text{ in}^3$$

In determining the engine displacement for multiple cylinder engines, Equations (5-1) and (5-2) usually are combined.

$$ED = \left(\frac{\pi B^2 S}{4}\right) x n \quad (5\text{-}3)$$

COMPRESSION RATIO

The compression ratio is an engine characteristic related to engine efficiency, that is, the ability of the engine to convert energy in the fuel to useful mechanical energy. The greater the compression ratio, the greater the potential efficiency of the engine is. The maximum compression ratio that can be obtained is a function of the type of fuel and the physical strength of the metal in the engine.

The compression ratio is the ratio of the total volume in a cylinder to the clearance volume. The total volume is the volume in the cylinder when the piston is at bottom dead center (BDC), or the piston displacement plus the clearance volume. The clearance volume is the volume above the piston when the piston is at top dead center (TDC). Expressed mathematically:

$$CR = \frac{PD + CV}{CV} \tag{5-4}$$

where:

CR = Compression ratio
PD = Piston displacement (in^3)
CV = Clearance volume (in^3)

Problem: What is the compression ratio for an engine with a B x S of 3.50 x 4.00 and a clearance volume of 7.20 in^3?

Solution: The first step is to calculate the displacement:

$$PD = \frac{\pi B^2}{4} \times S$$

$$= \frac{3.14 \times 3.50^2}{4} \times 4.00$$

$$= 38.5 \text{ in}^3$$

Then the compression ratio is:

$$CR = \frac{38.5 \text{ in}^3 + 7.2 \text{ in}^3}{7.2 \text{ in}^3}$$

$$= \frac{45.7}{7.2}$$

$$= 6.35 \text{ or } 6.35{:}1$$

Notice that the answer has no units. To have a ratio the units in the numerator and the denominator must be the same; thus the units cancel each other. A compression ratio of 6.35 would be expressed as 6.35 to 1 or 6.35:1.

PRACTICE PROBLEMS

1. Find the piston displacement for the following engines.
   A. B x S = 4.250 x 4.750
   B. B x S = 3.940 x 4.720
   C. B x S = 4.300 x 5.000
   Answers:
   A. 67.35 in^3; B. 57.52 in^3; C. 72.57 in^3
2. Find the engine displacement for the following engines.
   A. Four cylinders, B x S = 4 and 1/4 x 4 and 3/4.
   B. Three cylinders, B x S = 3.940 x 4.720
   C. Six cylinder with B x S = 4.300 x 5.000
   Answers:
   A. 269 in^3; B. 172.6 in^3; C. 435.4 in^3
3. Find the compression ratio for the following engines.
   A. B x S = 4 and 1/4 x 4 and 3/4, clearance volume of 9.6 in^3
   B. B x S = 3.940 x 4.720 and clearance volume of 3.59 in^3
   Answers:
   A. 8.02:1; B. 17.02:1

6
Power Trains

OBJECTIVES

1. Be able to describe a power train.
2. Be able to determine the appropriate size for a pulley, sprocket, or gear.
3. Be able to use speed ratios to determine pulley, sprocket, and gear sizes.
4. Be able to determine the speed and direction of rotation at any point in a power train.
5. Understand the relationship between speed and torque.
6. Be able to determine the torque and horsepower at any point in a power train.

INTRODUCTION

A power train is all of the mechanical devices used to transfer power through a machine. Common devices are pulleys, sprockets, shafts, bearings, gears, belts, and chains. These devices are used to deliver power to the individual components of a machine and to change it to meet each component's requirement. Changes in speed, direction of rotation, or torque may be needed. This chapter will illustrate some of the principles of power trains and provide examples of how these principles are used.

PULLEYS

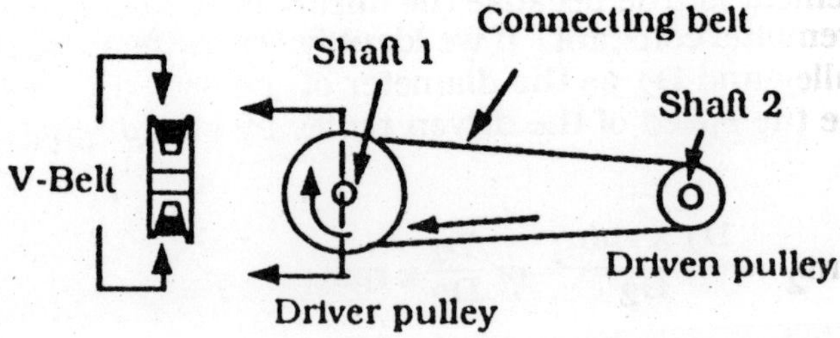

Figure 6.1. V-belt drive.

Pulleys are used in conjunction with V-belts. The V shape of the belt wedges in the V shape of the pulley, forming a contact resulting in a large amount of friction. A belt drive will always have at least two pulleys, the driver and the driven. Consider Figure 6.1, which represents two pulleys mounted on shafts and connected by a belt.

If we apply torque to the driver shaft and cause it to turn or rotate as indicated by the arrow on the pulley, a tension or force will be created in the belt. If the tension exceeds the load (torque) of the driven pulley and the friction of the drive train, it will cause the driven pulley and shaft to turn.

Drive trains using belts and pulleys may contain more than two pulleys. If more than two are used, one will be the driver and the others will be driven.

If the driver pulley in Figure 6.1 has a diameter of 10.0 inches and rotates at 100 revolutions per minute (rpm), and the driven pulley has a diameter of 5.0 inches, we can determine the speed of the driven pulley (and the shaft it is attached to) because the diameter of the driver pulley times the speed of the driver pulley is equal to the diameter of the driven pulley times the speed of the driven pulley. Expressed mathematically:

$$D_1 \times rpm_1 = D_2 \times rpm_2 \tag{6-1}$$

where:

D = Diameter of a pulley
rpm = revolutions per minute

This statement is true because the linear speed (feet per minute) of the belt remains constant. If we identify D_1 as the diameter of the driver pulley and D_2 as the diameter of the driven pulley, we can determine the speed of the driven pulley by rearranging Equation (6-1):

$$rpm_2 = \frac{D_1 \times rpm_1}{D_2} \text{ or } \frac{D_1}{D_2} \times rpm_1$$

$$= \frac{10.0 \text{ in} \times 100 \text{ rpm}}{5.0 \text{ in}}$$

$$= 200 \text{ rpm}$$

If you understand Equation (6-1), you should be able to state with confidence that when the driven pulley is smaller than the driver, the speed will increase, and when the driven pulley is larger than the driver, the speed will decrease. Thus by visual inspection and intuitive reasoning you should be able to tell if a pulley drive train will increase or decrease the speed. To determine the actual amount of change, use Equation (6-1).

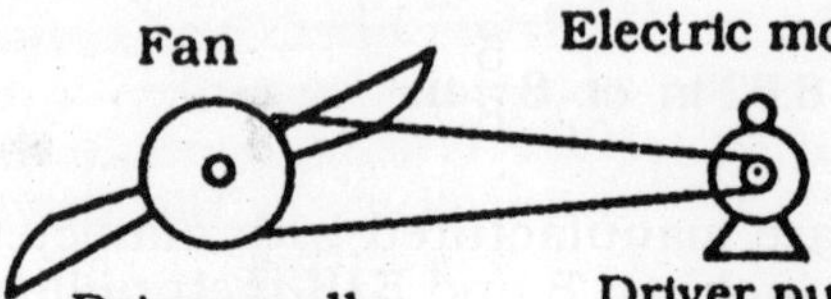

Figure 6.2. Calculating unknown diameters.

One application of this principle is represented in the fan drive in Figure 6.2. Large ventilation fans of this type are commonly used in greenhouses, animal buildings, and other agricultural applications.

Problem: Assume that you have a fan and an electric motor, but no pulleys. The fan is designed to operate at 500 rpm, and the electric motor operates at 1725 rpm. What sizes of pulleys will be needed to operate the fan?

Solution: First, intuitive reasoning tells us that a large change in speed will require a large difference in pulley diameters. Second, we know that Equation (6-1) includes four variables, and at this point we only know two, the pulley speeds. To find a solution we must select one of the pulley sizes and then determine the other.

We could begin by selecting a pulley for the fan, but because the fan speed (driven) is less than the motor speed (driver), we know that the pulley on the motor will be smaller than the pulley on the fan. If we selected a pulley for the fan that is too small, the calculated pulley size for the electric motor may be smaller than what is physically possible. Therefore, begin by selecting the pulley size for the electric motor, and then calculate the required pulley size for the fan. If we select a 2.5-inch pulley for the motor, then the size of the fan pulley can be determined by rearranging Equation (6-1):

$$D_2\ (\text{fan}) = \frac{D_1 \times \text{rpm}_1}{\text{rpm}_2}$$

$$= \frac{2.50\ \text{in} \times 1725\ \text{rpm}}{500\ \text{rpm}}$$

$$= 8.62\ \text{in or } 8\frac{5}{8}\ \text{in}$$

Because pulleys are manufactured with diameters in increments of fractions of an inch, an 8 and 5/8-inch pulley probably would be used.

Note that the ratios of the pulley diameters, D_2/D_1, will be equal to the ratios of the pulley speeds, $\text{rpm}_1/\text{rpm}_2 = 3.45$. Thus if for any reason the 2.5-inch pulley for the motor is not available, any combination of pulley diameters with a ratio of 3.45 (or ≅ 3.5) will provide the correct speed. For example, pulleys with diameters of:

$$\frac{D_2\ (\text{fan})}{D_1\ (\text{motor})} = \frac{8.625}{2.5} = \frac{17.25}{5.0} = \frac{34.5}{10.0} = 3.45$$

will produce the same change in speed. This ratio of two pulleys is called a speed ratio and will be discussed in more detail later in this chapter.

SPROCKET SIZES

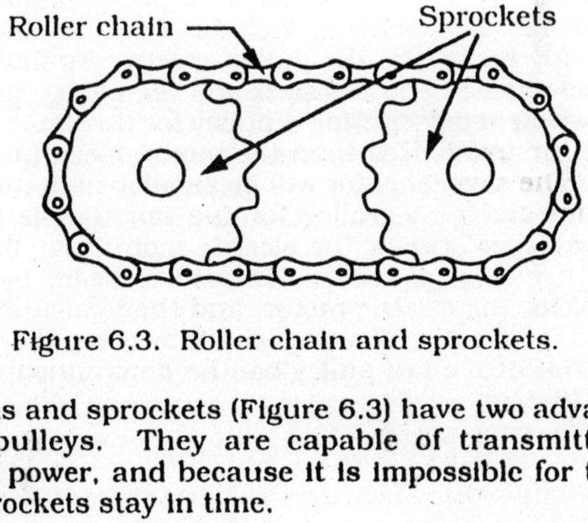

Figure 6.3. Roller chain and sprockets.

Roller chains and sprockets (Figure 6.3) have two advantages over belts and pulleys. They are capable of transmitting greater amounts of power, and because it is impossible for the chain to slip, the sprockets stay in time.

Equation (6-1) can be used to determine sprocket sizes with one modification. The diameter of the pulleys is replaced by the number of teeth for each sprocket. For sprockets, Equation (6-1) becomes:

$$T_1 \times rpm_1 = T_2 \times rpm_2 \qquad (6\text{-}2)$$

Problem: A hydraulic pump will be powered by a tractor power take-off (pto). The pump must turn at 2100 rpm, and the pto operates at 540 rpm. What sizes of sprockets are needed?

Solution: The first step is to select the size of one of the sprockets. For this example, we will assume that the pump came with an 18-tooth sprocket. We need to determine the size of the pto sprocket.

Rearranging Equation (6-2) for the number of teeth in the driver sprocket give us:

$$T_1 = \frac{T_2 \times rpm_2}{rpm_1}$$

$$= \frac{18 \text{ teeth} \times 2100 \text{ rpm}}{540 \text{ rpm}}$$

$$= 70 \text{ teeth}$$

The pump will turn at the correct speed if the pto sprocket of the tractor has 70 teeth.

GEAR SIZES

Gears are used in power trains when the shafts are very close together, when very large amounts of power are being transmitted, or in transmissions where selectable speed ratios are needed. The sizes of gears are determined in the same way as those of chains and sprockets. Equation (6-2) can be used without modification.

SPEED RATIOS

In some situations when the speeds of the driver and driven shafts are known, pulley, sprocket, and gear sizes can be determined by using speed ratios instead of Equations (6-1) or (6-2).

In the previous problem we determined that a 70-tooth sprocket was needed to power the pump. A 70-tooth sprocket will have a large diameter and may be too large to fit on a small tractor. Does this mean that the pump cannot be used?

The solution is to use a smaller sprocket on the pump and then determine the size of sprocket needed for the pto. In the original problem we saw that 18- and 70-tooth sprockets would provide the correct speed. Thus we know that the ratio of the two sprockets is 70/18 or 3.9:1. In other words, the sprocket on the pto must have approximately four times as many teeth as the sprocket on the pump.

With the speed ratio between the two shafts known, several different sprocket combinations could be used:

$$\frac{T_1}{T_2} = \frac{70}{18} = \frac{35}{9} \cong \frac{43}{11} \cong \frac{47}{12} = 3.9$$

Knowing the speed ratio makes it easier to select sprocket combinations that will operate the pump at the correct speed and still fit within the physical limitations of the machine.

DIRECTION OF ROTATION

A component on an agricultural machine may require a direction of rotation different from that of the engine or the motor. The two directions of rotation are clockwise (cw) and counterclockwise (ccw) when viewed from the end of the shaft. The direction of rotation can be changed through the use of belts and pulleys, chains and sprockets, and gears. We will illustrate each of these methods.

BELTS AND PULLEYS

Two different techniques can be used to change the direction of rotation (Figure 6.4).

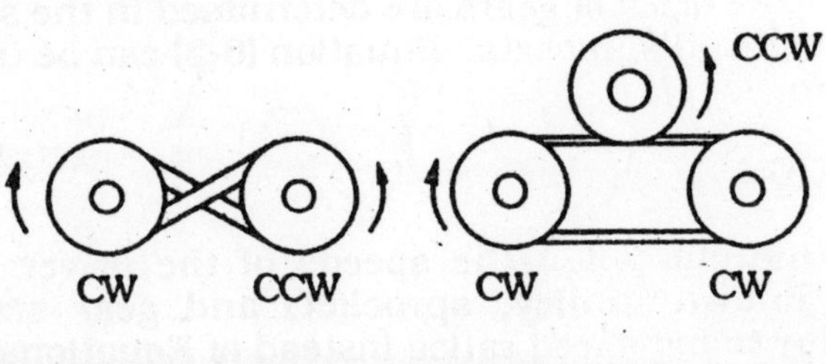

Figure 6.4. Reversing rotation with belts and pulleys.

Notice that twisting the belt changes the direction of rotation. This technique is acceptable if the pulleys are some distance apart. If the two pulleys are close together, the belt will rub at the crossover point. The friction produced from rubbing will shorten the life of the belt.

The addition of a third pulley also will reverse the direction of rotation. This requires a six-sided, or double-V, belt that is designed to engage the pulleys on both sides.

ROLLER CHAINS AND SPROCKETS

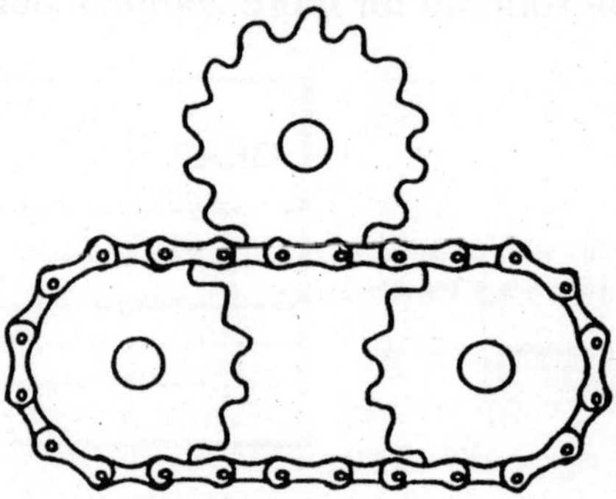

Figure 6.5. Changing the direction of rotation with a roller chain and sprockets.

Figure 6.5 shows that roller chains can be used to reverse the direction of rotation. Because roller chains cannot be twisted, changing the direction of rotation requires the use of a third sprocket.

GEARS

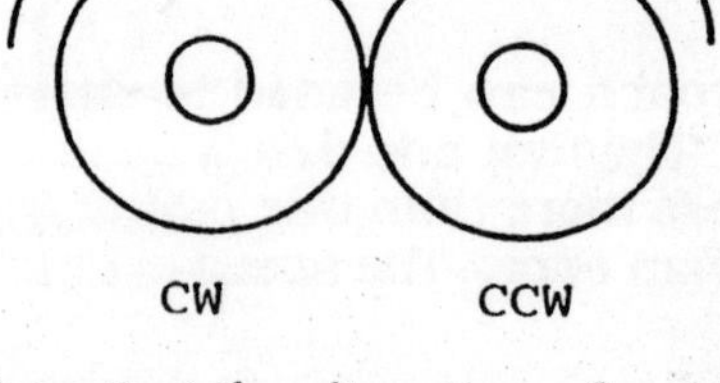

Figure 6.6. Changing the direction of rotation with gears.

Gears are unique in that each pair of gears will change the direction of rotation. (See Figure 6.6.)

COMPLEX POWER TRAINS

Many machines use power trains that are more complex than what has been discussed up to this point. Figure 6.7 represents a power train designed to allow an engine to supply the power for two different components. These components are attached to output shafts A and B. This figure illustrates the application of direction and speed of rotation for more complex power trains.

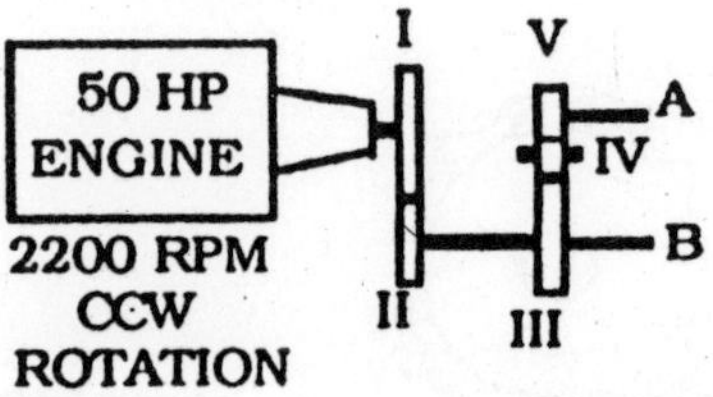

GEAR	NUMBER OF TEETH
I	24
II	12
III	16
IV	8
V	12

Figure 6.7. Shaft speed and direction of rotation in multiple shaft drives.

Problem: What are the speed and the rotation of shaft A and shaft B in Figure 6.7?

Solution: In this power train the output shaft of a 50-horsepower engine powers gear I. Gear II is powered by gear I, and because gear III is attached to the same shaft, it is powered by gear I also. Gear IV is powered by gear III, and gear V by gear IV. Shaft A will turn at the same speed and direction of rotation as gear V, and shaft B will turn at the same speed and direction of rotation as gears II and III.

More than one approach can be used to determine the speed of shaft A and shaft B. The first one that we will show uses Equation (6-2). Because there is more than one pair of gears, Equation (6-2) must be used more than once. The speed of gear II is:

$$rpm_2 = \frac{T_1 \times rpm_1}{T_2}$$

$$= \frac{24 \times 2200}{12}$$

$$= 4400 \text{ rpm}$$

Because gear II is fixed to shaft B, shaft B and gear III turn at 4400 rpm.

To determine the speed of shaft A, Equation (6-2) is used two more times, first to find the speed of gear IV:

$$rpm_2 = \frac{T_1 \times rpm_1}{T_2}$$

$$= \frac{16 \times 4400}{8}$$

$$= 9000 \text{ rpm}$$

and then the speed of gear V:

$$rpm_2 = \frac{T_1 \times rpm_1}{T_2}$$

$$= \frac{8 \times 9000}{12}$$

$$= 6000 \text{ rpm}$$

Therefore, shaft A turns at 6000 rpm.

Remembering the discussion of speed ratios, we can develop an alternative approach for solving this problem. If the speed of shaft B is determined by the speed of the driver gear times the gear ratio of the two gears, then the speed of shaft B can be determined by:

$$rpm_B = rpm_1 \times \frac{T_I}{T_{II}}$$

$$= rpm_1 \times \frac{24}{12}$$

$$= 2200 \times \frac{24}{12}$$

$$= 4400 \text{ rpm}$$

and the speed of shaft A can be determined by:

$$rpm_A = rpm_1 \times \frac{T_I}{T_{II}} \times \frac{T_{III}}{T_{IV}} \times \frac{T_{IV}}{T_V}$$

$$= 2200 \times \frac{24}{12} \times \frac{16}{8} \times \frac{8}{12}$$

$$= 6000 \text{ rpm}$$

When the speed ratio approach is used, we must remember to place the number of teeth of the driver in the numerator and the number of teeth of the driven in the denominator.

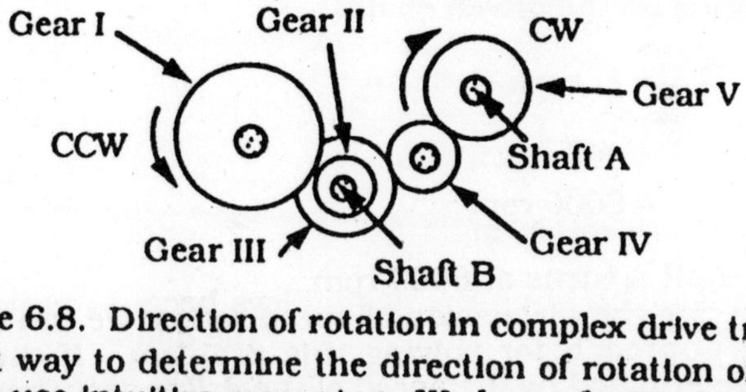

Figure 6.8. Direction of rotation in complex drive trains.

The best way to determine the direction of rotation of shafts A and B is to use intuitive reasoning. We know from our discussion of gears that the direction of rotation changes with every pair of gears in the power train. Thus, shaft B is driven by one pair of gears, and has one direction of rotation change. Shaft B turns clockwise. Shaft A is powered by three pairs of gears, and has three direction of rotation changes. Shaft A turns clockwise also. Study Figure 6.8 to check these answers.

SPEED AND TORQUE

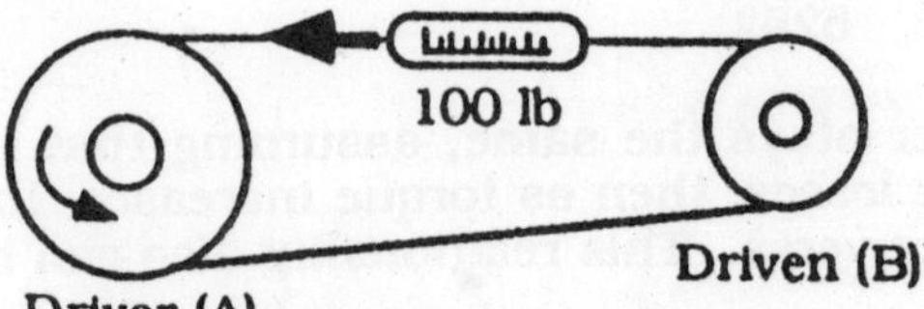

Figure 6.9. Speed and torque.

Suppose that we could attach a set of scales to the belt, as in Figure 6.9, and assume that the scale reads 100 pounds. Because the tension or force in the belt is constant along its length, there is 100 pounds of force pulling at the edge of both the driver(A) and the driven (B) pulley.

If the driver pulley has a diameter of 10 inches and that of the driven is 5 inches, then the torque on the driver pulley in Figure 6.9 is:

$$\begin{aligned} To &= \text{Force} \times \text{Radius}_A \\ &= 100 \text{ lb} \times 5 \text{ in} \\ &= 500 \text{ lb-in} \end{aligned}$$

and the torque on the driven shaft is:

$$\begin{aligned} To &= \text{Force} \times \text{Radius}_B \\ &= 100 \text{ lb} \times 2.5 \text{ in} \\ &= 250 \text{ lb-in} \end{aligned}$$

The torque is different on the two pulleys because pulleys behave as class one levers; the radius (one-half the diameter) is the length of the lever arm. A larger diameter pulley will have a longer lever arm. This example also illustrates that because the belt speed (in inches per minute) stays the same, the torque on the driven shaft is inversely proportional to the change in speed between the driver and driven pulleys. If the driven shaft turns at a higher speed, its torque is decreased relative to the driver shaft, and vice versa.

For every speed change, there is a change in the torque. This relationship can be shown by reviewing the pto horsepower equation:

$$hp = \frac{To \times rpm}{5252} \tag{6-3}$$

If the horsepower stays the same, assuming that there are no drive train power losses, then as torque increases, the rpm must decrease, and vice versa. This relationship also can be expressed as:

$$To_1 \times rpm_1 = To_2 \times rpm_2 \tag{6-4}$$

Problem: If the driver shaft of a belt power train turns at 300 rpm and applies 20 lb-ft of torque, and the driven pulley turns at 50 rpm, how much torque will be developed at the driven pulley?

Solution: Rearranging Equation (6-4) to solve for To_2 gives us:

$$To_2 = To_1 \times \frac{rpm_1}{rpm_2}$$

$$= 20 \text{ lb-ft} \times \frac{300 \text{ rpm}}{50 \text{ rpm}}$$

$$= 120 \text{ lb-ft}$$

Notice that the speed of the driven shaft is one-sixth that of the driver shaft, but the torque on the driven shaft is six times that on the driver shaft. This relationship suggests the reason for a tractor transmission. The engine turns at high speed with low torque, and the drive axle turns at low speed with high torque. The transmission uses several different gear pairs to produce different speed-torque combinations at the drive axle.

TRANSMISSION OF HORSEPOWER AND TORQUE

In managing agricultural machinery, it is sometimes useful to know the amount of torque being transmitted by a component of a power train. For example, it would be useful to know the amount of torque and the horsepower available at shafts A and B in Figure 6.8.

From the previous discussion of the relationship between torque and speed, we should be able to determine the torque available at each shaft:

$$To_B = To_I \times \frac{rpm_I}{rpm_{II}}$$

There is a slight problem--we do not know the amount of torque being produced by the engine. In Chapter 7 we will discuss horsepower in greater detail, but rotary horsepower can be determined by Equation (6-3):

$$hp = \frac{To \times rpm}{5252}$$

Because we know the horsepower and the rpm being produced by the engine, we can rearrange this equation to solve for the engine torque:

$$To_{eng} = \frac{hp \times 5252}{rpm}$$

$$= \frac{50 \text{ hp} \times 5252}{2200 \text{ rpm}}$$

$$= 119 \text{ lb-ft}$$

Now we can solve for the torque at shaft B:

$$To_B = To_I \times \frac{rpm_I}{rpm_{II}}$$

$$= 119 \times \frac{2200}{4400}$$

$$= 59.5 \text{ lb-ft}$$

and the torque at shaft A is:

$$To_A = To_{eng} \times \frac{rpm_{eng}}{rpm_A}$$

$$= 119 \text{ lb-ft} \times \frac{2200}{6000}$$

$$= 44 \text{ lb-ft}$$

Note that because we already knew the speed of shaft A, we used the speed ratio to solve for the torque. If we did not know the speed of shaft A, we would solve for it first.

POWER TRANSMISSION THROUGH POWER TRAINS

Power is transmitted through a power train. Study Figure 6.8 again. Can you predict how much power is available at either shaft A or shaft B? The answer 50 horsepower is correct. If we assume no frictional losses in the power train, we will get out all of the power we put in. This can be demonstrated by using Equation (6-3) to solve for the power available at shaft A.

$$hp = \frac{To \times rpm}{5252}$$

$$= \frac{44 \text{ lb-ft} \times 6000 \text{ rpm}}{5252}$$

$$= 50 \text{ hp}$$

PRACTICE PROBLEMS

1. Determine the missing information for the roller chain and sprocket drive train in Figure 6.10.

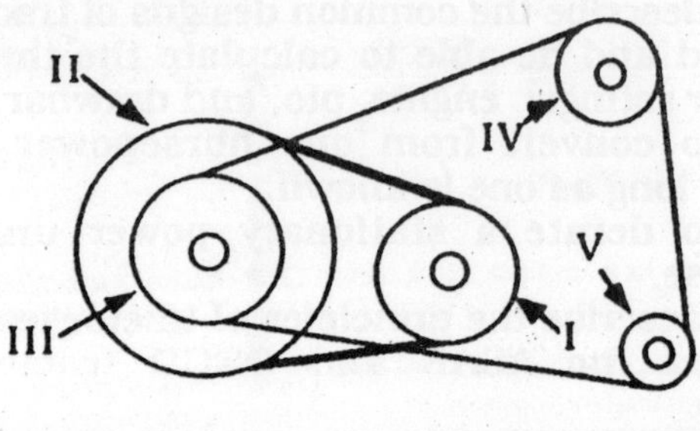

Sprocket	Teeth	Speed	Torque
I	12	480 rpm	20 lb-ft
II	20	A	B
III	40	A	B
IV	C	400 rpm	D
V	16	E	F

Figure 6.10. Multiple shaft sprocket and chain drive.

Answers:

A. 288 rpm
B. 33.33 lb-ft
C. 29 teeth
D. 24.0 lb-ft
E. 720 rpm
F. 13.3 lb-ft

2. If sprocket I rotates in a clockwise direction, in what direction will sprocket V rotate?
Answer: Clockwise

7
Tractors and Power Units

OBJECTIVES

1. Be able to describe the common designs of tractors.
2. Understand and be able to calculate the three tractor horsepower ratings: engine, pto, and drawbar.
3. Be able to convert from one horsepower rating to another as long as one is known.
4. Be able to derate a stationary power unit for the intended use.
5. Be able to describe the principles of tractor testing.
6. Understand the ASAE and OECD tractor testing procedures.

INTRODUCTION

Many different types of tractors and power units are used in agriculture. It is important, therefore, for the owner/manager to have a basic understanding of the types of tractors, how stationary engines and tractors are derated, and how tractors are tested.

TYPES OF TRACTORS

The diversity of modern agriculture requires many tractor designs. Historically, utility (use) has been the basis of tractor classification schemes. Based on utility, there are six types of tractors: general purpose, row crop, orchard, vineyard, industrial, and garden. This scheme is still workable if a subcategory is added for each type of propulsion system: rear wheel drive (RWD), four wheel drive articulating steering (4WDAS), four wheel drive four wheel steer (4WD), tracks (T), and rear wheel drive with front wheel assist (FWA).

GENERAL PURPOSE

The general purpose tractor is the traditional design with the rear wheels and the front wheels spaced the same distance apart. This type of tractor usually is built closer to the ground than the row crop design. The horsepower range of tractors of this type is very broad; sizes range from about 25 to over 300 horsepower. The use of a general purpose tractor is influenced by its horsepower. The smallest sizes are very popular for horticultural enterprises and for mowing. The mid-range sizes are used extensively for cultivating, spraying, tilling, and mowing, and for mobile and stationary pto power. The larger sizes normally are used for primary tillage and to provide pto power for larger mobile and stationary machines such as large balers, and forage harvesters and blowers.

General purpose tractors are available with all five types of propulsion systems. Historically, this tractor category has been dominated by the rear wheel drive, but in recent years the situation has changed. The propulsion system also is influenced by the horsepower. Smaller tractors use the rear wheel drive or the front wheel assist; in the middle of the horsepower range, all types can be found; and in the largest sizes, the most common type is the four wheel drive.

ROW CROP

Row crop tractors are designed with greater ground clearance than the general purpose tractors have. This gives them the ability to straddle taller crops with less plant damage. The size range of row crop tractors is narrower than that of the general purpose, as these tractors are usually 50 to 100 horsepower. Many are built with the front wheels closer together than the rear wheels (tricycle style). The narrow front wheels eliminate the use of tracks, front wheel assist, and articulating steering; but row crop tractors without narrow front wheels can be found with these configurations.

ORCHARD

Orchard tractors are not a separate type of design as general purpose and row crop tractors are, but are tractors that have been modified to reduce the possibility of tree limbs catching on them. Modifications usually include changing the location of the exhaust and the air intake and the addition of shields around the tires and other protuberances. Orchard work is not as power-demanding as primary tillage; therefore, these tractors are usually in the medium horsepower sizes.

VINEYARD

The vineyard tractor also is found in the smaller horsepower range. It has been designed or modified to reduce its width so that it can pass between narrow rows. It also may use shielding similar to that of the orchard tractor. The narrower size limits the propulsion system to the conventional rear axle drive, front wheel assist, and tracks.

INDUSTRIAL

These tractors look like general purpose agricultural tractors, but they have important differences. They will be equipped with tires designed for use on hard, smooth surfaces and the front axle and frame will be designed to withstand the weight and shocks of front loaders, backhoes, and other industrial equipment.

GARDEN

This tractor category has the greatest amount of variation in mechanical construction. These tractors usually are less than 25 horsepower. Some are manufactured to look like a small tractor, but others may look more like a riding lawn mower. They generally use the rear wheel drive system, with or without front wheel assist.

TRACTOR HORSEPOWER RATINGS

The discussion of horsepower determination in Chapter 4 is appropriate for calculating horsepower when distance, force, and time can be measured; but early in the development of engines it became apparent that it was necessary to measure the power being produced by engines. Because an engine produces a rotary mechanical force, a means had to be developed to measure this force. One of the first devices used for this purpose is the Prony Brake.

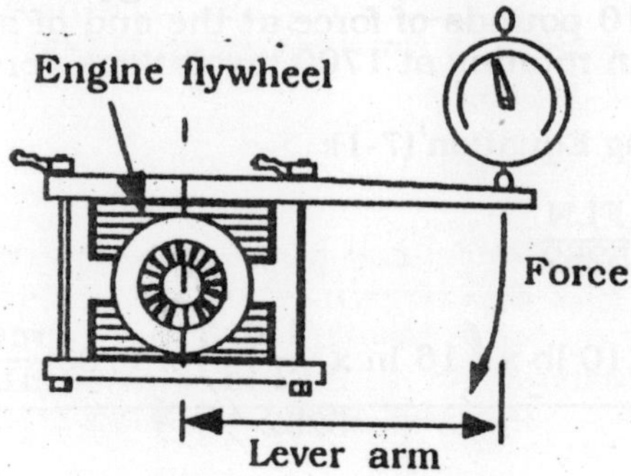

Figure 7.1. Prony Brake.

The early Prony Brake used the friction between a rotating flywheel and a stationary block of wood to produce a force on the lever arm (Figure 7.1). Once this force and the speed of rotation were known, the brake horsepower was determined. Mathematically brake horsepower is:

$$\text{Bhp} = \frac{FLN}{5252} \tag{7-1}$$

where:

F = Force produced (lb)
L = Length of the lever arm (ft)
N = Rotary speed of the Prony brake shaft (rpm)
5252 = Units conversion constant

This equation is derived from the horsepower equation:

$$1 \text{ hp} = \frac{\frac{2\pi}{\text{rev}} \times F \times D \times N}{\dfrac{1 \text{ hp}}{33{,}000 \frac{\text{ft-lb}}{\text{min}}}}$$

$$= \frac{F \times D \times N}{5252}$$

where the length of the lever arm equals the radius of the circle and the distance the force is working through.

Problem: How many horsepower are being produced by an engine if it produces 10 pounds of force at the end of an 18-inch Prony brake arm when rotating at 1700 revolutions per minute?

Solution: Using Equation (7-1):

$$Bhp = \frac{FLN}{5252}$$

$$= \frac{10 \text{ lb} \times \left(18 \text{ in} \times \frac{1 \text{ ft}}{12 \text{ in}}\right) \times 1700 \frac{\text{rev}}{\text{min}}}{5252}$$

$$= 4.9 \text{ Bhp}$$

Notice that Equation (7-1) contains a length and a force. We know from earlier discussions that if we have a force times a length, we are dealing with torque. Therefore, Equation (7-1) can be rewritten as:

$$Bhp = \frac{To \times N}{5252} \tag{7-2}$$

A Prony brake can still be used to measure the horsepower of engines, but electrical and hydraulic dynamometers are more accurate than the Prony brake. The rotary power of modern engines is measured at either the flywheel or the pto.

PTO HORSEPOWER

Power take-off horsepower (ptohp) is a rating of the horsepower available at the power take-off of an agricultural tractor. Power take-offs are used to supply rotary power to many different types of machines such as balers, pumps, and mowers. To determine power take-off horsepower, either Equation (7-1) or Equation (7-2) can be used.

DRAWBAR HORSEPOWER

If agricultural machinery is towed (has its own wheels), it is attached at the drawbar. Drawbar horsepower (Dbhp) is an evaluation of the amount of horsepower available at this point. During tractor testing a load cell is placed between the tractor and a load to measure the pounds of drawbar force the tractor is developing. In this situation Equation (4-4) is not appropriate.

Instead, because time is measured by the speed of travel (miles per hour) (Equation 4-4):

$$hp = \frac{F \times D}{T \times 33,000}$$

an equivalent equation is:

$$hp = \frac{F \times \frac{D}{T}}{33,000}$$

and because $1 \frac{mi}{hr} = 88 \frac{ft}{min} \left(\frac{D}{T}\right)$, then $1\ hp = \frac{F \times S \times 88}{33,000}$. Reducing the fraction $\frac{88}{33,000}$ gives us the common Dbhp equation:

$$Dbhp = \frac{F \times S}{375} \qquad (7\text{-}3)$$

where

F = Force (lb)

S = Speed (mph)

375 = Units conversion constant

Problem: How much drawbar horsepower is a tractor producing if it develops 1500 pounds of force at a speed of 5.5 miles per hour?

Solution: Using Equation (7-3):

$$Dbhp = \frac{F \times S}{375}$$

$$= \frac{1500\ lb \times 5.5\ \frac{mi}{hr}}{375}$$

$$= \frac{8300}{375}$$

$$= 22\ hp$$

CONVERTING TRACTOR HORSEPOWER RATINGS

Of the three different horsepower ratings, manufacturers usually advertise their products on the engine or brake horsepower basis. Unfortunately, this rating is not usable in determining the amount of power the tractor will produce at the pto or the drawbar. If the tractor is rated by engine or brake horsepower, the pto horsepower will be less because of the losses in the power train, and the drawbar horsepower will be less because a tractor is not able to apply all of the torque of the drive wheels to the soil.

Actual pto and drawbar horsepower ratings can be determined if the tractor has been tested by the Nebraska Tractor Test (NTT) Station or by the Organisation for Economic Cooperation and Development (OECD). If actual pto and drawbar ratings are not available, the *86% rule* can be used to estimate them from the engine rating.

Studies have shown that if a large number of tractors are compared over many different traction conditions, then the pto horsepower will be approximately 86% of the engine horsepower, and the drawbar horsepower will be approximately 86% of the pto. The 86% rule permits a good estimate of pto and drawbar horsepower. It is not intended to be a substitute for actual data.

Problem: Estimate the amount of horsepower available at the pto and the drawbar for a tractor rated at 125 engine horsepower (Ehp).

Solution: Using the 86% rule:

$$\begin{aligned} \text{ptohp} &= \text{Ehp} \times 0.86 \\ &= 125 \text{ Ehp} \times 0.86 \\ &= 108 \text{ ptohp} \end{aligned}$$

$$\begin{aligned} \text{Dbhp} &= \text{Ehp} \times 0.86 \times 0.86 \\ &= 125 \text{ Ehp} \times 0.86 \times 0.86 \\ &= 93 \text{ Dbhp} \end{aligned}$$

The 86% rule can be used in other ways also. For example, if the drawbar horsepower is known, the pto and engine horsepower can be estimated.

Problem: What is the estimated pto horsepower if the tractor produces 50.0 horsepower at the drawbar?

Solution: From the discussion of the 86% rule, we know that the pto horsepower will be larger than the drawbar. Therefore:

$$\text{ptohp} = \frac{\text{Dbhp}}{0.86}$$

$$= \frac{50.0\ \text{Dbhp}}{0.86}$$

$$= 58\ \text{ptohp}$$

DERATING POWER UNITS

Manufacturers of engines intended for stationary use, for example, to power a pump or a generator, usually can supply the purchaser of an engine with a performance curve for the engine (see Figure 7.2).

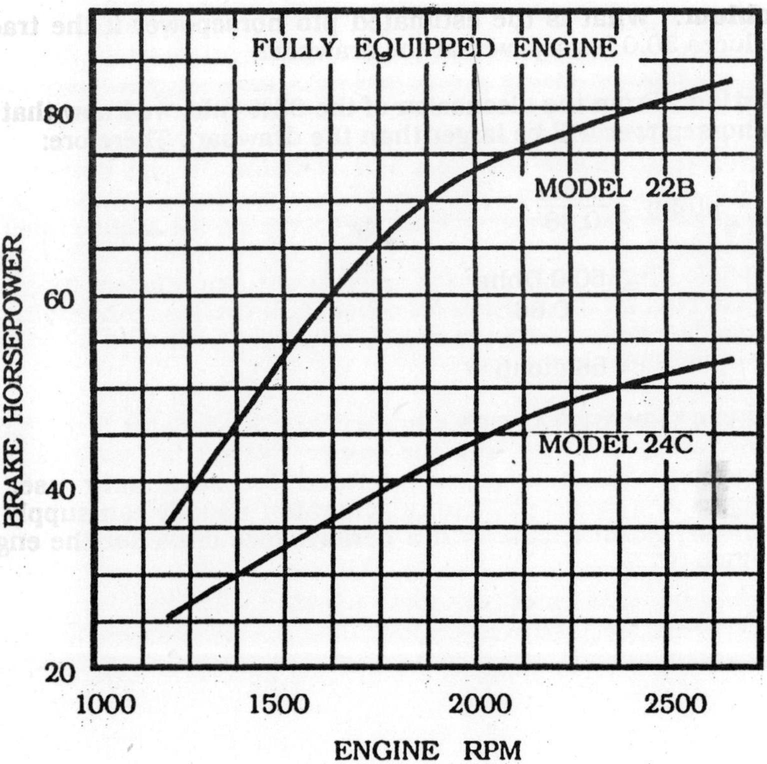

Figure 7.2. Engine performance curve.

The performance curve will show the rated horsepower for an engine for different engine speeds ranging from the minimum speed recommended for a load to the maximum. However, the usable horsepower is less than the rated horsepower if one of several conditions exists, as explained below. The adjustment from rated horsepower to usable horsepower is called derating. Failure to derate an engine could shorten the life of the engine.

The factors used for derating depend on the engine type and the operating environment. Spark ignition and diesel engines are derated to allow for the effect of accessories, temperature, altitude, and type of service.

ACCESSORIES

If the horsepower rating is reported for a *basic engine*, sometimes called the net horsepower rating, it was tested with all accessories removed. These accessories include the air cleaner, muffler, generator, governor, and fan and radiator. If the horsepower rating is for a *fully equipped engine*, sometimes called a gross horsepower rating, these accessories were on the engine when it was tested.

If basic engine horsepower is reported, the engine must be derated *10%* for all accessories other than the fan. An additional *5%* must be deducted if the engine will have a fan and a radiator instead of a heat exchanger.

Problem: How much usable horsepower is available if the basic engine rating is 75 hp, and the engine will use fan and radiator cooling?

Solution: Derating 10% for the accessories and 5% for the fan:

$$\text{hp} = 75 \text{ hp} \times \left(1.0 - (0.10 + 0.05)\right)$$

$$= 75 \text{ hp} \times 0.85$$

$$= 64 \text{ hp}$$

TEMPERATURE

The ambient temperature must be considered because as the temperature of the air that the engine breathes increases, the density decreases, and there is less oxygen per cubic foot of air. The decrease in oxygen decreases the efficiency of the engine. For spark ignition engines the horsepower rating must be reduced 1% for each 10°F ambient temperature rise above 85°F. For diesel engines the adjustment is 1% for each 5°F above 85°F.

Problem: How much usable horsepower will a 65 Bhp spark ignition engine produce if it will be operating in 100°F air temperature?

Solution: Using the recommended derating for temperature:

$$hp = 65\ hp \times \left(1.0 - \left(0.01 \times \frac{100\ ^{\circ}F - 85\ ^{\circ}F}{10\ ^{\circ}F}\right)\right)$$

$$= 65\ hp \times 0.99$$

$$= 64\ hp$$

ALTITUDE

As the altitude increases, the barometric pressure decreases. This reduction in pressure reduces the efficiency of naturally aspirated engines because as the elevation of the engine increases, the pressure difference is less between the air pressure inside the cylinder, on the intake stroke, and the atmospheric pressure. Decreasing the pressure difference decreases the amount of air that will flow into the engine on the intake stroke.

Altitude is not a problem for engines with turbochargers or superchargers because they increase the intake system pressure. For nonturbocharged spark ignition and diesel engines the horsepower rating must be adjusted (reduced) by 3% for each 1000 feet of elevation above 500 feet.

Problem: What is the usable horsepower rating for a 225-hp diesel engine operating at an elevation of 4500 feet?

Solution: Using the derating recommendation for altitude:

$$hp = 225\ hp \times \left(1 - \left(0.03 \times \left(\frac{4500\ ft - 500\ ft}{1000\ ft}\right)\right)\right)$$

$$= 225\ hp \times 0.88$$

$$= 198\ hp$$

TYPE OF SERVICE

The type of engine service is determined by the load--intermittent or continuous. An intermittent load on an engine is a load that varies in torque and speed; for example, tractors in tillage operations are subject to intermittent loads. Continuous loads provide little variation in the torque and speed demands placed on the engine; irrigation pumps are an example of a continuous load. Some manufacturers may indicate the type of service for the rated horsepower. If not, the engine should be derated for the type of service. Type of service derating must be completed *after* the adjustments have been completed for accessories, temperature, and altitude (A, T, & A). The available power must be reduced by 10% for intermittent loads and 20% for continuous loads.

Problem: What is the usable horsepower for an engine that has been derated for accessories, temperature, and altitude to 115.3 hp if it will be used for continuous duty?

Solution: Derating for continuous duty:

$$\text{hp} = 115.3 \text{ hp} \times \frac{100\% - 20\%}{100}$$

$$= 115.3 \text{ hp} \times .80$$

$$= 92 \text{ hp}$$

From this discussion it is evident an important difference may exist between rated horsepower and usable horsepower for stationary engines. Also note that if a tractor is being used for stationary power for an extended period of time, it should be derated. When derating a tractor, remember that the pto horsepower will be equal to that of a fully equipped engine.

TRACTOR TESTING

Early tractors were designed to deliver power in three ways: by belt pulley, drawbar, and power take-off. On newer tractors the belt pulley has been eliminated. One problem the owner/manager has faced since the first tractor was designed is lack of information on the power ratings of tractors. As a rule, tractor manufacturers do not advertise the drawbar or pto ratings of their tractors; instead many use brake horsepower or engine horsepower. If engine horsepower is used, it could be a theoretical horsepower rating for the engine.

In 1918, the Nebraska legislature passed a law that established the Nebraska Tractor Test Station. This law mandated that a typical model of tractor must be tested before it could be sold within the state of Nebraska, and that the manufacturer must maintain a parts supply depot within the state. This testing station has provided the only independent evaluation of tractors in the United States.

As time passed and a large percentage of tractor manufacturing moved outside the United States, a change was needed. Two changes have occurred: the Nebraska Law was changed to allow tractors to be sold in Nebraska with either a Nebraska test or an Organisation for Economic Cooperation and Development (OECD) test, and the Nebraska test was changed to match the standards established by the Society of Automotive Engineers (SAE) and the American Society of Agricultural Engineers (ASAE). Currently the Nebraska Tractor Test Station is qualified to conduct either test at the request of the tractor manufacturer. A full review of both testing standards is not possible in this text; instead the following is a discussion of the general principles of testing and the two test methods. Individual reports and additional information can be obtained from the testing stations.[1,2]

PRINCIPLES OF TESTING

Because of the important role tractors play in agricultural production, accurate information is a must for efficient management of the modern farm and ranch. Any information is usable, but the main objective of testing is to provide standardized results so that comparisons can be made between different models and different years. The primary purpose of tractor testing standards is to establish the test conditions and the rules of behavior for the manufacturer and the testing station.

It should be evident that engines are complex mechanisms with many different factors that influence the power produced and fuel efficiency. Because of the widespread use of the data, manufacturers want to be sure they get the best possible results. To provide standardized information, the testing environment must be consistent for every test, day after day, year after year, or changes must be thoroughly investigated so that the appropriate adjustments in the results can be made. In both tests, these factors are called test conditions.

---

[1] *OECD Standard Codes for the Official Testing of Agricultural Tractors*, Organisation for Economic Cooperation and Development, 1988. 2, rue Andre-Pascal, 75775 Paris CEDEX 16, France.

[2] Nebraska Test Station, Agricultural Engineering Department, University of Nebraska--Lincoln, Lincoln, Nebraska 68583.

Test conditions include the rules for the selection of the tractor and the control and/or recording of environmental conditions. During the pto test, air temperature, barometric pressure, fuel type, fuel temperature, fuel measurement, lubricants, and accessory equipment on the tractor must be either controlled or recorded to ensure that they are within acceptable limits. Strict control of these factors is important because many tests measure the maximum horsepower of the tractor. Each one of these factors will influence the horsepower produced.

For the drawbar test all of the environmental factors in the pto test must be accounted for, plus those that affect traction. The latter include tractor ballast, tires, and testing surface. The ballast, tires, and testing surface are critical because the amount of pull a tractor can produce at the drawbar is greatly influenced by the amount of traction.

Both the NTT station and the OECD station have strict standards on how all these factors are controlled and/or recorded.

In addition to the test conditions, the testing codes must establish rules governing such things as breakdowns, repeating tests, testing accessory systems such as hydraulic systems, safety standards, noise standards, and the method of reporting and publishing the results.

PRACTICE PROBLEMS

1. Determine the pto horsepower being developed if the dynamometer has a 24.0 inch lever arm and the tractor produces 23.0 pounds of force while operating at 2000 rpm.
   Answer: 17.5 hp
2. Determine the amount of drawbar horsepower being produced if the tractor is producing 2300 pounds of pull while traveling at 4.50 miles per hour.
   Answer: 27.6 hp
3. What is the usable power for a spark ignition basic engine rated at 115.5 horsepower that will be operated at an elevation of 3000 feet at 90°F air temperature, will use a radiator and a fan, and will operate at continuous duty?
   Answer: 72 hp
4. What is the usable power for the Model 24C diesel engine in Figure 7.2 operating at 2250 rpm and at an elevation of 2500.0 feet at 100°F temperature, with a fan and a radiator and intermittent duty?
   Answer: 34 hp

8
Equipment Efficiency and Capacity

OBJECTIVES

1. Understand the concept of efficiency and be able to apply it to agricultural operations.
2. Understand the concept of capacity and be able to apply it to agricultural machines.
3. Be able to calculate effective field capacity.
4. Be able to calculate the throughput capacity of agricultural machines.

INTRODUCTION

In this chapter we will be concerned with the efficiency and the capacity of machines. Efficiency is a determination of how well something is done. In referring to machinery, it is an evaluation of how well machines do the tasks that they are designed to perform. Capacity is a measurement of the amount of performance that has occurred.

EFFICIENCY

In this chapter we will use the concept of efficiency to evaluate how well a machine performs its designed task in terms of quantity and/or quality of performance. Owners and managers of farm enterprises are deeply concerned with efficient operation of equipment and other resources because inefficient operation leads to greater operating expenses and reduced profits.

In the most general terms, efficiency can be expressed as:

$$\text{Efficiency (E)} = \frac{\text{Output}}{\text{Input}} \qquad (8\text{-}1)$$

or, efficiency is the ratio of what we get out of something relative to what we put in. Because efficiency is a ratio of things having the same units, the units cancel. The results usually are multiplied by 100 and expressed as a percentage. If the output is 10 units (pounds, hours, etc.) and the input 10 units, the efficiency is:

$$\%E = \frac{\text{Output}}{\text{Input}} \times 100$$

$$= \frac{10 \text{ units}}{10 \text{ units}} \times 100$$

$$= 100\%$$

Or, if the output is 5 units and the input 10 units, the efficiency is:

$$\%E = \frac{\text{Output}}{\text{Input}} \times 100$$

$$= \frac{5 \text{ units}}{10 \text{ units}} \times 100$$

$$= 50\%$$

MECHANICAL EFFICIENCY

Mechanical efficiency has to do with how well machines convert energy from one form to another. For example, an engine converts the chemical or heat energy in fuel into mechanical power, torque, and rotation of the engine crankshaft. All the energy in fuel is not converted to torque and shaft rotation (the majority of the heat produced escapes through the radiator and out the exhaust); therefore, engines are not 100% efficient. A typical gasoline engine is about 35% efficient; a diesel engine is slightly better. An electric motor converts electrical energy into shaft rotation and torque with an efficiency of 95 to 98%.

PERFORMANCE EFFICIENCY

Performance efficiency refers to the *quality* of work done by a machine. For a harvesting machine, performance efficiency is a measure of the *actual* performance of the machine compared to the *desired* performance. For example, if the machine were a combine, we could measure the bushels of grain harvested compared to the total bushels of grain in the field. Combines also could be evaluated according to the amount of damaged grain. Other harvesting machines could be evaluated on the basis of the amount of bruising of fruit or on the number of cracked shells.

Problem: What is the performance efficiency (percent) in lost grain for the combine shown in Figure 8.1?

Solution: Figure 8.1 represents the results of measuring the losses from a combine. Before explaining the procedure of evaluating combine losses, we will review the basic principles of combine operation.

A combine can lose grain in three different ways: the gathering unit can shatter grain from the head or drop heads, the threshing unit can fail to remove grain from the head as it passes through the machine, and the separating and cleaning units can fail to separate the grain from the material other than grain (MOG).

Evaluating combine losses is a multiple-step problem. What we want to know is the efficiency of the combine expressed as the percent of grain loss. The first step in evaluating the performance of a combine is to determine if a problem actually exists. This is done by determining total losses.

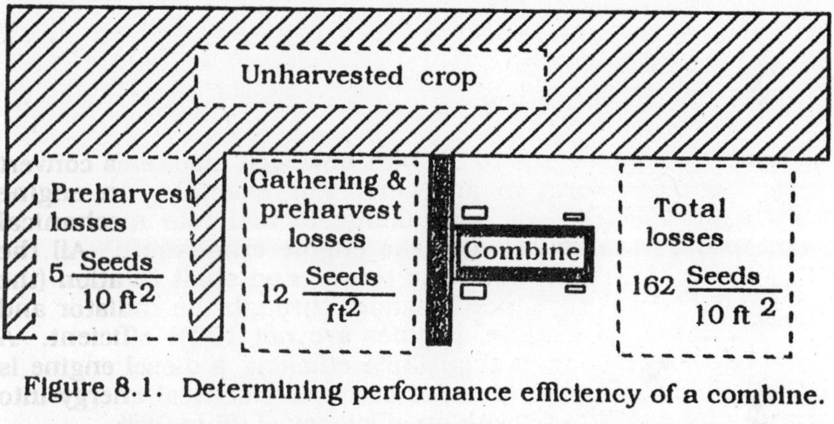

Figure 8.1. Determining performance efficiency of a combine.

To determine total losses, a known area is marked out, and grain is counted on the ground behind the combine. Losses at this point include grain on the ground before the combine started (preharvest losses) and grain loss by the combine (machine losses). For most cereal grains, losses are determined by counting the number of grains in a known area, for example, 10 or 100 square feet. This will provide data with units of seeds per area.

Next, because the amount of grain in the field usually is measured in units of bushels per acre, the grain count is converted into bushels per acre. In the example illustrated in Figure 8.1, 162 seeds of wheat were counted in a 10-square foot area behind the machine.

Table 8-1. Approximate number of kernels per square foot to equal one bushel per acre.

Crop	Seeds per square foot
Barley	13 -- 15
Beans-Red Kidney	1.2 -- 1.6
Beans-White	3 --4
Oats	10 -- 12
Rice	29 -- 30
Rye	21 -- 24
Sorghum	19 -- 22
Soybeans	4 -- 5
Wheat	18 -- 20
Corn	1 ear/435 ft^2 2 kernels/ft^2

By referring to Table 8-1 we can convert the total losses from seeds per 10 square feet to bushels per acre. Using 20 seeds per square foot equals one bushel per acre, and the units cancellation method:

$$\frac{bu}{ac} = \frac{162 \text{ seeds}}{10 \text{ ft}^2} \times \frac{1 \frac{bu}{ac}}{\frac{20 \text{ seeds}}{1 \text{ ft}^2}}$$

$$= 0.81 \frac{bu}{ac}$$

Now we must decide if this is an acceptable level of loss for the machine. It is generally accepted that an expert operator should be able to keep losses to 1%, but the typical operator will lose about 3%. To determine the percentage of loss we must know what the crop is yielding (bu/ac). For this example we will assume that the wheat is yielding 30 bu/ac. The total loss percentage (L_t%) is:

$$L_t\% = \frac{0.81\,\frac{bu}{ac}}{30\,\frac{bu}{ac}} \times 100$$

$$= 2.7\%$$

This loss would be acceptable for the average operator, but for this example we will assume that the operator is experienced.

At this point it is important to remember that total loss is a combination of machine loss and preharvest loss. If the total loss is unacceptable, we must determine if the machine is the cause of the loss, or if the grain is already on the ground as preharvest loss. Preharvest loss is measured by counting the grain on the ground in the standing crop that has not been harvested. In Figure 8.1 we note that preharvest losses are 5 seeds per 10 square feet. Therefore, the machine loss is:

$$\text{Machine loss } (L_m) = \text{Total loss } (L_t) - \text{Preharvest loss } (L_p) \quad (8\text{-}2)$$

$$= \frac{162 \text{ seeds}}{10 \text{ ft}^2} - \frac{5 \text{ seeds}}{10 \text{ ft}^2}$$

$$= \frac{157 \text{ seeds}}{10 \text{ ft}^2}$$

$$= 16 \frac{\text{seeds}}{\text{ft}^2}$$

Converting this value to bushels per acre:

$$L_m\left(\frac{bu}{ac}\right) = 16\frac{\text{seeds}}{\text{ft}^2} \times \frac{1\,\frac{bu}{ac}}{\frac{20 \text{ seeds}}{1 \text{ ft}^2}} = 0.80\frac{bu}{ac}$$

Converting this to a percent:

$$L_m\% = \frac{0.80\,\frac{bu}{ac}}{30\,\frac{bu}{ac}} \times 100 = 2.7\%$$

This indicates that the machine loss is equal to the total loss, 2.7%. This does not seem right unless we consider the preharvest loss as a percentage:

$$L_p\% = \frac{0.025 \frac{bu}{ac}}{30 \frac{bu}{ac}} = 0.08\%$$

The preharvest loss percentage is less than 1/10 of one percent. This is such a small portion of the overall loss that it can be ignored.

It is now safe to predict that the excessive losses are caused by the machine. The total loss is unacceptable (0.81 bu/ac = 2.7%) and the preharvest loss is small (0.025 bu/ac = 0.08%); so the majority of the losses are caused by the machine (2.7% - 0.08% = 2.62%). When this occurs, it is necessary to determine which component of the machine is the source of the loss.

The first step is to check the gathering unit. The performance of the gathering unit (header) is checked by counting the seeds on the ground between the header and the uncut crop. Figure 8.1 shows that the losses in this area are 12 seeds per 10.0 square feet. (Remember that this also includes the preharvest losses.) The gathering unit (L_g) losses are determined by subtracting the preharvest loss from seeds counted in the test area between the header and the uncut crop. Refer to Figure 8.1:

$$L_g = \frac{12 \text{ seeds}}{10.0 \text{ ft}^2} - \frac{5 \text{ seeds}}{10.0 \text{ ft}^2}$$

$$= \frac{7 \text{ seeds}}{10 \text{ ft}^2}$$

$$= 0.7 \frac{\text{seeds}}{\text{ft}^2}$$

Converting this value to bushels per acre:

$$\frac{bu}{ac} = 0.7\frac{seeds}{ft^2} \times \frac{1\frac{bu}{ac}}{\frac{20\ seeds}{1\ ft^2}}$$

$$= 0.04\frac{bu}{ac}$$

or as a percent:

$$\frac{0.04\frac{bu}{ac}}{30\frac{bu}{ac}} \times 100 = 0.13\%$$

This shows that the gathering unit losses are 0.13%, and are a very small part of the total machine losses.

If the gathering unit losses are subtracted from the total machine losses (16 seeds/ft^2 - 0.7 seeds/ft^2), what remains (15.3 seeds/ft^2) is the losses caused by the threshing and separating units. The threshing and separating losses are:

$$L_{t\&s}(\%) = \left(\frac{15.3\ seeds}{ft^2} \times \frac{1\frac{bu}{ac}}{20\frac{seed}{ft^2}} \times \frac{1}{30\frac{bu}{ac}}\right) \times 100$$

$$= 2.6\%$$

If the preharvest loss is insignificant, and the gathering unit losses are below 0.2%, then it is obvious that the excessive machine loss is caused by incorrect operation of the threshing and separating units.

Threshing losses are represented by heads or cobs on the ground behind the machine with grain still attached. Cleaning and separating losses are represented by grain on the ground behind the machine that is not pre-harvest or gathering unit loss. Cleaning and separating losses can be determined by subtraction:

$$L_{c\&S} = L_t - L_p - L_g - L_{th} \qquad (8\text{-}3)$$

where:

$L_{c\&s}$ = Cleaning and separating losses
L_t = Total losses
L_p = Pre-harvest losses
L_g = Gathering unit losses
L_{th} = Threshing losses

FIELD EFFICIENCY

Field efficiency is a comparison of the amount of "work" (volume of activity, not F x D) done by a machine compared to what it should be capable of doing. A machine is capable of covering ground at a rate determined by the width of the machine and the speed of travel. If the machine is operated with a consistent width and travels at a constant speed, it will operate at 100% field efficiency. A machine is capable of operating at 100% field efficiency for short periods of time, but as soon as the speed changes (slow down for turns, etc.), or the width changes (overlap width of the machine to prevent skips), it is operating at less than 100% efficiency. Field efficiencies less than 100% are caused by lost time (unproductive time) and by not using the full working width of the machine. Typical field efficiencies for common machines can be found in Appendix II. This concept is illustrated in more detail in the next section, on capacity.

CAPACITY

The term capacity is used to evaluate the productivity of a machine. In agriculture, two types of capacity are commonly used, *field capacity* and *throughput capacity*. Field capacity is used to evaluate the productivity of machines used to work the soil, such as plows, cultivators, and drills. Throughput capacity is used to describe machines that handle or process a product, such as grain augers, balers, forage harvesters, and combines.

An additional concept relating to both types of capacity is the difference between theoretical and actual productivity. If a tillage machine operates at 100% efficiency, it is operating at 100% capacity. This is called the *theoretical field capacity*.

$$\text{Theoretical field capacity } (C_T) = \frac{S \times W}{8.25} \qquad (8\text{-}4)$$

where:

C_t = Theoretical field capacity $\left(\frac{ac}{hr}\right)$

S = Speed of travel $\left(\frac{mi}{hr}\right)$

W = Width of the machine (ft)

8.25 = Units conversion constant $\left(43{,}560\,\frac{ft^2}{ac}\right) \div \left(5280\,\frac{ft}{mi}\right)$

This equation can be used as long as the speed and the width of the machine are entered with the correct units.

Problem: Determine the theoretical capacity for a machine that travels at 5.0 mph and has an operating width of 20 feet.

Solution: Using Equation (8-4):

$$C_T = \frac{S \times W}{8.25}$$

$$= \frac{5.0 \times 20}{8.25}$$

$$= 12\,\frac{ac}{hr}$$

If this machine travels at a constant speed and with a constant effective width, it has a capacity of 12 ac/hr.

Effective field capacity is the amount of productivity that actually occurred. Loss in productivity is caused by less than 100% efficiency in the operation. Lost capacity is an important concern for the machine operator and/or manager because it represents lost revenues or resources. Usually lost capacity is caused by lost time, time not operating, and operating the machine with less than the maximum working width. Common causes of lost capacity include:

1. Mechanical breakdowns.
2. Taking time to adjust the machine.
3. Stopping to fill seed hoppers, spray tanks, etc.
4. Failure to use the full width of the machine.
5. Slowing down to turn at the end of the row or crossing water ways, etc.
6. Operator rest stops.

The common equation for effective field capacity is:

$$C_E = \frac{S \times W \times E_f}{8.25} \qquad (8\text{-}5)$$

where:

C_E = Effective field capacity (ac/hr)
S = Average speed of travel (mph)
W = Effective width of the machine (ft)
E_f = Field efficiency (decimal form)

Problem: Assume that the operator in the previous problem averages 0.75 hour of lost time per 10.0-hour day. What is the effective field capacity?

Solution: The first step is to use Equation (8-1) to determine the efficiency:

$$E = \frac{\text{Output}}{\text{Input}} \times 100$$

$$= \frac{10.0 \text{ hr} - 0.75 \text{ hr}}{10 \text{ hr}} \times 100$$

$$= 92.5\%$$

The second step is to use Equation (8-5) to determine the effective capacity:

$$C_E = \frac{S \times W \times E_f}{8.25}$$

$$= \frac{5.0 \times 20.0 \times 0.925}{8.25}$$

$$= \frac{93}{8.25}$$

$$= 11.0 \frac{ac}{hr}$$

Now the effects of lost productivity are apparent. The theoretical capacity is 12 ac/hr, but because of lost time, the effective capacity is 11 ac/hr.

The concept of effective capacity also can be used to determine the amount of time it would take a machine to cover a field.

Problem: How many hours will it take to cultivate 200 acres with a field cultivator that is 24 feet wide?

Solution: The first step in this problem is to determine the effective capacity of the field cultivator. Once that is known, we can determine the hours it will take to cover the field.

Compare the information presented in the problem with Equation (8-5) and notice that two pieces of information are missing, the speed and the field efficiency. If the actual speed and the field efficiency are unknown, the typical values found in Appendix II can be used.

In this case we will use the typical values. In Appendix II the typical field efficiency for a field cultivator is 85%, and the typical speed is 5.5 mph. With these values, the problem can be solved:

$$C_E = \frac{S \times W \times E_f}{8.25}$$

$$= \frac{5.5 \frac{mi}{hr} \times 24 \text{ ft} \times 0.85}{8.25}$$

$$= \frac{120}{8.25}$$

$$= 14 \frac{ac}{hr}$$

Now that we know the effective field capacity for the field cultivator, we can determine the amount of time that it will take to cultivate the field using units cancellation:

$$hr = \frac{1 \text{ hr}}{14 \text{ ac}} \times 200 \text{ ac}$$

$$= 14 \text{ hr}$$

If the average field speed is 5.5 mph and the operator can maintain an 85% field efficiency, it will take 13 hours to cultivate the 200 acre field.

THROUGHPUT

The concepts of theoretical and effective capacity also are applicable to throughput capacity. Throughput is based on time, but because throughput usually refers to the flow of material through a machine, the units may be different from those used above. For example, if we were evaluating the performance of a hay baler, we could use units of bales per hour or tons per hour.

Problem: What would the throughput efficiency be of a new baler if it baled 150 tons in one week while operating an average of 6 hours per day?

Solution: With the information given, several different units could be used for the output. These include tons/week, tons/day, or bales/day. The "correct" units are the ones that match the input units. For this example, assume that the manufacturer advertises that the baler has a capacity of 6 tons/hr. This means we need to determine the output (effective throughput) in units of ton/hr.

$$\frac{\text{ton}}{\text{hr}} = \frac{150 \text{ tons}}{\text{week}} \times \frac{1 \text{ week}}{5 \text{ day}} \times \frac{1 \text{ day}}{6 \text{ hr}}$$

$$= \frac{150}{30}$$

$$= 5 \frac{\text{ton}}{\text{hr}}$$

Now we can determine the throughput efficiency for baling. The efficiency is:

$$E = \frac{\text{Output}}{\text{Input}} \times 100$$

$$= \frac{5 \frac{\text{ton}}{\text{hr}}}{6 \frac{\text{ton}}{\text{hr}}} \times 100$$

$$= 83\%$$

If the advertised throughput of the baler is a reasonable value, then this operation is only 83% efficient in baling hay.

The throughput of a baler also can be evaluated in units of bales per hour (bales/hr). To determine this value we need several values, including the weight of the hay (lb/bale) and two units conversion values.

Problem: If each bale weighs 1200 lb, what is the effective throughput in bales per hour?

$$\frac{\text{bales}}{\text{hr}} = \frac{150 \text{ ton}}{\text{week}} \times \frac{1 \text{ week}}{30 \text{ hr}} \times \frac{2000 \text{ lb}}{\text{ton}} \times \frac{1 \text{ bale}}{1200 \text{ lb}}$$

$$= \frac{3.0 \times 10^5}{3.6 \times 10^4}$$

$$= 8.3 \frac{\text{bales}}{\text{hr}}$$

Obviously, throughput can be expressed in many different ways depending on the values being compared. Remember that efficiency is a ratio--both values must have the same units. In addition, these examples illustrate the usefulness of units cancellation for solving problems of this type.

PRACTICE PROBLEMS

1. What is the work efficiency of an employee who behaves in the following manner (assuming an expected workday from 8:00 to 5:00 with two 15-minute breaks and a one-hour noon break)?

   Arrive at work: 8:02
   Morning break: 10:00 to 10:20
   Lunch hour: 11:58 to 1:05
   Afternoon break: 2:58 to 3:17
   Go home: 4:55

   Answer: 95%
2. During an evaluation of your lawn care business you discover that it takes one of your employees 2.5 hours to mow a 15,000-square-foot lawn. If the worker uses a 22-inch mower and walks at 2.5 miles per hour, what is the worker's mowing efficiency?
   Answer: 25%
3. Refer to Table 8-2, which contains the results of a performance evaluation for a combine operating in oats yielding 50 bushels per acre, and answer the following questions.

Table 8-2. Losses for Harvesting Oats.

Losses	Seeds/ft^2	bu/ac
Total	24	
Preharvest	10	
Gathering	2	

A. What is the percent of loss for the combine?
B. How many bushels per acre have been lost before the combine starts harvesting the field?
C. What percent of the machine loss is caused by the threshing, separating, and cleaning components of the combine?
Answers:
A. 3.0%; B. 1 bu/ac; C. 2.4%;

4. What is the theoretical capacity of a 45.0 foot field cultivator if it is operated at 6.75 miles per hour?
Answer: 36.8 ac/hr
5. What is the effective capacity for the field cultivator in problem 4 if the driver operates at typical efficiency?
Answer: 31.3 ac/hr
6. What is the throughput capacity (bu/hr) for a combine with a 24-foot header if it is operating at typical efficiency and at 6.50 miles per hour in wheat producing 50 bushels per acre?
Answer: 662 bu/hr

9
Machinery Calibration

OBJECTIVES

1. Understand the general principles of calibration.
2. Be able to calibrate a broadcast type fertilizer applicator.
3. Be able to calibrate a grain drill.
4. Be able to calibrate a row crop planter.
5. Be able to calibrate a field sprayer.
6. Be able to prepare the proper mix of chemicals and water for a sprayer.

INTRODUCTION

One important role of agricultural machinery is the dispensing of materials such as seeds, fertilizers, and sprays. If a machine fails to dispense the material at the desired rate and pattern, economic losses may occur. An insufficient amount of material will not produce the desired results, and excessive amounts are a lost resource that may result in crop damage and/or contribute to contamination of the environment.

Incorrect application of materials can have several causes. Manufacturers supply calibration charts or tables with each machine, but they can be lost or damaged, leaving the operator with no or incomplete information. A machine may have been damaged or modified in some way that renders the calibration chart or table inaccurate. Variations in the weight, size, moisture content, and cleanliness of the seed used or in the physical condition (lumpiness, flowability) of the fertilizer or chemical granules used can all contribute to an actual dispensing rate that varies considerably from the machine setting. The economic penalties and potential environmental damage from incorrect application of materials warrant the time and effort required to ensure that the machine is dispensing the desired amount.

Checking the application rate and patterns of dispersal of machines is called *calibration*. Although the exact procedure used to calibrate machines and other measuring devices varies from one situation to another, this chapter will illustrate the calibration of four common agricultural material dispensing machines.

PRINCIPLES OF CALIBRATION

All of the different techniques used to calibrate agricultural machines are based on two principles: (1) all dispensing machines meter (control the rate of) the flow of material at a predetermined rate selected by the operator, and (2) calibration occurs by collecting material dispensed by the machine in units of a *volume or weight per unit area.* For example, to calibrate a row crop planter it is necessary to determine the seeds per acre that the planter is planting. To calibrate a sprayer, the application rate is determined in units of gallons per acre. The unit of area used during calibration usually will be in square feet or a fraction of an acre. It is important to remember that the larger the area used, the greater the accuracy of the calibration procedure.

CALIBRATING FERTILIZER APPLICATORS

Fertilizers, which are mainstays of modern agriculture, are applied in liquid, gaseous, or granular form. In this section we will discuss the calibration of granular applicators.

Granular applicators will be one of two designs, broadcast or gravity flow. The procedures for their calibration are easily understood if we know how the granular applicators work; so the following section reviews the mechanisms used in granular applicators.

Broadcast spreaders consist of a hopper that holds the material, a metering mechanism, and a spreading mechanism. Metering usually is accomplished through the use of a variable-speed chain auger and an adjustable opening. The chain auger generally is operated by a drive train powered by one of the wheels of the spreader. Because the chain auger is driven by a ground wheel, the amount of material dispensed changes as the speed of the spreader changes. The application rate of the material usually is set by changing the speed ratio of the drive train that powers the metering device and/or changing the size of the opening. The process of using a variable opening for metering is called *bulk metering.* The material usually is spread as it drops onto one or more rotating disks, which sling it out in a wide pattern either behind or in front of the spreader.

Gravity flow applicators also use a hopper, but in this type of applicator the hopper extends across the width of the machine. The material is dispensed through adjustable openings along the bottom of the hopper. These spreaders usually use an agitator along the bottom to prevent the material from bridging across the hopper and to break up lumps, thus improving the uniformity of flow. The material flows through the openings and onto the soil surface.

Both types of spreaders may be calibrated either stationary or mobile. In both methods the application rate (lb/ac) is equal to the pounds of material collected per revolution of the drive wheel, divided by the area covered (width x distance) per revolution of the drive wheel. Or, the application rate is:

$$\frac{lb}{ac} = \frac{\frac{lb}{rev}}{\frac{ac}{rev}} \qquad (9\text{-}1)$$

or expressed in the units cancellation method:

$$\frac{lb}{ac} = \frac{lb}{rev} \times \frac{rev}{ac}$$

If checked while stationary, the drive wheel for the metering mechanism is elevated and rotated a number of turns as the material is being caught. The weight of the material collected divided by the number of turns equals the pounds per revolution. The acres per revolution are determined by multiplying the circumference of the drive wheel by the number of turns and the effective width of the spreader, and then converting this area to acres, or:

$$\frac{ac}{rev} = \frac{\frac{2\pi r}{1\ rev} \times W}{43{,}560\,\frac{ft^2}{ac}} \qquad (9\text{-}2)$$

where:

π = 3.14
r = Effective radius of drive wheel (ft)
W = Effective width of the spreader (ft)
43,560 = Number of square feet per acre

Combining the unchanging units to form a constant gives:

$$\frac{ac}{rev} = \frac{2\pi}{43{,}560} \times r \times W$$

$$= (1.442 \times 10^{-4}) \times r \times W$$

Therefore, when a spreader is calibrated in a stationary position, the pounds per acre can be determined by:

$$\frac{lb}{ac} = \frac{lb\ collected}{(1.442 \times 10^{-4}) \times r \times W \times n} \quad (9\text{-}3)$$

where:

n = Number of revolutions of the drive wheel
r = Effective radius of the drive wheel (ft)
W = Effective width of the broadcast (ft)

Problem: You wish to apply 1400 lb/ac of fertilizer with your neighbor's broadcast applicator. The machine is set according to the manufacturer's chart, and during a stationary calibration of the applicator 100.0 pounds of fertilizer were collected as the drive wheel was turned 15 revolutions. If the effective diameter of the drive wheel is 21.0 inches and the effective width of the spreader is 30.0 feet, is the application rate correct?

Solution: Using Equation (9-3):

$$\frac{lb}{ac} = \frac{lb\ collected}{(1.442 \times 10^{-4}) \times r \times W \times n}$$

$$= \frac{100.0\ lb}{\left(1.442 \times 10^{-4}\right) \times \left(\frac{\frac{21.0\ in}{2}}{1\ rev} \times \frac{1\ ft}{12\ in}\right) \times 30.0\ ft \times 15\ rev}$$

$$= \frac{100}{0.05677}$$

$$= 1761.222\frac{lb}{ac} \text{ or } 1760\frac{lb}{ac}$$

Note that the radius of the wheel is multiplied by the units conversion of 1 foot equals 12 inches to convert the units to feet.

In this problem the spreader is applying 360 lb/ac more than the desired amount. Is this an acceptable level of accuracy? Should the spreader metering unit be adjusted and rechecked? These are the questions the operator must answer. In this example the amount of error was 26% [(360 lb/1400 lb) x 100]. This is an excessive amount of error for this type of fertilizer spreader.

The one major disadvantage of the stationary method of calibrating broadcast applicators is the practical problem of collecting the fertilizer during the calibration process (100 pounds in this example). The quantity of material that must be collected will be greater if the desired application rate (lb/ac) is increased, or if the number of revolutions is increased. The primary advantage of this method is that it can be performed when it is impossible to have the applicator in the field, for instance, because of muddy ground or inclement weather.

The alternative is to complete a mobile calibration. This can be accomplished in two ways. In the first method, collectors (flat pans or pieces of plastic or tarp) are randomly placed in the distribution path of the spreader. After the spreader is driven over the collectors, the material is weighed. The actual application rate (lb/ac) can be computed by dividing the amount of material collected, by the area of the collectors, and then converting the answer from pounds per square foot to pounds per acre.

$$\frac{\text{lb}}{\text{ac}} = \frac{\text{material collected (lb)}}{\text{area (ac)}} \qquad (9\text{-}4)$$

Problem: What is the application rate of a spreader if 23.5 pounds of material is collected on two tarps, each measuring 10.0 ft x 12.0 ft?

Solution: Using Equation (9-4):

$$\frac{\text{lb}}{\text{ac}} = \frac{23.5 \text{ lb}}{2 \times \left(\dfrac{10.0 \text{ ft} \times 12.0 \text{ ft}}{43{,}560 \dfrac{\text{ft}^2}{\text{ac}}} \right)}$$

$$= \frac{23.5 \text{ lb}}{5.51 \times 10^{-3} \text{ ac}}$$

$$= 4260 \frac{\text{lb}}{\text{ac}}$$

This method does not require a spreader wheel to be elevated, but you must be able to drive the spreader in the field or over an area as wide as the dispersal pattern. If the spreader is dispensing an excessive amount of material, the test area will be over fertilized.

The second mobile method can be used if it is certain that the spreader is reasonably accurate. First, weigh the spreader, and then drive it over a measured area. Then reweigh the spreader. The difference between the before and after weights is the amount of material applied. The area is already known, so it is easy to find the application rate using Equation (9-4).

Gravity flow fertilizer spreaders can be calibrated by using any of these methods. Because of the difficulty in collecting the material for a mobile calibration, the stationary method usually is used.

CALIBRATING GRAIN DRILLS

Grain drills also use bulk metering, but they use a metering device for each row of seeds planted (6-10 inches apart). Equation (9-3) can be used if the drill is calibrated stationary, or Equation (9-4) can be used if the drill is calibrated in the field. The units cancellation method can be used in either situation.

The calibration of grain drills is more critical than the calibration of fertilizer spreaders because the drills are dispensing seeds. A small error can have a great impact on the yield. In addition, uniformity of dispensing is more important for drills. Grain drills usually are calibrated by attaching a container to each metering unit. The drill then is driven a measured distance, or the drive wheel is turned for a selected number of revolutions.

Problem: An 18-6 (18 metering units spaced 6 inches apart) drill is set to apply 1.0 bu/ac of wheat. The amounts of seed collected during calibration are shown in Table 9-1. If the diameter of the drive wheel is 26 inches, and the drive wheel was turned 25 revolutions, is the drill planting the correct amount of seed (bu/ac)? (*Note*: Because each end wheel of a grain drill powers half of the metering units, only nine units are shown.)

Table 9-1. Pounds of wheat collected from nine grain drill metering units.

Unit	1	2	3	4	5	6	7	8	9
lb	0.11	0.11	0.12	0.10	0.11	0.11	0.11	0.15	0.13

Solution: The first step is to determine the total amount of seed collected.

$$0.11 + 0.11 + 0.12 + 0.10 + 0.11 + 0.11 + 0.11 + 0.15 + 0.13 = 1.05 \text{ lb}$$

The next step is to determine the bushels per acre. To solve this step, units cancellation can be used. In an earlier section, Equation (9-1) was written in units form. If we change the pounds to bushels, then:

$$\frac{bu}{ac} = \frac{bu}{rev} \times \frac{rev}{ac}$$

and then using the standard conversion for wheat of 1 bu = 60 lb:

$$\frac{bu}{ac} = \left(\frac{1\ bu}{60\ lb} \times \frac{1.05\ lb}{25\ rev}\right) \times \frac{1\ rev}{\left(\dfrac{\pi \times 26\ in}{12\ \dfrac{in}{1\ ft}}\right) \times \left(\dfrac{9\ units}{1} \times \dfrac{6\ in}{unit} \times \dfrac{1\ ft}{12\ in}\right)} \times \frac{43{,}560\ ft^2}{ac}$$

$$= \frac{1\ bu}{60\ lb} \times \frac{1.05\ lb}{25\ rev} \times \frac{1\ rev}{6.8\ ft \times 4.5\ ft} \times \frac{43{,}560\ ft^2}{ac}$$

$$= \frac{1\ bu}{60\ lb} \times \frac{1.05\ lb}{25\ rev} \times \frac{1\ rev}{31\ ft^2} \times \frac{43{,}560\ ft^2}{ac}$$

$$= \frac{45{,}700}{46{,}500}$$

$$= 0.983\ \frac{bu}{ac}$$

The desired planting rate is 1 bu/ac. Is an error of 0.017 bu/ac (1.02 lb/ac) acceptable for planting wheat? Some seed companies publish acceptable seeding rates or this information may be found in an extension bulletin. One rule of thumb to use if such information is not available is that the seeding rate of the drill should be within 5% of the desired rate. One method that is used for this type of problem is to set an acceptability limit on each side of the desired rate. If the actual rate falls within this limit, it is acceptable. The limits can be set by using plus or minus 5% of the desired rate. In this case the upper limit (L_u) is:

$$L_u = 1.0\frac{bu}{ac} + \left(1.0\frac{bu}{ac} \times 0.05\right)$$

$$= 1.05\frac{bu}{ac}$$

and the lower limit (L_l) is:

$$L_l = 1.0\frac{bu}{ac} - \left(1.0\frac{bu}{ac} \times 0.05\right)$$

$$= 0.95\frac{bu}{ac}$$

Using this rule, the accuracy of the grain drill is acceptable (1.05 > 0.983 > 0.95).

One other aspect of the drill that should be checked is the uniformity of the distribution. This can be accomplished by using the same rule and setting the limits around the mean amount of seeds collected from the metering units. This will give:

$$\text{Mean} = \frac{1.05 \text{ lb}}{9 \text{ units}} = 0.12\frac{\text{lb}}{\text{unit}}$$

The upper limit is:

$$L_u = 0.12 \text{ lb} + (0.12 \text{ lb} \times 0.05)$$

$$= 0.13 \text{ lb}$$

and the lower limit is:

$$L_l = 0.12 \text{ lb} - (0.12 \text{ lb} \times 0.05)$$

$$= 0.11 \text{ lb}$$

A comparison of these limits to the calibration results shown in Table 9-1 indicates that although the grain drill seeding rate is acceptable, the distribution is not. The rate for metering unit #8 is excessive and the rate for unit #4 is insufficient. Both metering units should be readjusted before the drill is used.

CALIBRATING ROW CROP PLANTERS

Row crop planters are used to plant crops in wider rows than those planted by grain drills. The planters will use one of two types of metering--mechanical or air. Mechanical metering units have been traditionally used to plant crops such as corn, and grain sorghum. This type of unit selects ("singulates") and plants individual seeds. The seeds are deposited in holes (cells) on the rim of a ground driven metering plate, and as the metering plate rotates, the seeds leave the plate and fall into a furrow that has been opened in the soil. The seeding rate is changed by using a plate with a different number of cells, or by changing the drive train speed ratio between the drive wheel and the metering unit.

Air metering units also singulate seeds, but pressurized air is used to hold the seed in a vertical seed plate or drum and when the air is shut off, the seeds drop into the opened furrow or are blown into tubes which deliver them to the opened furrow.

A few manufacturers also produce an optional bulk type metering unit, which also is ground driven. The seeding rate (seeds/acre) is determined by the speed at which the metering unit operates in relation to the ground speed of the planter.

Both bulk and singulating row crop planters can be calibrated stationary by following the procedure used for stationary calibration of fertilizer applicators or grain drills. If the stationary method is used for a row crop planter, the seeding rate is calculated by dividing the seeds planted per revolution of the drive wheel by the acres covered per revolution of the drive wheel, or:

$$\frac{\text{seeds}}{\text{ac}} = \frac{\dfrac{\text{seeds}}{\text{rev}}}{\dfrac{\text{ac}}{\text{rev}}} \qquad (9\text{-}5)$$

In the next section we will discuss an alternative method for calibrating a singulating type of metering unit. The singulating metering unit is very easy to calibrate if the planter is mobile because there is a unique spacing between the seeds in the row for every combination of seeding rate and planter row spacing.

Problem: What is the spacing in the row (in/seed) for 40,000 plants per acre if the planter plants rows 28 inches apart?

Solution: Using units cancellation:

$$\frac{\text{in}}{\text{seed}} = \frac{1\ \text{ac}}{40{,}000\ \text{seed}} \times \frac{43{,}560\ \text{ft}^2}{1\ \text{ac}} \times \frac{144\ \text{in}^2}{1\ \text{ft}^2} \times \frac{1\ \text{row}}{28\ \text{in}}$$

$$= \frac{6{,}272{,}640}{1{,}120{,}000}$$

$$= 5.6 \frac{\text{row-in}}{\text{seed}}$$

Is this the correct answer? The units in the answer do not match the desired units we started with, but the answer is correct. For convenience it is common practice to drop off the unit of row in the answer and just use in/seed.

If the consistent units in the previous problem are combined ($43{,}560\ \text{ft}^2 \times 144\ \text{in}^2$), the seed spacing in the row can be found by the equation:

$$SS = \frac{6.27 \times 10^6}{POP \times RS} \qquad (9\text{-}6)$$

where:

SS = Seed spacing in the row (in)
POP = Population, planting rate (seeds/ac)
RS = Row spacing (in)

If this method is used, the planter is set according to the manufacturer's recommendations (found in the owner's manual) and driven for a short distance. The seeds are carefully dug out, and the distances between several seeds are measured. The average distance between seeds is compared to the required distance.

If the seeding rate is not correct, further evaluation of the planter must be made. Because the metering unit is ground driven, the source of the error may be in the drive train between the drive wheel and the metering unit.

CALIBRATING SPRAYERS

Accurate calibration of spray equipment is very important because with only slight changes the application rate may cause chemical damage to the crop or the environment, be wasteful of materials, or be ineffective. There is one important distinction in the procedure used to calibrate most sprayers: the application rate (gal/ac) is a function of the flow rate of the nozzles (gal/min) and the speed of the sprayer (mi/hr). This is so because both the size of the nozzle (diameter of the orifice) and the pressure of the spray must be regulated to control the flow rate, and the flow is produced by a pump that is not ground driven. The flow rate does not change as the ground speed changes. Therefore, the speed of the sprayer must be considered in calculating the application rate.

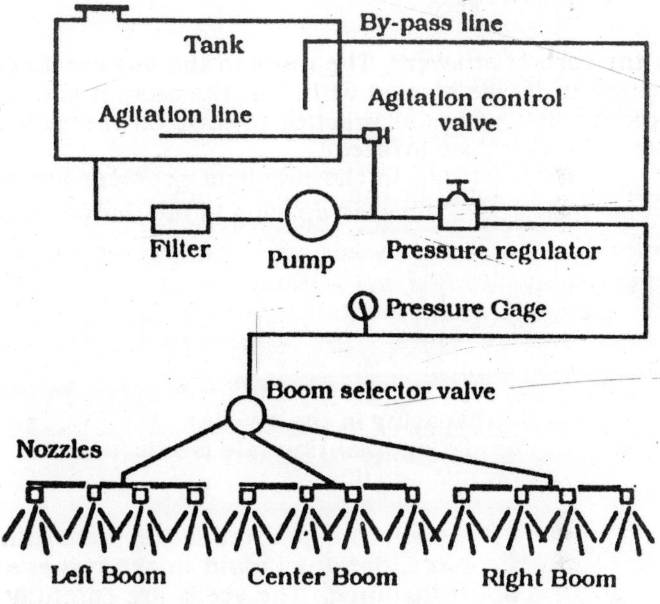

Figure 9.1. Schematic diagram of a boom sprayer.

To understand how a sprayer works, study Figure 9.1 and the following description. Figure 9.1 is a diagram of an overlapping boom sprayer. This sprayer consists of tank, filter, pump, means to control the pressure, three sections of nozzles, and boom selection valve. The mixture in the tank flows through the filter to remove any particles that might plug the orifice in the nozzles, and then to the pump. One of several different types of pumps is used, depending on the flow (gal/min) and the pressure (psi) needed by the system. From the pump the mixture goes to the pressure regulating valve. In some sprayer designs a portion of the flow from the pump is returned to the tank for agitation to prevent the spray materials from separating. Any excess flow produced by the pump also is returned to the tank by the pressure regulating valve. From this valve the fluid is pumped to the boom selector valve. At some point in this line a connection is made for a pressure gage. The boom selector valve directs the flow of the mixture to the different sections of the boom, and in some types of valves provision is made for a hand gun. A hand gun is very useful for spraying skips or along fence rows and other obstructions.

One popular selector valve design has seven positions:

1. All outlets off
2. All booms on
3. Left boom on
4. Center boom on
5. Right boom on
6. Hand gun on
7. Booms and hand gun on

In this type of system the pump is either engine, pto, or electric motor driven. As long as the pump is operating, the spraying system can function, whether the sprayer is moving forward or not. Thus it is easy to see what effect ground speed has on the spray application rate (gal/ac). When a sprayer operating in the field slows down, the application rate increases; conversely, if the sprayer moves faster, the application rate decreases. Therefore, precise control of the sprayer speed is very important.

The design shown in Figure 9.1 often is modified to meet the demands of different types of plants or application methods. Two additional examples are shown in Figures 9.2 and 9.3.

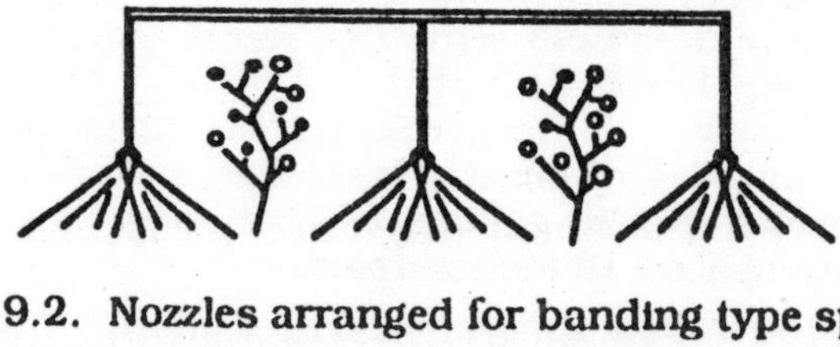

Figure 9.2. Nozzles arranged for banding type sprayer.

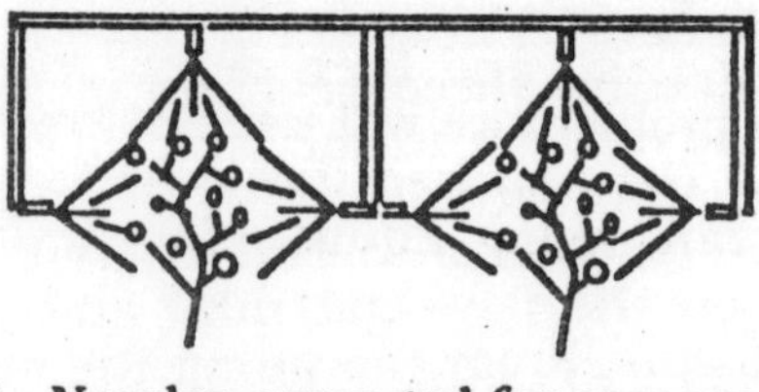

Figure 9.3. Nozzles arranged for row crop sprayer.

The application rate (gal/ac) of a field sprayer is controlled by three factors:

1. The speed of the sprayer (mi/hr).
2. The rate of discharge from the nozzle (gal/min).
3. The width covered by one nozzle (nsi).

Arranging these variables into one equation gives:

$$\frac{gal}{ac} = \frac{5940 \times \frac{gal}{min}}{\frac{mi}{hr} \times nsi} \tag{9-7}$$

where:

gal/ac = application rate
5940 = units conversion constant
gal/min = flow rate per nozzle
nsi = nozzle spacing (in)

Note: Use either the gal/min from one nozzle and the nsi per nozzle, *or* the flow from all nozzles (gal/min x number of nozzles) and the total width of the sprayer (nsi x number of nozzle). In either case, the application rate (gal/ac) will be the same. *Do not interchange these values.*

The calibration of a sprayer is a multiple-step process. In addition, the process can be started at different points, depending on which one of the three variables (speed, nozzle flow rate, or application rate) is selected first.

Problem: What size of nozzles (gal/min) is required for a boom type sprayer to apply 20 gallons of spray per acre? The sprayer has 24 nozzles spaced 18 inches apart.

Solution: Because the application rate of field sprayers is speed-dependent, begin by selecting a reasonable speed that can be maintained in the field, and then determine the size of nozzles needed. For this problem we will use the typical speed (Appendix II) of 6.5 mi/hr. The required flow rate for the nozzles can be determined by rearranging Equation (9-7) to solve for the flow rate (gal/min).

$$\frac{gal}{ac} = \frac{5940 \times \frac{gal}{min}}{\frac{mi}{hr} \times nsi}$$

$$\frac{gal}{min} = \frac{\frac{gal}{ac} \times \frac{mi}{hr} \times nsi}{5940}$$

$$= \frac{\frac{20\ gal}{1\ ac} \times \frac{6.5\ mi}{1\ hr} \times \frac{18\ in}{1}}{5940}$$

$$= \frac{2300}{5940}$$

$$= 0.39\ \frac{gal}{min}$$

For this application rate and nozzle spacing, nozzles with a capacity of 0.39 gal/min should be installed on the sprayer. Then before it is used, the sprayer should be calibrated to ensure that the application rate is correct because small variations in the construction of the nozzles or in the pressure at the nozzles can cause an unacceptable error in the application rate.

Assume the operator installed the 0.39 gal/min nozzles on the sprayer and proceeded with the calibration.

Problem: A container placed under all 24 nozzles of the sprayer collected 14.40 gallons of spray in 2 minutes of operation. If the desired application rate was 20 gal/ac, is the sprayer accurate?

Solution: In this example only the total volume is known. To arrive at a solution we must use the total volume and the width of the sprayer, *not* the volume per nozzle and the distance between nozzles. One alternative is to determine the average flow rate per nozzle and then use Equation (9-7), but this process will not be as accurate as using units cancellation:

$$\frac{gal}{ac} = \frac{14.40\ gal}{2.0\ min} \times \frac{60.0\ min}{1\ hr} \times \frac{1\ hr}{6.5\ mi} \times \frac{1\ mi}{5280\ ft}$$
$$\times \frac{43{,}560\ ft^2}{1\ ac} \times \frac{12.0\ in}{1\ ft} \times \frac{1\ nozzle}{18\ in} \times \frac{1}{24\ nozzles}$$

$$= \frac{4.52 \times 10^8}{3.0 \times 10^7}$$

$$= 15 \frac{gal}{ac}$$

The desired application rate was 20 gallons per acre, but the calibration indicates that the application rate is 5 gallons per acre less than this (20 gal/ac - 15 gal/ac). It is important to check the label of the chemical to determine if this is an acceptable application rate. If the error is unacceptable, how do we reduce it? The first step is to check the filters and nozzles of the sprayer to make sure that one or more were not slightly restricted. If all of the nozzles are in proper working order, the sprayer must be adjusted to apply the correct rate.

Adjustments can be made in the speed and the system pressure. Equation (9-6) can be rearranged to calculate the adjustment in the speed of travel. Only a small amount of change in the application rate can be made by adjusting the pressure. The pressure must be doubled to increase the flow rate by 50 percent, and modern boom type sprayers operate within a narrow pressure range. In this problem we will adjust the speed of travel.

Units cancellation could be used, but this time we will rearrange Equation (9-6) to solve for the speed of travel. Because Equation (9-6) requires the flow rate per nozzle, we will determine the average flow rate per nozzle. This average provides an acceptable level of accuracy.

$$\frac{gal}{nozzle} = \frac{14.4 \text{ gal}}{24 \text{ nozzles}}$$

$$= 0.60 \frac{gal}{nozzle}$$

and because the spray was collected for 2 minutes:

$$\frac{gal}{min} = \frac{\frac{0.60 \text{ gal}}{\text{nozzle}}}{2 \text{ min}}$$

$$= 0.30 \text{ gal/min/nozzle}$$

For convenience, the unit "nozzle" usually is not used; gpm = 0.30. Then:

$$\frac{mi}{hr} = \frac{5940 \times \frac{gal}{min}}{\frac{gal}{ac} \times nsi}$$

$$= \frac{5940 \times \frac{0.30\ gal}{1\ min}}{20\ \frac{gal}{ac} \times 18}$$

$$= \frac{1800}{360}$$

$$= 5.0 \frac{mi}{hr}$$

If the speed of the sprayer is changed from 6.5 to 5.0 miles per hour, the sprayer will apply the correct rate.

Although the preferred way of calibrating a sprayer is to determine the nozzle size first, this method requires the purchase of a new set of nozzles if the correct size is not available. In some situations the nozzle size is selected first (the best available), and then the required speed of travel is determined. If this method is used, the calculated speed of travel may be unrealistic.

Problem: We need to apply 15 gallons of spray per acre. Only one set of nozzles is available, and they have a capacity of 0.25 gallon per minute. If the sprayer has 35 nozzles spaced 24 inches apart, what speed will be required to apply the correct rate?

Solution: Equation (9-7) could be rearranged to solve for speed. Instead we will use the units cancellation method.

$$\frac{mi}{hr} = \frac{1\ mi}{5280\ ft} \times \frac{43{,}560\ ft^2}{1\ ac} \times \frac{1\ ac}{15\ gal} \times \frac{\frac{0.25\ gal}{1\ min}}{nozzle} \times \frac{1\ nozzle}{2\ ft} \times \frac{60\ min}{1\ hr}$$

$$= \frac{6.5 \times 10^5}{1.6 \times 10^5}$$

$$= 4.1 \frac{mi}{hr}$$

In this problem, if the sprayer is operated at 4.1 mi/hr, the correct rate will be applied.

Other types of sprayers can be calibrated by using these methods if the appropriate adjustments are made for differences in how the area and the application rate are determined. For example, to calibrate the row crop sprayer in Figure 9.3, the width becomes the distance between the rows, and each nozzle should apply one-third of the required flow (gal/min) per row.

Sprayers used for banding also can be calibrated. In checking a sprayer used for banding, the nozzle spacing (nsi) becomes the width of the band (see Figure 9.2).

PREPARING SPRAY MIXES

A very important part of chemical application is the proper preparation and mixing of the chemical and the carrier (usually water). The application rates of most chemicals are given in terms of *pounds of active ingredient* to be applied per acre. The pounds of active ingredient (AI) per gallon of solution in the container usually is found on the label. A typical material might contain 4 pounds of active ingredient per gallon. Wettable powders (WP), on the other hand, are specified as a certain percent strength, such as a 50% or an 80% WP, which means that 50% or 80% of the weight of the material in the container is the active ingredient. The rest is inert material (carrier).

Problem: You need to apply 2.0 pounds of active ingredient of an 80% wettable powder in a 30 gallon per acre dilution. If the sprayer has a 100-gallon tank, how many pounds of wettable powder are required to mix 100-gallon of spray?

Solution: To obtain 2.0 pounds of active ingredient, 2.5 pounds of powder would be required (80% of 2.5 = 2.0). If the solution is to be applied at 30 gallons per acre, mix 2.5 pounds of 80% wettable powder in each 30 gallons of water. The tank holds 100 gallons or 3.33 units of 30 gallons. Because 2.5 pounds of wettable powder should be added to each 30 gallons of water, you should add 3.33 x 2.5 or 8.33 pounds of wettable power to each 100 gallons. Or by ratio:

$$\frac{2.5 \text{ lb of WP}}{30 \text{ gal } H_2O} = \frac{? \text{ lb of WP}}{100 \text{ gal } H_2O}$$

$$? \text{ lb of WP} = \frac{2.5 \times 100.0}{30}$$

$$= 8.33 \text{ lb } 80\% \text{ WP}$$

To mix the spray, add 8.33 pounds of wettable powder to a partially filled tank, mix it thoroughly, and add water to make 100 gallons of mixture. During spraying this mixture must be continuously agitated to prevent the wettable powder from settling.

Preparing a mix using liquid chemicals can be accomplished with the same procedures.

Problem: A liquid contains 2.0 pounds of active ingredient per 5.0 gallons. It is desired to apply 1.0 pound of active ingredient per acre at a rate of 20.0 gallons per acre. If the sprayer tank holds 180 gallons, how much water and spray should be used for each tank full?

Solution: If the liquid contains 2.0 pounds of active ingredient per 5.0 gallons, then 2.5 gallons would contain 1.0 pound of active ingredient. Thus, for each acre 2.5 gallons is mixed with 17.5 gallons of water (20 - 2.5) to get 20 gallons of spray. By ratio:

$$\frac{2.5 \text{ gal}}{20 \text{ gal}} = \frac{? \text{ gal}}{180 \text{ gal}}$$

$$? \text{ gal} = \frac{2.5 \times 180}{20}$$

$$= 22.5 \text{ gal concentrate}$$

and 180 gal - 22.5 gal = 157.5 gal. Thus, for every tank 22.5 gallons of chemical is mixed with 157.5 gallons of water.

PRACTICE PROBLEMS

1. One half of a gravity flow fertilizer applicator is driven by a wheel of 67-inch circumference and operates 16 outlets spaced 3.5 inches apart. When the drive wheel is turned 40 revolutions, 14.35 pounds of fertilizer is collected. What is the application rate (lb/ac)?
Answer: 598 lb/ac
2. When the drive wheel of a row crop fertilizer unit is turned 50 times, 4.0 pounds of fertilizer is collected. If the drive wheel is 16 inches in diameter, and the crop row spacing is 40 inches, what is the application rate?
Answer: 250 lb/ac
3. A broadcast spreader is driven over two 10.0 ft x 12.0 ft tarps placed on the ground. If 14.36 pounds of fertilizer was collected on each tarp, what is the application rate (lb/ac)?
Answer: 2610 lb/ac
4. A grain drill is equipped with wheels with an effective diameter of 23 inches. When it is calibrated at the desired setting, 5.50 pounds of seed is collected from 10 metering units spaced 6 inches apart as the wheel is turned 50 revolutions. Before the drill can get to the field, the tire is punctured and is replaced with a wheel having an effective diameter of 24.5 inches. For the same setting, what change in seeding rate (lb/ac) would occur because of using the new wheel (assuming 1 bu = 60 lb)?
Answer: 21.73 lb/ac less (Units cancellation method)
5. The information shown in Table 9-2 was developed from the stationary calibration of an 18-7 grain drill. What is the seeding rate if the effective diameter of the drive wheel is 36 inches and the material was collected during 25 revolutions?
Answer: 77 lb/ac

Table 9-2. Results of grain drill calibration.

Unit	1	2	3	4	5	6	7	8	9
lb	0.24	0.24	0.25	0.23	0.24	0.24	0.24	0.26	0.25

6. Is the uniformity of the metering units in problem 5 acceptable? Why?
Answer: No. Unit #8 is outside the acceptability range of 0.23 to 0.25 pound per unit.
7. During the mobile calibration of an 18-10 grain drill 2.60 pounds of seeds was collected as the drill traveled 100 feet.

If the desired seeding rate is 1.25 bushels per acre, is the drill calibrated? Why?
Answer: Yes. The seeding rate is 1.27 bushels per acre, which is within the acceptability range of 1.31 to 1.19 bu/ac.

8. What is the seed spacing in the row for a row crop planter that plants 32-inch rows when the desired planting rate is 45,000 seeds per acre?
Answer: 4.4 in
9. What size of nozzles (gal/min) will be required to apply 9.5 gallons per acre if the sprayer has 13 nozzles spaced 21 inches apart and travels at 6.25 miles per hour?
Answer: 0.21 gal/min
10. How fast should a row crop sprayer with three nozzles per row travel to apply 25.5 gallons per acre if the nozzle capacity is 0.024 gallon per minute, and the rows are spaced 28 inches apart?
Answer: 0.60 mi/hr
11. How many pounds of 75% WP should be added to a 50-gallon spray tank to apply 0.50 pound of active ingredient per acre if the application rate is 10 gallons per acre?
Answer: 3.4 lb
12. How many gallons of water and how many gallons of spray should be added to a 50-gallon spray tank if the dilution rate is one part concentrate to four parts of water?
Answer: 10 gallons of concentrate and 40 gallons of water

10
Economics of Agricultural Machinery

OBJECTIVES

1. Be able to list the criteria for selecting tractors and machines.
2. Be able to determine optimum machine size.
3. Be able to calculate ownership and operating costs of agricultural equipment.
4. Understand ways to reduce the costs of owning and operating tractors and machinery.
5. Understand the concept of break-even use for a machine.
6. Be able to calculate break-even use for a machine.
7. Understand the importance of regular maintenance of agricultural machinery.

INTRODUCTION

Machinery is one of the largest investments for agricultural enterprises. Selecting the wrong manufacturer, design, or size for a tractor or a machine may have seriously affect on the profitability of the enterprise. After studying this chapter, you should have a better understanding of the criteria to use when selecting tractors and machines, and be able to match tractor and machine sizes.

SELECTION CRITERIA

Some of the characteristics or capabilities of a machine that make it more attractive than another are abstract, but they can have a tremendous bearing on the quality of the machine and/or the quality of its performance. We will discuss some of the criteria that are commonly used and illustrate their importance in the selection of agricultural machines.

COMPANY NAME

The company name should be considered in machinery selection. Manufacturers spend years and multitudes of resources establishing a reputation. A company's reputation is based on the quality and durability of its products, service to its customers, or a combination of both. It is important to know if a manufacturer will stand behind its product and warranties.

The importance of selecting tractors and machinery from reputable companies cannot be overstated. In some situations the best economic decision would be to choose one tractor or machine over another, even though it did not have the better durability record, just because the reputation of the manufacturer was better.

REPAIRS

All machines will break down at some time. If you purchase a particular machine because it is the least expensive, but parts are not available locally or are very expensive to purchase and replace, it may not be a good buy, especially if it breaks down during a prime use time. Evaluate the machine not only on its quality and durability but also on the amount of time and money that will be required to have it repaired.

DESIGN

The design of the machine is an important consideration. Because of the diversity of agricultural machinery, several different designs might produce an acceptable level of performance, yet small variations in design may make one more suitable than the others for a given situation. For example, for fields that are large and relatively flat, tillage equipment with wide rigid sections is suitable. But if the fields are terraced, the same type of machine must be more flexible to produce the same quality of results. More flexibility will probably cost more money, however. It is difficult to know what features of a design improve the value of a machine for a particular situation.

CAPACITY

Increased capacity has been a constant trend in agricultural machinery. As we learned in a previous chapter, to increase capacity we must use a wider width or a faster speed (both requiring more horsepower) and/or increased efficiency.

It also is important to be able to complete the operation in a timely fashion. Unfortunately, information on the timeliness of agricultural operations is limited. Some concepts of timeliness and the effect of machine size are discussed in the next section.

THE OPTIMUM MACHINE SIZE

The optimum machine size can be selected from two different points of view: it can be based on the amount of time available to complete an operation, or it can be based on the amount of power available from the tractor. If the machine is too small, the operating costs will be higher, and its reduced capacity will require a greater number of hours to complete an operation. If the machine is too large, it will not produce the results it was designed for, or it may shorten the life of modern tractors designed to operate at lighter drafts and faster speeds than older tractors.

The recommended procedure is to use the available time (timeliness) for selecting the capacity of the machine, and then to determine the size of tractor needed. Timeliness refers to the optimum amount of time that should be spent to complete any single operation. For example, the longer a crop stands in the field waiting to be harvested, the greater the potential is for losses due to weather and pests. Therefore, there is an optimum capacity for the machine that will provide the most timely harvest. A full discussion of timeliness is beyond the scope of this text, but we will illustrate this concept for determining the size of machine and tractors.

As we learned earlier, the unit of measure of capacity will not be the same for all machines. We first will illustrate the selection of machines and tractors based upon the width of the machine.

Problem: It is recommended that for optimum results you should be able to complete in one week the primary tillage for planting corn. If you anticipate planting 500.0 acres of corn and only work 12.0 hours per day and 6 days per week, what size of moldboard plow do you need if you can plow at typical speed and efficiency?

Solution: The first step is to determine the capacity (ac/hr) required to plow the ground in the available time. This can be accomplished by using units cancellation:

$$\frac{ac}{hr} = \frac{500\ ac}{1\ wk} \times \frac{1\ day}{12\ hr} \times \frac{1\ wk}{6\ day}$$

$$= 6.9\,\frac{ac}{hr}$$

To plow the 500 acres in one week, the plow must have a width and be operated at a speed that will produce a capacity of 6.9

ac/hr. The second step is to determine the width of the plow. You will recall from Chapter 8 that the capacity of field equipment can be determined by using Equation (8-5):

$$C_E = \frac{S \times W \times E_f}{8.25}$$

Rearranging this equation to solve for W and looking up the typical speed and efficiency in Appendix II gives us the width of the plow:

$$W = \frac{C_E \times 8.25}{S \times E_f} \qquad (10\text{-}1)$$

$$= \frac{6.90 \frac{ac}{hr} \times 8.25}{4.5 \frac{mi}{hr} \times 0.80}$$

$$= \frac{56.9}{3.6}$$

$$= 16 \text{ ft}$$

To be able to plow the field in one week, assuming that the plow will be operated at typical speed and efficiency, you will require a plow with an effective width of 16 feet. Plows are not usually sized by feet of width; instead they are sized by the effective width of each bottom and the number of bottoms. Sixteen feet is the same as a 12-16 plow (12 bottoms with 16 inches per bottom).

The next step is to determine the size of the tractor needed to pull the plow. This is accomplished by determining the drawbar horsepower required. The first step is to replace the term force in Equation (7-2) with the term draft.

$$Dbhp = \frac{D \times S}{375} \qquad (10\text{-}2)$$

The term draft is used to describe the amount of force required to pull a machine. Appendix III gives the ASAE standard values for the draft of agricultural machines. Notice that more than one type of unit is used for draft. That is, the draft of plows is listed as pounds of force per square inch (cross sectional area) plus a speed factor, spring tooth harrows are listed as pounds per foot of width, and some rotary power machines are given in horsepower. One must be careful to understand the units.

Problem: What size tractor (Dbhp) will be required to pull the 12-16 plow?

Solution: To complete this problem, find the draft of the plow in Appendix III. Notice that the draft for a plow varies with soil type. We will assume that the plow will be used in a silty clay soil [draft = 10.24 lb/in^2 + (0.185 x S^2)]. In addition, we will also discover that it is very useful to modify Equation (10-2) to show the total draft as the product of the draft per unit times the number of units:

$$D\,(\text{lb}) = D\left(\frac{\text{lb}}{\text{unit}}\right) \times \text{Number of units}$$

To arrive at the total draft(D_T) for the plow, multiply the cross--sectional area of the soil worked by the plow by the total draft per area (lb/in^2 + speed factor). Therefore:

$$\text{Dbhp (plow)} = \frac{D_T\left(\frac{\text{lb}}{\text{in}^2}\right) \times A\,(\text{in}^2) \times S\left(\frac{\text{mi}}{\text{hr}}\right)}{375} \qquad (10\text{-}3)$$

where:

D_T = Total draft of the plow
A = Area (width x depth)
S = Speed

If we assume that the plow will be operated 6.00 inches deep, then the required drawbar horsepower for the plow is:

$$\text{Dbhp} = \frac{D_T\left(\frac{\text{lb}}{\text{in}^2}\right) \times A\,(\text{in}^2) \times S\left(\frac{\text{mi}}{\text{hr}}\right)}{375}$$

$$= \frac{\left(\frac{10.24\ \text{lb}}{1\ \text{in}^2} + \left(0.185 \times 4.50^2\right)\right)}{375}$$

$$\times \frac{\left(\frac{6.00\ \text{in}}{1} \times \frac{12\ \text{bottoms}}{1} \times \frac{16.0\ \text{in}}{\text{bottom}}\right) \times 4.50 \frac{\text{mi}}{\text{hr}}}{375}$$

$$= \frac{\frac{14.0\ \text{lb}}{1\ \text{in}^2} \times 1150\ \text{in}^2 \times 4.50 \frac{\text{mi}}{\text{hr}}}{375}$$

$$= \frac{16{,}100\ \text{lb} \times 4.50 \frac{\text{mi}}{\text{hr}}}{375}$$

$$= \frac{72{,}400}{375}$$

$$= 193\ \text{Dbhp}$$

With typical speed and efficiency and operating 6 inches deep in clay soil, the 12 16 plow will require a tractor with 193 drawbar horsepower.

One disadvantage of using this method to determine the optimum size of machines is now apparent. The calculated tractor size may be larger than what you have. What do you do if you do not want to purchase a larger tractor? You could lease a tractor for a short period or hire someone else to do the plowing. Another option, which will allow you to complete the plowing with the tractor available, is to adjust one or more of the factors in Equation (10-2). A common practice is to extend the amount of time available to complete the tillage operation. It also is possible to reduce the draft of the plow by reducing the operating depth or to reduce the speed. In some situations one of these two choices is the best option, but for this problem we will determine the additional time needed if a smaller plow is used.

Problem: Assume that the largest tractor you have available to pull the plow in the previous example is 100 drawbar horsepower. If this tractor is used, how many 12 hour days will it take to plow the 500 acres?

Solution: This approach to the problem uses the previous steps. The first step is to determine the size of plow the 100 Dbhp tractor can pull. This is accomplished by rearranging Equation (10-3) to solve for width [because A = Width (W) x Depth (d)]:

$$W = \frac{\text{Dbhp} \times 375}{D \times d \times S}$$

$$= \frac{100 \text{ hp} \times 375}{\frac{14 \text{ lb}}{1 \text{ in}^2} \times \frac{6 \text{ in}}{1} \times \frac{4.50 \text{ mi}}{1 \text{ hr}}}$$

$$= \frac{37{,}500}{378}$$

$$= 99.2 \text{ in or } 8.27 \text{ ft}$$

If only 100 Dbhp is available, the size of the plow is reduced to 8.26 feet; or if the bottoms are 16 inches, a 6-16 plow (8.00 ft) is used. The next step is to determine the capacity of a plow 8.00 feet wide. Using Equation (8-5):

$$C_E = \frac{S \times W \times E_f}{8.25}$$

$$= \frac{4.50 \frac{\text{mi}}{\text{hr}} \times 8.00 \text{ ft} \times 0.80}{8.25}$$

$$= \frac{28.8}{8.25}$$

$$= 3.49 \frac{\text{ac}}{\text{hr}}$$

Now that we know the capacity (3.49 ac/hr), we can determine the number of days it will take to plow 500 acres. Using units cancellation:

$$\text{days} = \frac{1 \text{ day}}{12 \text{ hr}} \times \frac{1 \text{ hr}}{3.49 \text{ ac}} \times \frac{500 \text{ ac}}{1}$$

$$= \frac{500}{42}$$

$$= 12 \text{ days}$$

This means if the 100 Dbhp tractor is used instead of the 193 Dbhp that is the optimum, it will take 6 extra days (12 days – 6 days = 6 days) to plow the field.

MATCHING TRACTORS AND MACHINES

The previous section illustrated a method for determining the optimum size of a machine. Use of this method normally is restricted to situations where both the tractor and the machine will be purchased at the same time, and/or where timeliness is an important factor. The more common situation is to select a machine to match a tractor or to select a tractor to match a machine. For these two situations slightly different methods are used.

Problem: It becomes necessary to increase the field capacity of your farming enterprise and the opportunity to buy a 185 pto horsepower tractor is too good to pass up. What size (width) of heavy duty disk harrow (W_{dh}) and field cultivator (W_{fc}) will you need for your new tractor? Assume a clay soil and the lowest typical value for speed and efficiency.

Solution: We noted earlier that Appendix III does not use the same units of draft for each type of machine. These differences serve to improve the accuracy of the data. Equation (10-3) must be modified to fit the units of draft used for each machine. Because the draft of disk harrows is listed as a factor times the mass (weight), to determine the size of the disk harrow, Equation (10-3) must be modified to solve for the weight. Company literature or a local equipment dealer then must be consulted to determine what width (ft) of disk harrow has the calculated weight. For the heavy disk, Equation (10-3) becomes:

$$M_{dh} = \frac{\text{Dbhp} \times 375}{\text{DF} \times \text{S}}$$

where:

M_{dh} = Mass of disk (lb)
Dbhp = Horsepower of tractor
DF = Draft factor
S = Speed (mi/hr)

The mass (lb) of the disk is (remember to convert from pto horsepower to drawbar horsepower):

$$lb = \frac{(185 \text{ hp} \times 0.86) \times 375}{1.5 \times 3.50}$$

$$= \frac{160 \text{ hp} \times 375}{1.5 \times 3.50}$$

$$= \frac{60{,}000}{5.25}$$

$$= 11{,}000 \text{ lb}$$

The 185 pto horsepower tractor will be able to pull a heavy duty disk harrow that weights up to 11,000 pounds in clay soil if it is operating at the low end of the typical speed and efficiency ranges.

The draft of the field cultivator is listed as pounds of force per tool (shovel, sweep etc.). Therefore, the size of the cultivator is determined by the number of tools. For the cultivator, Equation (10-3) becomes:

$$Dbhp = \frac{D\left(\frac{lb}{ft}\right) \times W\,(ft) \times S\left(\frac{mi}{hr}\right)}{375}$$

where the draft (D) becomes $\left(\frac{\text{lb of force}}{\text{tool}} + \text{speed factor}\right)$, and the width (W) becomes the number of tools (T_n).

$$Dbhp = \frac{\left(\frac{lb}{tool} + \text{speed factor}\right) \times T_n \times S}{375}$$

Solving for the number of tools, using the draft from Appendix III (D = 111 lb/tool + 12 x S):

$$T_n = \frac{\text{Dbhp} \times 375}{\left(\frac{\text{lb}}{\text{tool}} + (12 \times S)\right) \times S}$$

$$= \frac{160 \text{ hp} \times 375}{\left(111 \frac{\text{lb}}{\text{tool}} + (12 \times 3.5)\right) \times 3.5}$$

$$= \frac{160 \text{ hp} \times 375}{153 \frac{\text{lb}}{\text{tool}} \times 3.5}$$

$$= \frac{60{,}000}{536}$$

$$= 112 \text{ Tools}$$

The 185 pto horsepower tractor will be able to pull a field cultivator with 112 soil-engaging tools. The width of the cultivator depends on the number of rows of tools and the spacing between each tool, or shank. For example, one possible arrangement would be a cultivator with three rows of staggered shanks, the second row aligned between the front row shanks, spaced 2.0 feet apart. This arrangement would have 112 shanks (37, 38, and 37), and be 76 feet wide.

Appendix III presents the draft of equipment in the form found in the American Society of Agricultural Engineers (ASAE) Standards. Other sources may provide draft figures for machines in pounds per foot. If these values are used, Equation (10-3) does not need to be modified each time, but the calculations will not be as accurate as this example problem.

COSTS OF MACHINERY

This section discusses those elements that contribute to the cost of owning and operating agricultural machinery. An understanding of the types of costs and their impact on the profitability of the enterprise improves our ability to make meaningful decisions regarding the management of agricultural equipment.

It is best to base decisions on the actual costs of the machine. Unfortunately, actual costs are not known until a machine has reached the end of its serviceable life, that is, until the machine wears out or is sold or traded in. Therefore, cost determinations must be based on estimations. To make these estimations realistic and reliable, they must be based on past machine performance and cost records. We will discuss the typical costs of owning and operating machinery as well as a method that can be used to estimate the costs of agricultural equipment.

Generally, machinery costs are classified into two groups:

FIXED COSTS	*VARIABLE COSTS*
1. Depreciation	6. Repair and maintenance
2. Interest on investment	7. Fuel
3. Taxes	8. Oil
4. Shelter	9. Labor
5. Insurance	

FIXED COSTS

Fixed costs are independent of machine use, and occur whether or not the machine is used. They are referred to as the *cost of ownership*. Each fixed cost is estimated on a calendar-year or an annual basis. The common fixed costs are:

1. *Depreciation*: Depreciation is the loss in value of a machine with the passage of time, whether or not it is used. Depreciation can be regarded as the amount of money that should be saved each year as a machine is used so that, at the end of its useful life, this money along with the remaining value of the machine (salvage value) could be used to replace it. Several choices exist in the way by which depreciation can be figured for cost and/or tax purposes. All depreciation methods require an estimation for the service life of the machine. The simplest method is straight line depreciation:

$$\frac{\$}{yr} = \frac{P - SV}{yr}$$

where:

$\$/yr$ = Annual depreciation
P = Purchase price
SV = Salvage value
yr = Years of service

2. *Interest on investment*: The interest rate depends on whether the machine is paid for, or payments are being made. If money is owed on a machine the actual interest rate can be used. If not, an interest charge should be

included because money tied up in equipment could be otherwise invested to provide a return. The interest returned on investment is used as part of the fixed costs if the machine is paid for.

3. *Taxes*: Any property and sales taxes paid on the equipment must be included as a fixed cost.
4. *Shelter*: A cost of shelter should be assigned to machinery. If a shelter is used, the cost can be determined and assigned over the life of the machine. If the machine is not sheltered, a cost still should still be assigned for shelter because the resale value of the machine will be less than that of a sheltered machine.
5. *Insurance*: Any liability or replacement insurance carried on the machine should be included.

The annual cost of owning a piece of equipment, then, is the sum of the fixed costs listed above. Notice that at this point no mention has been made of machine use.

If you have accurate records, the annual cost of a machine can be determined by figuring the cost in dollars per year for each of the five fixed costs. Another approach is to combine the five items into an annual fixed cost percentage (FC%). Cost analysis of data indicates that the FC% times the purchase price of the machine is an acceptable estimate for the annual ownership costs of a machine.

$$\text{Annual Owning Cost (AOC)} = \text{FC\%} \times P \qquad (10\text{-}4)$$

Problem: What is the annual ownership cost for a $150,000.00-dollar combine if the fixed cost percentage is 18%?

Solution:

$$\text{AOC} = \text{FC\%} \times P$$

$$= 0.18 \times \$150{,}000.00$$

$$= 27{,}000.00 \frac{\$}{\text{yr}}$$

VARIABLE COSTS

Variable costs are associated with the operation of a machine and occur only when the machine is used. The term *operating costs* frequently is used to describe variable costs. Variable costs are usually figured on an hourly basis. Continuing the above list, variable costs are:

6. *Repairs and maintenance (RM%)*: estimated by taking a percentage of the purchase price. The product of RM% x P is expressed as dollars per hour. An RM% of 0.01 to 0.03 is acceptable for most machines.
7. *Fuel (F)*: The fuel cost in dollars per hour will be the product of the fuel consumption (gal/hr) and the fuel price ($/gal).
8. *Oil (O)*: The oil cost in dollars per hour will be the product of the oil consumption (qt/hr) and the oil price ($/qt).
9. *Labor (L)*: the hourly wage for labor to operate the equipment in dollars per hour.

Thus, the total hourly operating cost (THOC), in dollars per hour, of a machine is the sum of items 6, 7, 8 and 9 above:

$$THOC = (RM\% \times P) + F + O + L \qquad (10\text{-}5)$$

Problem: What is the total hourly operating cost for a $12,000 tractor if the RM% = 0.015, the fuel consumption is 5.75 gal/hr, the fuel price is 1.25 $/gal, the labor costs are 10.00 $/hr, the oil consumption is 0.10 qt/hr, and the oil cost is 1.00 $/qt?

Solution: Using Equation (10-5):

$$THOC = (RM\% \times P) + F + O + L$$

$$= (0.00015 \times \$12{,}000) + \left(5.75\,\frac{gal}{hr} \times 1.25\,\frac{\$}{gal}\right)$$

$$+ \left(0.10\,\frac{qt}{hr} \times 1.00\,\frac{\$}{qt}\right) + 10.00\,\frac{\$}{hr}$$

$$= 1.80\,\frac{\$}{hr} + 7.19\,\frac{\$}{hr} + 0.10\,\frac{\$}{hr} + 10.00\,\frac{\$}{hr}$$

$$= 19.09\,\frac{\$}{hr}$$

Notice that it was necessary to convert all of the costs to a dollars-per-hour basis. For this tractor, the hourly operating costs will be $19.09 per hour.

To make decisions on machinery costs, the total annual cost (TAC) often is needed. The total annual cost is the sum of the annual ownership costs (AOC) and the total hourly operating costs (THOC):

$$TAC = AOC + THOC \qquad (10\text{-}6)$$

One difficulty exists here. The total annual cost is in units of dollars per year ($/yr), and the total hourly operating costs are in units of dollars per hour ($/hr). Before the total annual cost can be determined, a units conversion must be done. In this situation a conversion unit that includes hours and years is needed.

$$\frac{\$}{yr} = \frac{\$}{hr} \times \frac{hr}{yr}$$

If the annul use (AU), in hours, is known for the machine, the conversion is:

$$TAC\left(\frac{\$}{yr}\right) = AOC\left(\frac{\$}{yr}\right) + \left(THOC\left(\frac{\$}{hr}\right) \times AU\left(\frac{hr}{yr}\right)\right) \qquad (10\text{-}7)$$

If the annual use in hours is not known, it can be estimated by modifying Equation (8-6):

$$AU\left(\frac{hr}{yr}\right) = \frac{8.25 \times A}{S \times W \times Ef} \qquad (10\text{-}8)$$

where:

AU = Annual use (hr/yr)
A = Number of acres per year (ac/yr)
S = Average speed of travel (mi/hr)
W = Average effective width (ft)
Ef = Average field efficiency (decimal)

Thus the equation for total annual cost(TAC) becomes:

$$TAC = (FC\% \times P) + \left(\left(\frac{8.25 \times A}{S \times W \times Ef}\right)[(RM\% \times P) + F + O + L]\right) \qquad (10\text{-}9)$$

If the machine is towed by a tractor, Equation (10-9) is changed. The fuel (F) and the oil (O) are replaced by the cost of operating the tractor (T) in dollars per hour.

Problem: Calculate the total annual cost (TAC) of owning and operating a towed machine with the following characteristics:

AU = 200 ac/yr	RM% = 0.020%
FC% = 20%	L = 10.00 \$/hr
P = \$2500	F = 0
S = 3.5 mi/hr	O = 0
W = 6 ft	T = 8.50 \$/hr
Ef = 80%	

Solution: Notice that it is a towed machine. Then:

$$TAC = (FC\% \times P) + \left(\left(\frac{8.25 \times A}{S \times W \times E_f}\right) [(RM\% \times P) + L + T]\right) \qquad (10\text{-}10)$$

$$= (0.20\,\% \times \$2500) + \left(\frac{8.25 \times 200 \frac{ac}{yr}}{3.50 \frac{mi}{hr} \times 6.0\text{ ft} \times 0.80}\right)$$

$$\times \left((0.0002\,\% \times \$2500) + 10.00 \frac{\$}{hr} + 8.50 \frac{\$}{hr}\right)$$

$$= 500 \frac{\$}{yr} + \left(98 \frac{hr}{yr} \times \left(0.50 \frac{\$}{hr} + 10.00 \frac{\$}{hr} + 8.50 \frac{\$}{hr}\right)\right)$$

$$= 500 \frac{\$}{yr} + 1900 \frac{\$}{yr}$$

$$= 2400 \frac{\$}{yr}$$

This machine will cost \$2400 per year to own and operate.

If you were involved in custom farming or wanted to determine the profitability of one part of a diversified enterprise, you would need to know the total costs of a machine on a per hour or a per acre basis. Determination of costs on a per-hour or a per acre basis can be accomplished by using one of two methods. One way is to divide the total annual cost, as figured in the previous problem, by the acres or hours per year.

Problem: What would the per-acre and per-hour costs be for the machine in the previous problem?

Solution: Using Equation (10-9):

$$\frac{\$}{ac} = 2400\frac{\$}{yr} \times \frac{1\ yr}{200\ ac}$$

$$= 12\frac{\$}{ac}$$

Before the dollars per hour can be determined we must know how many hours the machine is used per year. This value is part of Equation (10-9):

$$\frac{hr}{yr} = \frac{8.25 \times A}{S \times W \times E_f}$$

$$= \frac{8.25 \times 200\ ac}{3.50\frac{mi}{hr} \times 6.0\ ft \times 0.80}$$

$$= 98\frac{hr}{yr}$$

Then total dollars per hour are:

$$\frac{\$}{hr} = 2400\frac{\$}{yr} \times \frac{1\ yr}{98\ hr}$$

$$= 24\frac{\$}{hr}$$

The best estimate for this machine is that it will cost $24.00 per hour to operate.

The second way to determine the total cost on a per-hour or per-acre basis is to convert the total fixed costs and total variable costs to the same units, using the appropriate conversion units, and then to add all of the costs.

At this point it is appropriate to show the effect of annual use on the per acre cost of using equipment.

Problem: What would the total costs per acre be for the machine in the original problem if it were used 500 acres per year instead of 200?

Solution: The first step is to solve for the total annual cost. Using Equation (10-10):

$$TAC = (FC\% \times P) + \left(\left(\frac{8.25 \times A}{S \times W \times Ef} \right) [(RM\% \times P) + L + T] \right)$$

$$= (0.20\,\% \times \$2500) + \left(\frac{8.25 \times 500\ ac}{3.50 \frac{mi}{hr} \times 6.0\ ft \times 0.80} \right)$$

$$\times \left((0.0002\,\% \times \$2500) + 10.00 \frac{\$}{hr} + 8.50 \frac{\$}{hr} \right)$$

$$= 500 \frac{\$}{yr} + \left(245 \frac{hr}{yr} \times \left(0.50 \frac{\$}{hr} + 10.00 \frac{\$}{hr} + 8.50 \frac{\$}{hr} \right) \right)$$

$$= 500 \frac{\$}{yr} + 4660 \frac{\$}{yr}$$

$$= 5160 \frac{\$}{yr}$$

If the machine is used on 500 acres per year, the total annual cost increases to $5160. The total cost per acre is determined by:

$$\frac{\$}{ac} = \frac{\$}{yr} \times \frac{yr}{ac}$$

$$= 5160 \frac{\$}{yr} \times \frac{1\ yr}{500\ ac}$$

$$= 10.32 \frac{\$}{ac}$$

This problem illustrates the principle that the cost per unit decreases if the number of units per year increases. In this example, the total costs in dollars per acre decreased from $12.00 per acre to $10.32 per acre. This principle is true because the fixed costs, which are independent of use, are spread out over more acres.

WAYS TO REDUCE COSTS

No single factor will keep ownership and operating costs of tractors and machinery to a minimum, but the following suggestions will be helpful in keeping production costs at a reasonable level.

WIDTH UTILIZATION

The effective width is always less than the width of the machine, except for row crops, because most operators overlap each round slightly to prevent skips. Any excessive overlap reduces the effective capacity of the machine and increases the cost per acre.

TIME UTILIZATION

Any time that a machine is not performing its designed task when it could be means lost productivity. Several practices can be used to reduce lost time. First, adjusting and lubricating of the machine should be kept to a minimum consistent with the need for service. Even better, do as much of the maintenance as possible when conditions prevent the machine from being in the field.

Second, breakdowns can be minimized by avoiding overloads and by a complete preventive maintenance program. Any machine is more likely to break down or to need additional maintenance if it is overloaded.

Third, a proper field layout will keep turning at the end of the row or round to a minimum. There is an optimum pattern for every field shape and size of machine. Machinery management texts provide more information on this topic.

Another idea is to reduce the time required to refill seed, fertilizer, and chemicals by using the largest practical size of hopper or tank. In addition, the equipment used to load the tank or the hopper should have the capacity to fill it in a reasonable time.

MATCHING TRACTORS AND MACHINES

Tractors furnish power most economically when operated at or near the rated load. If the load is too small, it may be increased by widening the machine or by using two machines in tandem. Increasing the speed also increases the effective tractor load. If all of the tractor power is not being utilized and it is not feasible to increase the speed, fuel costs can be reduced by shifting up into a higher gear and reducing the throttle. (Check the owner's manual before attempting this.)

REDUCING ORIGINAL INVESTMENT

The initial cost of a machine is a major factor in determining the fixed cost of owning and operating farm machinery. The initial cost can be reduced by buying used equipment or by building equipment and machinery in the farm shop. Both of these strategies substitute human labor for some of the initial cost.

INCREASING ANNUAL USE

As we discovered in the section on calculating costs, the more a machine is used, the less the cost per unit will be. Usage can be increased by joint ownership, by increasing the size of the enterprise, by doing custom work, or by increasing the working season by diversifying production.

INCREASING SERVICE LIFE

Ensuring that the machine lasts as long as possible is one way of reducing the need for the initial cost of a new machine. The service life can be extended through proper maintenance, careful adjustments, avoidance of overloads, and using skilled operators. The useful life also is extended through proper storage during the off-season.

BREAK-EVEN USE

In the previous section we introduced the notion that the total cost per acre or hour deereases as annual use increases. This is the basis of break-even use. For some operations it may be more profitable to consider hiring contract workers instead of owning and operating one's own machine. The decision to hire may hinge on the break-even usage, that is, the amount of use for which the costs of owning a machine are the same as the costs of hiring a custom operator.

Suppose for a given machine that the product of FC% and P equals \$1000. Also suppose that the operating costs are \$4.00 per acre. The TAC equation would be:

$$TAC = \$1000 + (\$4.00 \times A)$$

where A = acres of use. Next calculate the values of TAC for acre (A) values of 10, 50, 100, 200, and 500 acres:

$$TAC = \$1000 + (\$4.00 \times 10 \text{ ac})$$

$$= \$1000 + \$40.00$$

$$= \$1040$$

Table 10-1. Break-even use.

Acres	Total annual cost
10	$ 1040
50	1200
100	1400
200	1800
500	3000

We complete the calculations for the remaining acres to obtain Table 10-1.

Table 10-2. Cost per acre in Table 10-1.

Acres	TAC	Cost per acre
10	$ 1040	$ 104.00
50	1200	24.00
100	1400	14.00
200	1800	9.00
500	3000	6.00

Then if we wish to determine the cost of using the machine on a per-acre basis, we divide the TAC by the acres for each situation, and get the values shown in Table 10-2. A comparison of the various levels of use shows that the cost per year decreases as use increases. It is more economical to hire a custom operator for $22.00 per acre to cover 50 acres, rather than do the work yourself. For 75 acres or more, it is more economical to own the machine and do the work yourself.

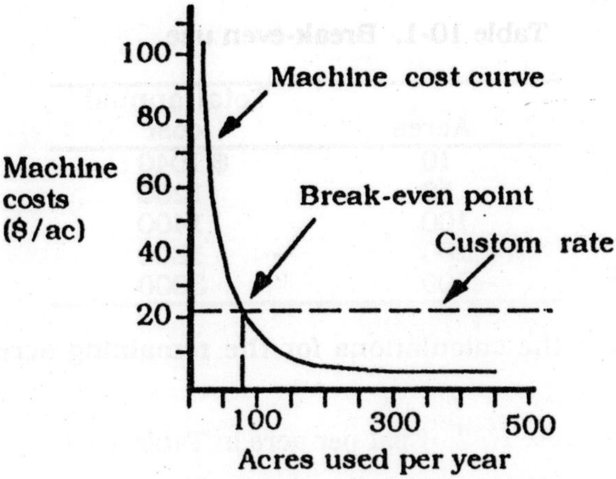

Figure 10.1. Break-even point.

The same relationship can be shown graphically by plotting the cost per acre versus acres covered, as in Figure 10.1.

Although this analysis indicates a hard-and-fast decision for a particular amount of use, the ownership--custom hiring decision should be tempered by other factors. Table 10-3 lists some advantages and disadvantages of custom hiring of farm equipment.

Table 10-3. **Advantages and disadvantages of custom hiring farm equipment.**

Advantages	Disadvantages
1. No ownership costs.	1. May not be possible to schedule when needed.
2. Cost of equipment can be invested in other enterprises.	2. Less control of quality of work.
3. Hired equipment usually supplies labor.	3. Increased potential for losses because of delays.
4. Less equipment is needed by owner, particularly specialized.	4. Increased risk of spreading weed seeds and diseases.
5. Owner can take advantage of newest machinery and techniques.	5. Costs for large jobs may be higher than owning machines.
6. Producer with small jobs can gain benefits of large machines.	6. Small jobs have a greater chance of being postponed.
7. Custom operator is responsible for repairs, maintenance, and materials.	7. Producer may not be able to utilize own labor freed up by custom hiring.

The break-even use (BEU) can be determined by the following equation:

$$BEU = \frac{AOC}{CR - OPC} \qquad (10\text{-}11)$$

where:

BEU = Break-even use (unit of use)
AOC = Annual ownership costs ($/yr)
CR = Custom rate ($/unit of use)
OPC = Operating costs ($/unit of use)

It is most important to use consistent units with each of the terms. If the custom rate is in dollars per acre, the operating cost must be in dollars per acre. In this case the units of the answer will be in acres per year.

Problem: What is the break-even use in acres for a $20,000 machine if the FC% is 22%, the operating costs are estimated to be $9.00 per hour, and the custom rate is $9.60 per acre?

Solution: Using Equation (10-11):

$$BEU = \frac{AOC}{CR - OPC}$$

$$= \frac{\$20{,}000 \times 0.22}{9.60 \frac{\$}{ac} - 9.00 \frac{\$}{hr}}$$

Because the custom rate and the operating costs are not in the same units, to determine the break-even use in acres the operating costs must be converted to $/ac. To do this we must know the effective capacity of the machine. If we assume an effective capacity of 2.50 acres per hour, then:

$$BEU\ (ac) = \frac{\$20{,}000 \times 0.22}{9.60 \frac{\$}{ac} - \left(9.00 \frac{\$}{hr} \times \frac{1\ hr}{2.50\ ac}\right)}$$

$$= \frac{\$4400}{9.60 \frac{\$}{ac} - 3.6 \frac{\$}{ac}}$$

$$= \frac{\$4400}{6.0 \frac{\$}{ac}}$$

$$= 730\ ac$$

To determine the break-even use in hours, the custom rate must be converted to dollars per hour.

MAINTENANCE SCHEDULES

Maintenance is the care given to a machine to ensure that it operates correctly and that it receives the required lubrication and adjustments. All machines require maintenance. Failure to provide adequate maintenance can shorten the life of the machine and/or increase its operating costs. Manufacturers consider the amount of resources that a machine will need to maintain its operation. The owner/operator's responsibility is to ensure that the maintenance is accomplished on schedule, based on the manufacturer's recommendations in the owner's manual. This schedule must be followed for the machine to reach its designed potential in performance and longevity.

PRACTICE PROBLEMS

1. What size of machine is required when it is necessary to cover 150 acres in 10 hours at 3.5 miles per hour and to operate with a field efficiency of 60%?
   Answer: 59 ft
2. Thirty hours are expected to be available to plant 125 acres. A planter can average 3 miles per hour and can operate with a field efficiency of 70%. What size of planter (rows) is required if the crop is planted in 32 inch rows?
   Answer: 6 rows (nearest size)
3. What size of tractor (ptohp) will be needed to pull a 7 shank subsoiler 24.0 inches deep and 3.25 miles per hour in a tight sandy loam soil?
   Answer: The answer will range from 118 to 186 hp depending on the value used for the draft.
4. Determine the total annual cost of owning and operating a tractor with the following characteristics:

AU = 600 hr	L = $8.50/hr
RM% = 0.015 %	FC% = 22%
P = $45,000	F = $20/hr
S = 4.75 mph	O = $0.10/hr

   Answer: $31,110/yr
5. Determine the break-even use for the tractor in problem 4 if a tractor can be leased for $55.00/hr.
   Answer: 500 hr

11
Sound and Noise

OBJECTIVES

1. Understand the nature of sound and the basis of sound measurement, the decibel (db).
2. Be able to compare different environmental sounds.
3. Understand how humans are affected by noise.
4. Become familiar with noise exposure standards and protection from excessive noise.

INTRODUCTION

Humans live in a world of sound. Many sounds are quite pleasant, and persons who are not hearing impaired enjoy hearing voices, music, and many sounds of nature. People often listen for sounds that could warn of danger or the malfunctioning of equipment. Individuals have differing abilities to detect sound of varying intensities and frequencies, and differ as well in their personal tolerance of and appreciation of sound.

Sound that is harsh and unpleasant (or unhealthy) commonly is referred to as noise. In recent years the subject of noise has been given considerable attention, especially as it affects human health and behavior. The federal government, through OSHA (the Occupational Safety and Health Administration), has established noise exposure limits to prevent worker hearing loss and/or psychological stress due to excessive exposure to noise. We need a understanding of sound and noise so that we can know when unhealthy environments may exist due to undesirable or unwanted sound.

WHAT SOUND IS

The sound that people hear is due to vibrations in air or substances that are transmitted to the hearing organs. What are perceived as sounds are sonic pressure waves that travel through the air (or different substances) and interact with the eardrum by entering the ear canal or by passing through the body. Thus the eardrum responds to "sound pressure." There is a very, very large change in sound pressure (perhaps as much as 10,000,000 times) as sounds vary from the "threshold of hearing" (the intensity of sound just barely detected by an average human ear) to the sound pressure created by a large jet engine operating nearby. People can "feel" sound when they touch a vibrating body and the vibrations pass through the body to the eardrum.

The sense of hearing also responds to sound frequency (or pitch), that is, the number of vibrations or cycles per second (hertz, abbreviated Hz). The range of sound frequencies that can be heard varies from about 20 to 20,000 Hz, depending on the individual. As the intensity of sound is increased to an appropriately high level for a given frequency, the hearing sensation becomes painful, and the "threshold of pain" is reached.

Human hearing also can distinguish between sounds that differ in quality, those combinations of frequencies and intensities that produce squealing, grating, grinding, or rasping sounds. When the frequencies and intensities are combined in suitable proportions, pleasant musical or vocal sounds result. Thus, the sounds that are heard can be quite complex, but their effects on humans are well established.

In this chapter our concern is with noise and how it may affect workers and their work. Generally, excessive noise can lead to hearing impairment, fatigue, annoyance, and interference with performance. Noise also can serve as a warning of equipment malfunction or a signal of needed maintenance. We frequently rely on sounds (or no sound) to tell us that equipment is performing satisfactorily.

HOW SOUND IS MEASURED

To simplify the measurement of sound, an exponential scale of sound pressure levels was developed that uses a unit called the *decibel (dB)*, whose values range from 0, a reference level referred to as the "threshold of hearing," to 100 or more. Note that the decibel is *not* an absolute measure of the sound pressure, but rather is a ratio of a *measured* sound pressure to a *reference* sound pressure. Also, because this sound scale is exponential, a sound of 10 dB has an intensity 10 times greater than a sound of 0 dB, and a sound of 20 dB is 100 times more intense than 0 dB. Thus, a 10 dB difference in sound pressure level changes the intensity by 10 times, a 20 dB difference changes the intensity by 100 times, a 30 dB difference changes the intensity by 1000 times, and so on.

The basic instrument used to measure continuous sound is the sound-level meter. It consists of a microphone to pick up the sound, an amplifier, one or more frequency weighting networks, and a meter to display the sound level. Sound-level meters usually are self-contained (they operate on internal batteries) and are small enough to be hand-held although tripod mounting generally is preferred.

Proper sound-level meter use involves careful placement of the microphone to avoid sound reflections that influence the readings. In measuring the noise exposure of an individual (his or her work environment), the microphone is placed as close as possible to the subject's ear (or where the ear would be in the work environment). Prior to use the instrument must be calibrated against a known stable sound source.

For many measurements, the dB(A) frequency weighting network (or A-weighted sound level) is commonly used. The frequency weighting is done because the apparent loudness that people attribute to a sound varies not only with the sound pressure but also with the frequency. The A-weighted sound level measurement is used mainly to measure outdoor, non-directional sound sources and in rating ambient noises for possible human reactions.

COMPARING DIFFERENT SOUNDS

Table 11-1 shows some common sounds and the approximate sound pressure level associated with them.

Note that the values shown in the table are average values. Also notice that (almost) identical sounds may come from different machines and situations. Further, individuals may differ in their tolerance of and classification of different sounds and noises.

Table 11-1. Decibel rating of common sounds.

Sound Pressure Level (db)		Sound Description
188		Apollo lift-off, close
150		Jet engine, 10 feet away
140	Pain threshold	
130		Warning siren
125		Chain saw
120	Discomfort threshold	Loud thunder
115	Max under federal law	
110		Very loud music
105		Loud motorcycle or lawn mower
100	Very loud	Pneumatic air-hammer
90		Cockpit of light plane, heavy truck
85		Average street traffic
80		Lathe, milling machine, loud singing
75		Vacuum cleaner, dishwasher
70		Average radio, noisy restaurant
65	Annoying	
60		Normal conversation, air conditioner
50		Light traffic, average office
40		Library, quiet office
30		Quiet room in home, audible whisper
20		Electric clock, faint whisper
10	Barely detectable	Rustle of leaves
0	Hearing threshold	

This chart may help you to identify and classify sounds that you normally encounter; and if they are disturbing or otherwise unhealthy, you can avoid them or properly protect yourself from any of their adverse effects.

THE EFFECT OF NOISE

As suggested previously, noise can have both psychological and physiological effects on people. *Psychologically* adverse noise mainly affects a worker's performance and state of well-being. Direct exposure to excessive noise may cause fatigue, distraction, annoyance, interference with communication, reduction in the memory function, and disturbance of rest and relaxation. Some or all of these effects may be involved in decreased performance in the workplace.

The main *physiological* effect of adverse noise is noise-induced hearing loss, which is irreversible damage to one or more parts of the hearing organs. However, high sound levels also can induce responses in other parts of the body, such as reduced blood circulation, change on the skin's resistance to electric current and a corresponding activation of the nervous system, increased muscle tension, changes in the breathing pattern, and disturbance of sleep. These non-hearing-related noise responses are considered reversible and soon disappear when the noise source is removed.

Not all adverse noise is encountered in the workplace. We are surrounded by such sound generators such as outdoor and indoor equipment and appliances (lawn mowers, chain saws, sink disposals, blenders, clothes washers, and the like) and recreation and hobby equipment (gas-powered model planes and cars, unmuffled racing car and boat engines, firearms and explosive devices, high power stereo amplifiers and speaker systems, trail motorcycles, snowmobiles, and pleasure aircraft, among other things). Many of these items generate unusually intense sounds, but when we are pre-occupied with the utility and the joy of using them, we are seldom aware of the noise they create or their potential for damaging our hearing.

PROTECTION FROM NOISE

We must become more aware or our "sound" environment, determine acceptable exposure limits, and take any steps necessary to avoid overexposure and potentially adverse psychological and physiological effects.

Some guidelines exist for exposure limits. Workplace exposure (time) standards have been established by OSHA, as shown in Table 11-2.

Table 11-2. Workplace maximum permissible noise exposure level versus daily exposure time.

Duration (hr/day)	Sound level db(A)
8	90
6	92
4	95
3	97
2	100
1.5	102
1	105
0.5	110
0.25 ≤	115

The Occupational Safety and Health Act makes provisions for employers to make accurate sound measurements in their places of business, to determine whether the workplace is safe for workers; the sound level should not exceed 90 dB(A) during an 8-hour work period. For sound levels above 90 dB(A), reductions in exposure time are required, with a limit of 15 minutes of exposure per day to a sound level of 115 dB(A). A further aspect of the Act is that no impulsive or impact noise should exceed 140 dB(A). Also, noise abatement in excessively noisy work areas is required. If a workplace is deemed excessively noisy, workers must be provided with safety equipment *and* be required to use it.

Besides the OSHA regulations and the regulations set forth under the Federal Noise Control Act (administered by EPA), several other federal agencies oversee noise control in related industries such as aviation, residential and commercial construction, all aspects of ground transportation, and mining. References to these regulations can be found in different volumes of the CFR (Code of Federal Regulations) that involve noise control.

Several things can be done. Once objectionable, excessive or unhealthy noise situations are identified in any environment, a course of action should be taken to eliminate or reduce the noise (through design changes or the use of sound-absorbing materials), or if that is not possible, to provide human protective equipment such as ear plugs, ear muffs, and specially designed helmets. Further, using Table 11-2 as a guide, one can identify and avoid prolonged exposure to, places where excessive noise is expected.

TOPICS FOR DISCUSSION

1. In your daily activities, identify and list the places where you believe that sounds (noise) are excessive.
2. For places that you deem to have excessive noise, make an estimate of the time you would want to spend in each place.
3. For places that you deem to have excessive noise, describe any changes that you might make to reduce the noise level.
4. There will be some places that you consider to have excessive noise where you need to be, and where you cannot reduce the noise level in any significant way. Describe how you would protect yourself in such an environment.

12
Measuring Distance

OBJECTIVES

1. Understand the advantages and disadvantages of the six common methods of measuring distance.
2. Be able to use the six common methods of measuring distance during surveying.

INTRODUCTION

Measuring distance and angles with simple instruments involves two of the most common procedures used in agricultural surveying. Even though the instruments are simple, a high degree of accuracy can be achieved with practice and careful work. In this chapter you will become acquainted with the basic methods and techniques of measuring distances. The layout and measurement of angles is covered in Chapter 13.

MEASURING DISTANCES

The principal methods of measuring distance are the (1) pacing, (2) odometer, (3) taping or "chaining," (4) stadia, (5) optical range finder, and (6) electronic distance measuring (EDM) methods. We will illustrate each of them in this chapter.

First it will be helpful to review the common units of distance (displacement). The common English units are as follows:

1 foot (ft) = 12 inches (in)
1 yard (yd) = 3 feet (ft)
1 rod = 16.5 feet (ft) = 5.5 yards (yd)
1 mile (mi) = 5280 feet (ft) = 1760 yards (yd) = 320 rods

The units cancellation method is very useful for converting from one unit of measure to another.

PACING

Pacing is the simplest and easiest method for measuring distance. With practice it is possible to pace a distance with an error of less than 2 feet per 100 feet. Frequently, this is all the precision that is necessary in agricultural work. The distance is determined by multiplying the number of steps taken between two points by one's *pace factor*. Each person must determine his or her own pace factor because pace factors will be different for each individual and change with time. Several factors can cause variations in pace factors, such as the roughness of the surface, the slope of the ground, and the type of vegetation. Care must be taken to ensure that a consistent pace factor is used. A pace factor is determined by pacing (walking) a measured distance, usually 300 to 500 feet, several times and determining the average length of pace (step).

Problem: An individual paces a 200-foot distance three times and counts 62, 60, and 64 paces. What is the person's pace factor (PF)?

Solution: The average number of steps is:

$$\bar{x} = \frac{62 + 60 + 64}{3}$$

$$= 62 \text{ steps}$$

and the pace factor is:

$$PF = \frac{200 \text{ ft}}{62 \text{ paces}}$$

$$= 3.23 \text{ ft}$$

Once the pace factor is known, the length of an unknown distance can be determined by counting the number of paces required to cover the distance and multiplying the number of paces by the pace factor.

Problem: If the individual in the previous problem paces the distance between two points and counts 375 paces, what is the distance in feet?

Solution: The distance, in feet, equals the number of paces times the pace factor. Or:

$$\text{ft} = 3.23 \frac{\text{ft}}{\text{pace}} \times 375 \text{ paces}$$

$$= 1210 \text{ ft}$$

ODOMETER

An odometer is a mechanical device that measures distance. An odometer wheel is used in surveying; this device counts the revolutions of a wheel and shows the distance traveled on a multiple dial readout (Figure 12.1). Any type of wheel can be used, including a bicycle or a vehicle wheel.

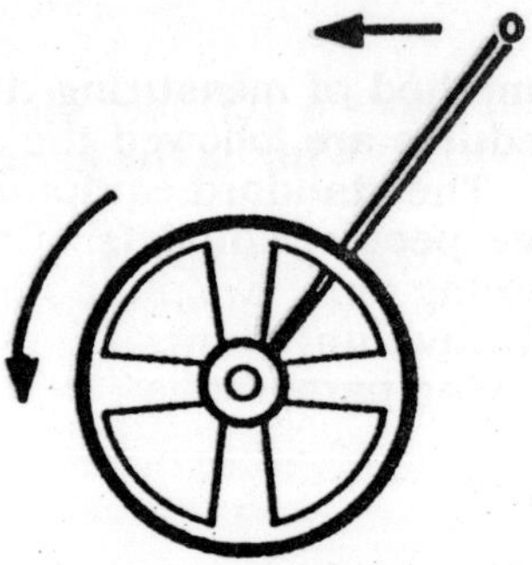

Figure 12.1. Odometer wheel.

If used correctly, a wheel is more accurate than pacing. An error of 1 foot per 100 feet can be expected. To be accurate, the wheel must roll along the ground without slipping. When an odometer is used, the readout should be reset to zero before starting; then the distance traveled can be read directly. If another type of wheel is being used, the distance traveled is equal to π times the diameter multiplied by the number of revolutions:

$$MD\ (ft) = \pi D \times N \qquad (12\text{-}1)$$

where:

MD = Measured distance
π = 3.14
D = Wheel diameter (ft)
N = Number of wheel revolutions

Problem: A bicycle wheel made 155.2 revolutions as it was rolled along the boundary of a field. If the wheel diameter is 2.16 ft, what is the length of the field (ft)?

Solution: Using Equation (12-1):

$$MD = \pi D \times N$$

$$= 3.14 \times 2.16 \text{ ft} \times 155.2$$

$$= 1050 \text{ ft}$$

TAPING

The most accurate method of measuring distances uses a steel tape. If proper procedures are followed the error will be less than 1.0 foot in 3000 feet. The standard equipment for a taping party, usually at least three people, consists of steel tape, two range poles, a set of 11 chaining pins, two plumb bobs, a hand level, and a field notebook. Individual items of taping equipment are described in the following paragraphs.

SURVEYOR'S STEEL TAPE

Standard steel tapes are 100 feet long and 3/8 inch wide, and weigh 2 to 3 pounds per 100 feet. They are graduated with marks set in babbitt-metal bosses with each foot marked, from 0 to 100 feet. Usually only the first foot and/or the last foot of the tape are subdivided, with the subdivisions usually in tenths or hundredths of a foot. Some tapes have an extra graduated foot at each end beyond the 0- and 100-foot marks.

METALLIC TAPE

Metallic tapes are handy for making rough measurements or when great accuracy is not needed. These tapes are constructed of several different materials but usually are available in 50-foot and 100-foot lengths and usually are hand-wound.

CHAINING PINS

Chaining pins are made of heavy gauge wire and are 12 to 15 inches long, are painted red and white, and sometimes have a bright cloth attached to help locate them in tall grass. They are used to mark the end of each tape length and come with 11 pins in a set; one pin is used to mark the start of the chaining (taping), and the remaining 10 pins are used to mark lengths of tape. When all 11 pins have been used, assuming a 100 foot tape, 1000 feet has been measured.

RANGE POLES

Range poles are 1-inch-diameter tubular steel or nonmetallic shafts 6 to 10 feet long with one pointed end. They are alternately painted red and white and are used for "lining in" when one is taping or measuring angles.

PLUMB BOBS

Plumb bobs with 6 to 10 feet of cord attached are used when one is taping on sloping or irregular ground to transfer the distance from the horizontally held tape to a point on the ground. They also are attached to a surveyor's level, to locate the level over a stake, when one is measuring distances accurately or laying out angles.

HAND LEVEL

A hand level consists of a small sighting tube 5 to 6 inches long equipped with a spirit level, a glass tube filled with a liquid and a bubble. The image of the bubble is reflected by a prism and can be observed by looking through the tube. The instrument is held to the operator's eye and is leveled by raising or lowering the end until the cross-hair intersects the image of the spirit-level bubble. This is a low-precision instrument used to make rough measurements of the slope and as an aid in keeping the surveyor's tape level. Newer models may also include stadia cross-hairs and direct-reading angle scales.

TAPING PROCEDURES

There are six basic steps involved in taping: (1) lining in, (2) applying tension, (3) plumbing, (4) marking tape lengths, (5) reading the tape, and (6) recording the distance.

All distances in surveying are measured by stations. A distance of 100 feet is called a *full station* and is written as 1+00 ft. A distance of 123 feet is written as 1+23 ft.

For most surveys the intent is to discover the true horizontal distance between two points. Two methods are used: (1) tape and plumb bob or (2) tape and calculation. If the latter method is used, the percent slope must be measured and the horizontal distance calculated by trigonometry or obtained from tables.

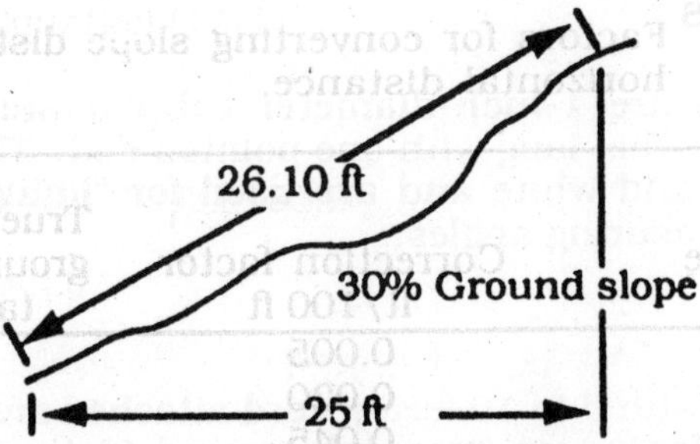

Figure 12.2. Effect of ground slope on true horizontal distance.

The need for horizontal measurements is illustrated in Figure 12.2. If measured along the surface of the ground, the distance would be 26.10 feet, whereas the true horizontal distance is 25.00 feet.

If a slope distance is measured, the percent slope also must be measured and the true horizontal distance determined from tables or calculated by trigonometry. The percent slope can be measured by a hand level or a surveying level. Table 12-1 shows the correction factors for various slopes up to 30%. Note that for slopes less than 2% the correction factor is very small, but for greater slopes it becomes significant.

Table 12-1. Factors for converting slope distance to true horizontal distance.

Slope %	Correction factor ft/100 ft	True distance on ground for 100 ft tape length
1	0.005	99.995
2	0.020	99.980
3	0.045	99.955
4	0.080	99.920
5	0.125	99.875
6	0.180	99.820
7	0.245	99.755
8	0.320	99.680
9	0.405	99.595
10	0.500	99.500
11	0.605	99.395
12	0.720	99.280
15	1.130	99.870
18	1.620	98.380
20	2.020	97.980
25	3.190	96.810
30	4.220	95.780

If true horizontal distance is determined by using method number two, the correction factor per 100 feet is multiplied by the slope distance and divided by 100, and the product is *subtracted* from the slope distance. It is important to remember that the correction factors are for 100 feet of distance. You must *divide* the slope distance by 100 first:

$$THD = SD - \left(\left(\frac{SD}{100}\right) \times CF\right) \quad (12\text{-}2)$$

where:

THD = True horizontal distance
SD = Slope distance
CF = Correction factor

Problem: What is the true horizontal distance (THD) if the slope distance (SD) is 623.82 feet and the slope is 12%?

Solution: Using Equation (12-2) and a correction factor:

$$THD = SD - \left(\left(\frac{SD}{100}\right) \times CF\right)$$

$$= 623.82 \text{ ft} - \left(\left(\frac{623.82 \text{ ft}}{100}\right) \times 0.720\right)$$

$$= 623.82 \text{ ft} - 4.49 \text{ ft}$$

$$= 619 \text{ ft}$$

If the ground slope is not uniform, the slope and the slope distance for each segment of the line must be determined and a separate correction applied to each segment.

With the horizontal tape method (number 1), one end of the tape is held on the ground, while the other end is raised until the tape is horizontal. The true distance is transferred to the ground from the elevated end of the tape by a plumb bob. If the slope is more that 5%, it is necessary to use a process known as "breaking chain." In this method the head chainman lays out the full length of the tape. The 100-foot length then is divided into convenient increments, usually 25 or 50 feet, with the chainman holding the tape horizontal and plumbing down to the ground at each increment. This process is illustrated in Figure 12.3. In this example the chain was "broken" into 25-foot sections. Every 25 feet a plumb bob and line was used to set a pin.

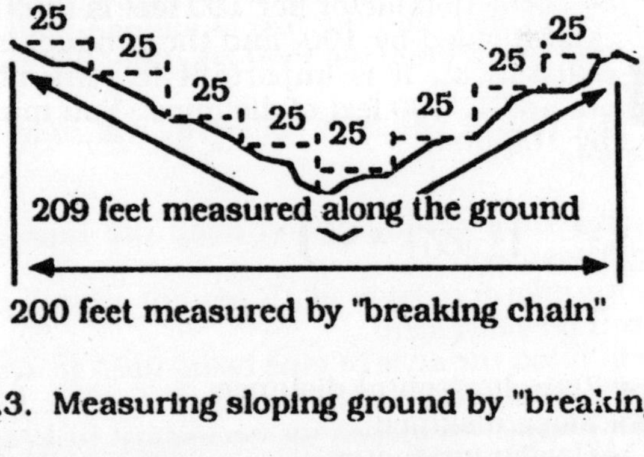

Figure 12.3. Measuring sloping ground by "breaking chain."

For accurate results, a taping activity must be very carefully thought out and well organized. The following procedure for taping is recommended to ensure accurate results. A taping party consists of at least three people: the head chainman, the rear chainman, and a note keeper. An axeman also may be necessary in brushy areas. The 11 chaining pins serve as temporary in brushy areas. The 11 chaining pins serve as temporary markers for each station, and also help to count the number of full stations measured.

The head chainman begins by setting a pin for the starting point and then leads off with the zero end of the tape. After one full station has been measured, the head chainman will have placed one pin in the ground at the beginning and one to mark the end of the first station. At this point he or she will have 9 pins left on the ring. As the chain is moved to the next station, the rear chainman pulls the pin used to start the chaining. After two full stations, the head chainman will have placed three pins in the ground and have 8 pins on the ring, and the rear chainman will have one in hand and one in the ground. If this system is carefully followed, the number of full stations measured will always be the same as the number of pins held by the rear chainman.

As described above, most surveyor's tapes are graduated in feet throughout their full length, with the first and/or last foot of the tape graduated in tenths of a foot. A special procedure is required for measuring a distance shorter than a full tape length. When the party nears the end of the line and the remaining distance is less than 100 feet, the head chainman moves the tape along the line until less than one foot of tape extends beyond the end point, and the rear chainman holds a whole foot mark beside the chaining pin marking the last full station. They both read the tape and the head chainman's reading is subtracted from the rear chainman's reading. For example, suppose that the head chainman reads 0.21 feet, and the rear chainman reads 53 feet. If the rear chainman has 6 pins, the total length of the line is 652.79 feet [600 ft + (53 ft - 0.21 ft)].

The following rules, if carefully followed, will help guarantee accuracy in taping.

1. Align the tape carefully, and keep the tape on the line being measured.
2. Keep a uniform tension of 15 pounds of pull on the tape for each measurement.
3. Keep in mind the style of tape being used to avoid an error of 1 or 2 feet at each end of the tape.
4. "Break chain" on slopes as necessary to keep the tape level, or calculate the percent slope if measuring with the tape on the ground.
5. Carefully mark each station and keep an accurate count of the stations.

STADIA

If one needs to measure distance very rapidly but with accuracy than taping, the stadia method may be used. "Stadia" comes from an early Greek word for a unit of length. Surveying instruments equipped for stadia measurement have two additional horizontal cross-hairs, called *stadia hairs*. They are placed equidistant above and below the horizontal leveling cross-hair. The distance between the stadia hairs and the horizontal cross-hair is fixed by the manufacturer to provide a constant *stadia interval factor* (SIF) for the instrument. The most common stadia interval factor is 100. If an instrument has an SIF of 100, there will be a one foot *stadia interval*, that is the difference between the top stadia reading (TSR) and the bottom stadia reading (BSR), when the rod is held 100 feet away from the instrument.

When the stadia method is used to measure a distance, the instrument person reads the TSR and the BSR, and then multiplies the difference by the stadia interval factor.

$$D\ (ft) = (TSR - BSR) \times 100 \qquad (12\text{-}3)$$

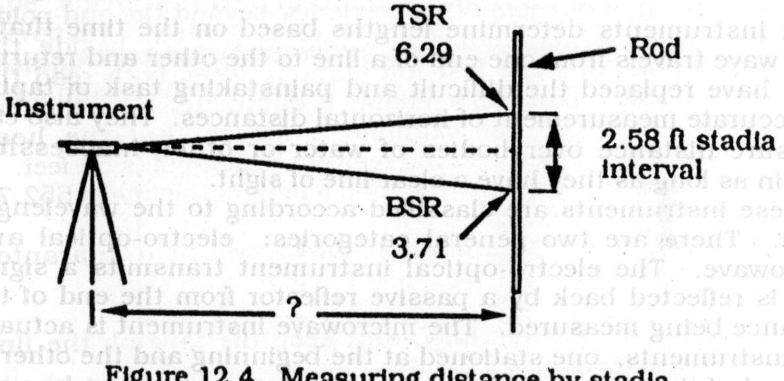

Figure 12.4. Measuring distance by stadia.

Refer to Figure 12.4. The top stadia hair reading (TSR) is 6.29, and the bottom stadia hair reading (BSR) is 3.71. Thus the stadia interval is equal to 6.29 minus 3.71, or 2.58 feet. The distance from the instrument to the rod is equal to 2.58 multiplied by 100, or 258 feet.

Problem: What is the distance to the rod if the stadia readings are 6.07 and 3.02?

Solution: Using Equation (12-3):

$$
\begin{aligned}
D\ (ft) &= (TSR - BSR) \times 100 \\
&= (6.07\ ft - 3.02\ ft) \times 100 \\
&= 3.05\ ft \times 100 \\
&= 305\ ft
\end{aligned}
$$

OPTICAL RANGE FINDERS

These instruments operate on the same principle as range finders on cameras. The operator looks through the eyepiece and adjusts the focus until two images are in coincidence, superimposed on top of each other. The distance is read from a scale on the instrument. Optical range finders have an acceptable level of accuracy for reconnaissance or sketching purposes for short distances, but the error increases as the distance increases.

ELECTRONIC DISTANCE MEASUREMENT (EDM)

EDM instruments determine lengths based on the time that a light wave travels from one end of a line to the other and returns. They have replaced the difficult and painstaking task of taping for accurate measurement of horizontal distances. They also can measure distance over bodies of water or other inaccessible terrain as long as they have a clear line of sight.

These instruments are classified according to the wavelength used. There are two general categories: electro-optical and microwave. The electro-optical instrument transmits a signal that is reflected back by a passive reflector from the end of the distance being measured. The microwave instrument is actually two instruments, one stationed at the beginning and the other at the end of the distance. The microwave instrument can be used when the line of sight is obscured by fog or light rain.

PRACTICE PROBLEMS

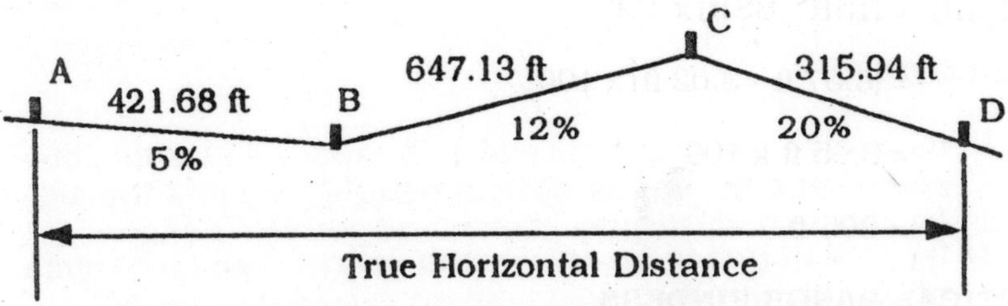

Figure 12.5. Diagram for true horizontal distance problem.

1. Find the true horizontal distance for Figure 12.5.
   Answer: 1400 ft (Using Table 12.1)
2. If the head chainman has 3 pins, how far has the chaining party traveled?
   Answer: 700 ft
3. What is the horizontal distance if the TSR is 8.35 ft and the BSR is 4.86 ft?
   Answer: 349 ft
4. A tractor tire 6.0 feet in diameter is rolled 20 revolutions. How far has the tire traveled?
   Answer: 380 ft

13
Angles and Areas

OBJECTIVES

1. Be able to use the three common methods of laying out and measuring angles without using a level or a transit.
2. Be able to find the area of standard geometric shapes.
3. Be able to determine the area of irregular-shaped tracts of land by division into standard geometric shapes.
4. Be able to determine the area of irregular-shaped tracts of land using the two trapezoidal equations.

INTRODUCTION

The layout and measurement of angles is a very important part of agricultural surveying. In this section you will learn, using simple tools and procedures, two methods that can be used to lay out a perpendicular (90°) angle and one method that can be used to lay out and measure any angle between 0° and 90°. These procedures are useful in planning buildings and fences and in determining the corner angles of irregular-shaped tracts, fields, and/or smaller areas. Angles are used to determine the areas of fields and the location of property lines.

ANGLES

The two methods limited to 90° angles are the chord method and the 3-4-5 method. The method that can be used with any angle between 0° and 90° is the tape-sine method. The following discussion illustrates all three methods.

CHORD METHOD

A chord is a line connecting any two points on a circle. This geometric principle can be used to lay out a line at a 90° angle to a base line. The method is illustrated in Figure 13.1.

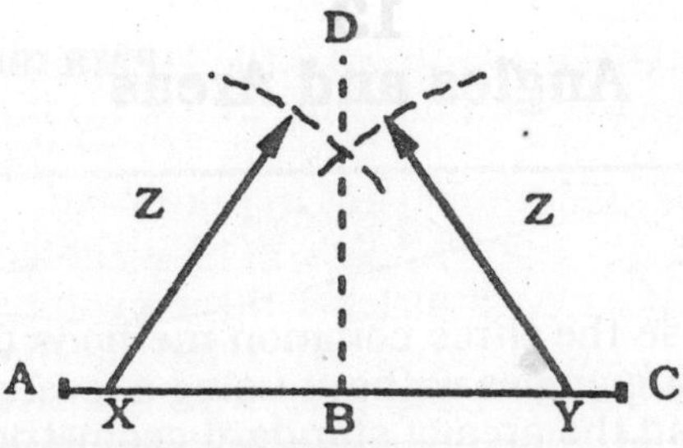

Figure 13.1. Laying out a right angle by the cord method.

The line BD is established at a 90° angle by completing the following steps:

1. Establish the base line AC if it is not in existence (fence or road edge, etc.).
2. Establish the turning point at B.
3. Set points X and Y equidistant from point B and on line AC.
4. Use a length greater than the distance XB or YB, and scribe an arc from X and Y as shown.
5. Set a stake at the intersection of the two arcs.
6. The line established by this stake and B will be at 90° with the base line AC.

This method is very simple and actually can be accomplished with two different lengths of string or even tree branches. The one disadvantage is that the base line must be extended past the turning point (B).

3-4-5 METHOD

The 3-4-5 method of laying out a right angle is based on the Pythagorean theorem: for any right triangle, the square of the hypotenuse is equal to the sum of the squares of the other two sides. In this method, if any multiples of 3 and 4 are used as the sides of a right triangle, the hypotenuse will be a multiple of 5. To prove this, study the following equation:

$$5 = \sqrt{3^2 + 4^2}$$

$$= \sqrt{25}$$

$$5 = 5$$

This method has three requirements: (1) the same units (feet, yards, etc.) must be used on all three sides; (2) the same multiples of 3, 4, and 5 are used for the lengths of the three sides; (3) the longest length is used for the hypotenuse. If these three requirements are met, a 90° angle will be established.

This method works best if at least three people and one or more tapes are used. If *three* tapes are used, either the 3 or the 4 dimension is used as the base line, and the two corners on the base line are marked. Then two people, one standing at each base line corner, hold two tape ends together at the correct dimensions, and a third person holds the remaining tape ends together at the correct dimensions and moves the third corner until the tapes are all at equal tension.

This process also may be accomplished by using a 100-foot tape. Because surveyor's steel tapes are not designed to be bent at a sharp angle, loops must be formed at two of the corners. It is recommended that at least a 5-foot loop be used. Study Figure 13.2.

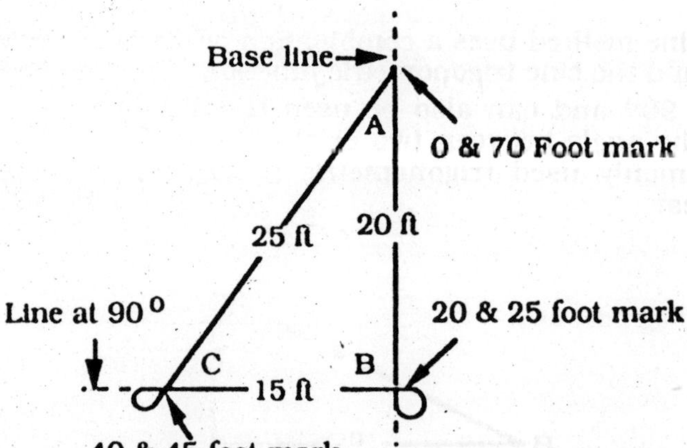

Figure 13.2. Laying out a right angle by the 3-4-5 method and a 100-foot tape.

By completing the following steps, a 90° angle may be laid out using the 3-4-5 method. This procedure will require three people.

1. Establish the base line (AB) and corner B.
2. Lay out the tape along the base line with the 20-foot mark (4 ft x 5) at corner B and the zero mark at corner A.
3. Set corner A, and have a person hold the zero mark on the corner.

4. Form a 5-foot loop in the tape, and have a person hold the 20-foot mark over the 25-foot mark, and align these marks over corner B.
5. Lay out the remaining tape in the direction of corner C.
6. Note the position of the 40foot mark (25 ft + 15 ft) (15 ft = 3 ft x 5), and form a 5-foot loop in the tape. Hold the 40- and 45-foot marks on corner C.
7. Extend the tape back to corner A.
8. Hold the 70-foot (45 ft + 25 ft) (25 ft = 5 ft x 5) and 0 marks together at corner A.
9. If the individuals at A and B hold their positions carefully while the individual at C tightens the tape in both directions, a 90° angle will be made at B.

This process will work for any combination of lengths as long as they are multiples of 3, 4, and 5. One advantage of this method is that the base line does not need to extend past the 90° corner.

TAPE-SINE METHOD

The tape-sine method uses a combination of distances measured by a tape and the sine trigonometric function. This method is not limited to 90° and can also be used to lay out an angle and measure the angle between two existing lines. A review of the three commonly used trigonometric functions will make this method clear.

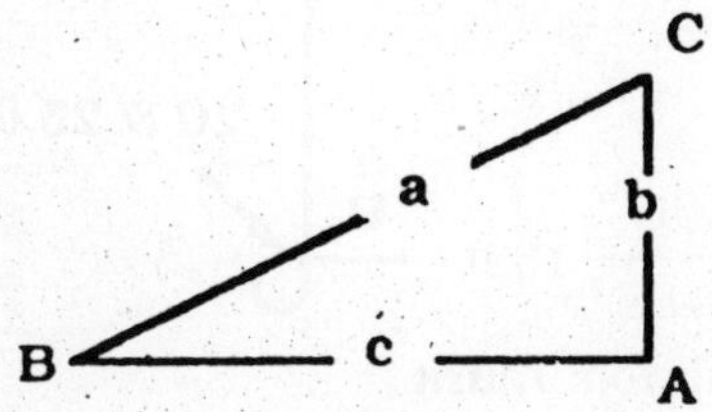

Figure 13.3. Notation for a right triangle.

Trigonometric functions are based on the principle that one unique ratio exists between the lengths of any two sides for angles B and C (Figure 13.3). Because a right triangle has three sides, each angle (B and C) has six possible combinations of two sides. Each one of these combinations has been given a name. The three common ratios are:

$$\text{Sine B} = \frac{\text{Opposite side (b)}}{\text{Hypotenuse (a)}} \tag{13-1}$$

$$\text{Cosine B} = \frac{\text{Adjacent side (c)}}{\text{Hypotenuse (a)}} \tag{13-2}$$

$$\text{Tangent B} = \frac{\text{Opposite side (b)}}{\text{Adjacent side (c)}} \tag{13-3}$$

The same relationships are true for angle C. Each of these functions forms an equation with three variables--the function of the angle and the lengths of two sides. If any two of the variables are known, the third can be determined.

In the tape-sine method, only the sine function is used. The procedure for laying out an angle (ø) is different from the procedure for measuring the angle between two lines.

We will discuss the procedure for measuring an existing angle first. Using the example illustrated in Figure 13.4, the first step is to form two right triangles. This is accomplished by laying out an equal distance along each side AB and AC (100 feet if possible) and measuring the distance BC (see Figure 13.4).

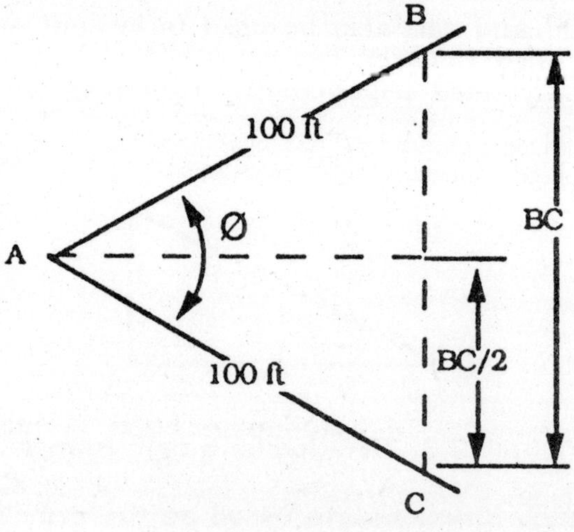

Figure 13.4. Diagram of the tape-sine method.

The distances BC/2 and AC are two sides of a right triangle. For this example we will assume that the distance BC = 61.8 feet. The angle for either triangle can be found by using Equation (13-1):

$$\text{Sine A} = \frac{\text{Opposite side (b)}}{\text{Hypotenuse (a)}}$$

$$= \frac{\text{Distance BC/2}}{\text{Distance AC}}$$

$$= \frac{30.9 \text{ ft}}{100 \text{ ft}}$$

$$= 0.309$$

The value 0.309 is the sine ratio of angle A. The next step is to determine the angle having a sine ratio of 0.309.

If you have a calculator with trigonometric functions, enter 0.309 and the inverse of the sine function. If you cannot use your calculator, consult Table 13-1.

Table 13-1. Sine values.

Angle 0°	Sine of the angle	Angle 0°	Sine of the angle	Angle 0°	Sine of the angle
0	0.000	31	0.515	61	0.875
1	0.017	32	0.530	62	0.883
2	0.035	33	0.545	63	0.891
3	0.052	34	0.559	64	0.899
4	0.070	35	0.574	65	0.906
5	0.087	36	0.588	66	0.914
6	0.105	37	0.602	67	0.921
7	0.122	38	0.616	68	0.927
8	0.139	39	0.629	69	0.934
9	0.156	40	0.643	70	0.940
10	0.174	41	0.656	71	0.946
11	0.191	42	0.669	72	0.951
12	0.208	43	0.682	73	0.956
13	0.225	44	0.695	74	0.961
14	0.242	45	0.707	75	0.966
15	0.259	46	0.719	76	0.971
16	0.276	47	0.731	77	0.974
17	0.292	48	0.743	78	0.978
18	0.309	49	0.755	79	0.982
19	0.326	50	0.766	80	0.985
20	0.342	51	0.777	81	0.988
21	0.358	52	0.788	82	0.990
22	0.375	53	0.799	83	0.993
23	0.391	54	0.809	84	0.995
24	0.407	55	0.819	85	0.996
25	0.423	56	0.829	86	0.998
26	0.438	57	0.839	87	0.999
27	0.454	58	0.848	88	0.999
28	0.469	59	0.857	89	1.000
29	0.485	60	0.866	90	1.000
30	0.500				

Either source should give an angle of 18°. Because we used the distance BC/2 to solve for the angle, the angle ABC is actually 18° x 2, or 36°.

The same procedures can be used to lay out an angle. For example, suppose you need to establish a fence at 40° to an existing fence. How would the tape-sine method be used? Study Figure 13.6.

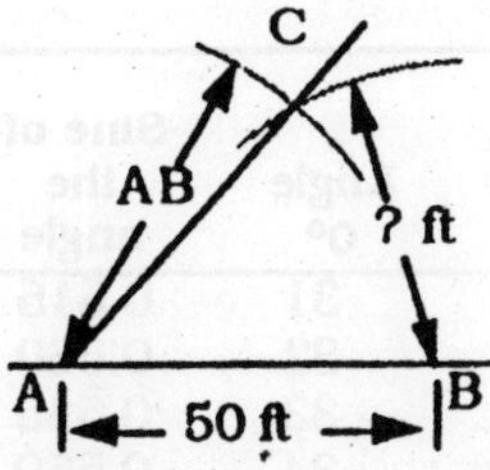

Figure 13.5. Laying out an angle by the tape-sine method.

To lay out an angle we mentally form two right triangles, solve for the length of the opposite side of one, and then double the distance. This distance can be used to lay out the arc needed to locate point C. A line from point A through C will establish the fence at the correct angle. The first step is to measure a distance along the present fence (AB). In this example we have used 50.0 feet. Next, we determine the unknown distance (? ft) that, when combined with the hypotenuse (50 feet), will form the correct ratio for 40°. For this type of problem we need to rearrange the sine function Equation (13-1) to solve for the length of the opposite side:

$$\text{Sine A} = \frac{\text{Opposite}}{\text{Hypotenuse}}$$

$$\text{Opposite} = \text{Sine A} \times \text{Hypotenuse}$$

$$= \text{Sine } 20^o \times 50.0 \text{ ft}$$

$$= 0.342 \times 50 \text{ ft}$$

$$= 17.1 \text{ ft}$$

The unknown distance is equal to 17.1 ft x 2 = 34.2 ft. To lay out the angle, mark an arc, with a radius of 34.2 feet, from point B and another arc, with a radius of 50, from point A, and set a pin at the intersection of the two arcs (point C). A line drawn from point A through point C will establish a line at a 40° angle to the base line (AB).

AREAS OF STANDARD GEOMETRIC SHAPES

One of the most common applications of surveying is to measure the area of a lot, field, farm, or ranch. If great accuracy is required, a professional engineer or a land surveyor should be employed. If this level of accuracy is not required, many areas can be determined with nothing more elaborate than a steel tape and the application of area formulas from geometry. The area of irregularly shaped fields can be found by subdividing them into standard shapes, determining the areas of the subdivisions by calculation, and then summing the areas of the subdivisions to find the total area. For example, the irregular-shaped field shown in Figure 13.6 has been subdivided (using dashed lines) into common geometric shapes. This activity should be done first to determine what measurements are needed to calculate the area.

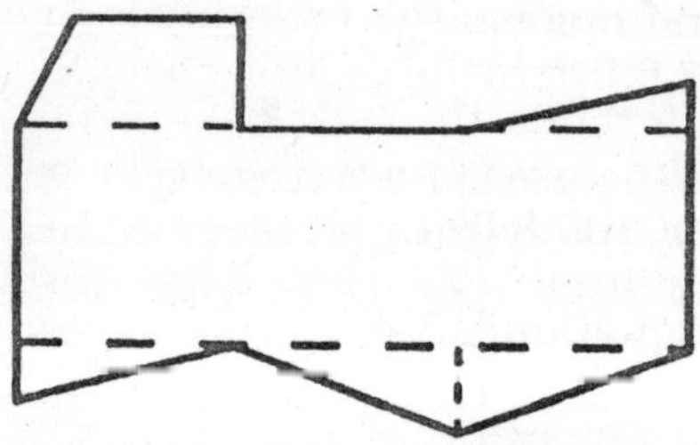

Figure 13.6. Irregular shaped field divided into common geometric shapes.

To use this method it is necessary to apply the correct area formula for each common geometric shape. We will illustrate the common shapes and the area formula for each.

TRIANGLE

Three different equations are used, based upon the known dimensions of the triangle. The first formula is used when the base and height are known (see Figure 13.7).

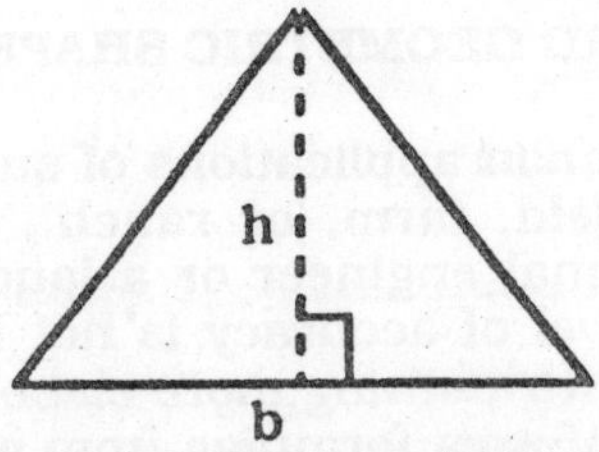

Figure 13.7. Triangle with base and height known.

$$A = \frac{1}{2} \times (b \times h) \qquad (13\text{-}4)$$

where:

A = Area
b = Length of base
h = Height perpendicular to base

Problem: What is the area of a triangle (ac) with a base 150.0 feet long and a height of 100.0 feet.

Solution: Using Equation (13-4):

$$A = \frac{1}{2} \times (b \times h)$$

$$= \frac{1}{2} \times (150.0 \text{ ft} \times 100.0 \text{ ft})$$

$$= 7500 \text{ ft}^2$$

Converted to acres this is:

$$A \text{ (ac)} = 7500 \text{ ft}^2 \times \frac{1 \text{ ac}}{43{,}560 \text{ ft}^2}$$

$$= 0.172 \text{ ac}$$

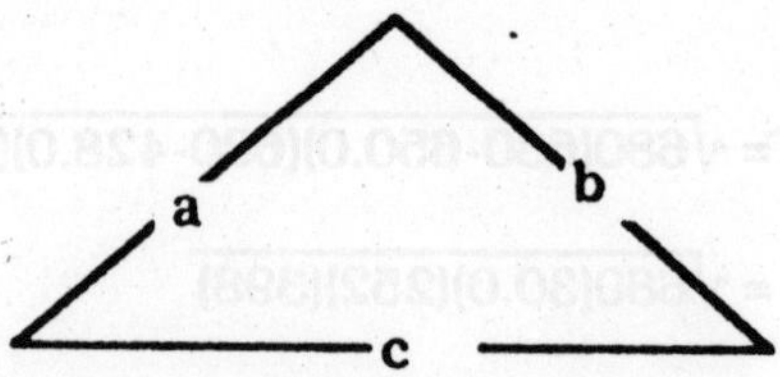

Figure 13.8. Triangle with three sides known.

The second type of triangle is one where the lengths of the three sides are known (Figure 13.8). The equation for area is:

$$A = \sqrt{S(S-a)(S-b)(S-c)} \qquad (13\text{-}5)$$

where a, b, and c are the lengths of the three sides and:

$$S = \frac{a+b+c}{2}$$

Problem: Determine the area (ft^2) for a triangle having sides measuring 650.0 feet, 428.0 feet and 282.0 feet.

Solution: Using Equation (13-5):

$$A = \sqrt{S(S-a)(S-b)(S-c)}$$

Solving for S:

$$S = \frac{a+b+c}{2}$$

$$= \frac{650.0\text{ ft} + 428.0\text{ ft} + 282.0\text{ ft}}{2}$$

$$= \frac{1360}{2}$$

$$= 680\text{ ft}$$

and the area is:

$$A = \sqrt{680(680-650.0)(680-428.0)(680-282.0)}$$

$$= \sqrt{680(30.0)(252)(398)}$$

$$= \sqrt{20.5 \times 10^8}$$

$$= 4.53 \times 10^4 \text{ ft}^2$$

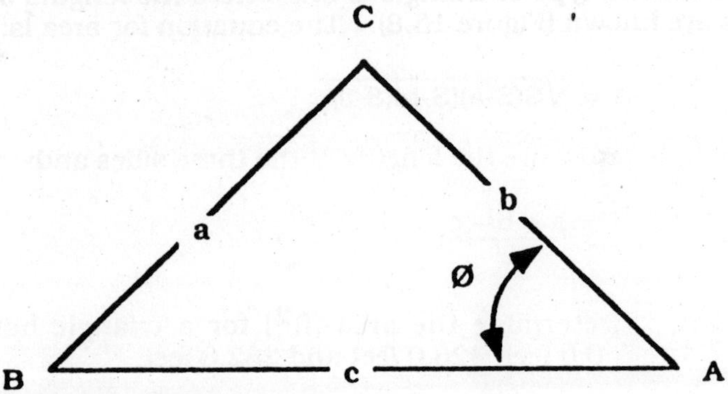

Figure 13.9. Triangle with two sides and one angle known.

The third type of triangle illustrated is one in which an angle and the adjacent sides are known, and the angle is less than 90° (Figure 13.9). The equation for area (A) is:

$$A = \frac{1}{2} \times (b \times c \times \sin ø) \quad (13\text{-}6)$$

where:

A = Area
b = Known side
c = Known side
ø = Angle between sides b and c
sin = Sine trigonometric function

Problem: Determine the area (ft^2) of a triangle given sides of 350.0 feet and 555.0 feet and the included angle of 45°.

Solution: Using Equation (13-6) and the sine value for the angle:

$$A = \frac{1}{2} \times (a \times b \times \sin \varnothing)$$

$$= \frac{1}{2} \times (350.0 \text{ ft} \times 555.0 \text{ ft} \times 0.707)$$

$$= \frac{1}{2} \times 1.373 \times 10^5 \text{ ft}^2$$

$$= 6.87 \times 10^4 \text{ ft}^2$$

RECTANGLE, SQUARE AND PARALLELOGRAM

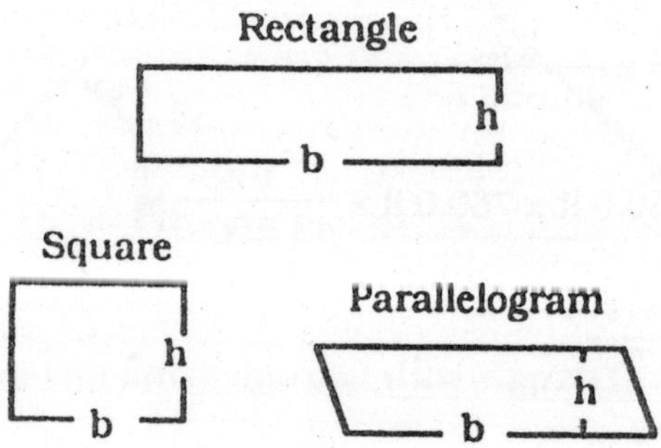

Figure 13.10. Dimensions of rectangle, square, and parallelogram.

These shapes are considered together because their areas are calculated by the same equation. Remember that the height (h) for a parallelogram is perpendicular to the base (b) (see Figure 13.10). The equation for area is:

$$A = b \times h \qquad (13\text{-}7)$$

where:

A = Area
b = Length of base
h = Height perpendicular to base

Problem: What is the area (ft^2) of a rectangle measuring 1320.0 feet by 660.0 feet?

Solution: Using Equation (13-7):

$$A = b \times h$$

$$= 1320.0 \text{ ft} \times 660.0 \text{ ft}$$

$$= 8.712 \times 10^5 \text{ ft}^2$$

Problem: What is the area (ac) of a parallelogram where the base measures 1050.0 feet, and the height measures 750.0 feet?

Solution: Equation (13-7) could be used to solve for the square feet and the answer converted to acres, but it is acceptable to attach the units conversion to the equation:

$$A\ (ac) = b \times h \times \frac{1 \text{ ac}}{43{,}560 \text{ ft}^2}$$

$$= 1050.0 \text{ ft} \times 750.0 \text{ ft} \times \frac{1 \text{ ac}}{43{,}560 \text{ ft}^2}$$

$$= \frac{788{,}000}{43{,}560}$$

$$= 18.1 \text{ ac}$$

CIRCLE OR SECTOR

The area of a circle, in a slightly different form, was used in Chapter 5 in figuring engine displacement.

$$A = \pi r^2 \qquad (13\text{-}8)$$

where:

A = Area
π = 3.14
r = Radius of the circle

A sector is slice of a circle. The known dimensions, the angle or the arc length, dictate the equation used to solve for the area of the sector. Study Figure 13.11.

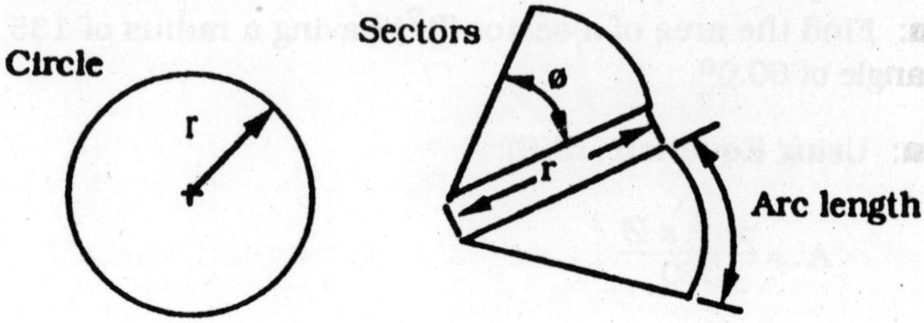

Figure 13.11. Circle and sectors.

If the angle is known, the equation is:

$$A = \frac{\pi r^2 \times \varnothing}{360} \qquad (13\text{-}9)$$

where:

A = Area
π = 3.14
Ø = Included angle of the sector
r = Radius of sector

If the length of the arc is known, the equation is:

$$A = \frac{r \times \text{Arc length}}{2} \qquad (13\text{-}10)$$

Problem: Find the area of a circle (ft^2) having a radius of 75.0 feet.

Solution: Using Equation (13-8):

$$A = \pi r^2$$

$$= 3.14 \times (75.0 \text{ ft})^2$$

$= 3.14 \times 5620$

$= 17,600 \text{ ft}^2$

Problem: Find the area of a sector (ft^2) having a radius of 135.0 ft and an angle of 60.0°.

Solution: Using Equation (13-9):

$$A = \frac{\pi r^2 \times Ø}{360}$$

$$= \frac{3.14 \times (135.0 \text{ ft})^2 \times 60.0°}{360}$$

$$= \frac{3.43 \times 10^6}{360}$$

$$= 9.53 \times 10^3 \text{ ft}^2$$

Problem: What is the area of a sector (ac) if the radius is 100.0 feet and the arc length is 210.0 feet?

Solution: Using Equation (13-10) (and adding the conversion value from square feet to acres):

$$A = \frac{r \times \text{Arc length}}{2} \times \frac{1 \text{ ac}}{43,560 \text{ ft}^2}$$

$$= \frac{100.0 \text{ ft} \times 210 \text{ ft}}{2} \times \frac{1 \text{ ac}}{43,560 \text{ ft}^2}$$

$$= \frac{21,000 \text{ ft}^2}{2} \times \frac{1 \text{ ac}}{43,560 \text{ ft}^2}$$

$$= 0.241 \text{ ac}$$

TRAPEZOID

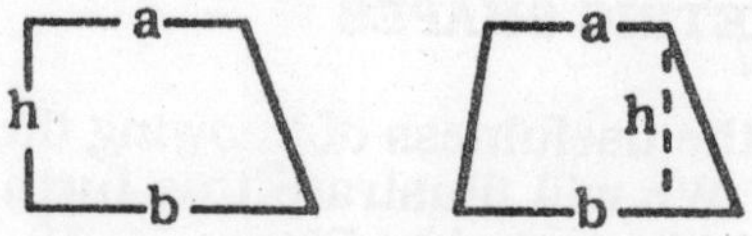

Figure 13.12. Trapezoids.

A trapezoid is a four-sided figure with only two parallel sides (see Figure 13.12). The area of a trapezoid is determined by the equation:

$$A = h \times \left(\frac{a + b}{2}\right) \qquad (13\text{-}11)$$

where:

A = Area
h = Height (distance between the parallel sides)
a = Length of one parallel side
b = Length of the second parallel side

Problem: What is the area (ac) of a trapezoid with parallel sides of 300.0 feet and 450.0 feet, and with a height of 120 feet?

Solution: Using Equation (13-11) (plus conversion to acres):

$$A = h \times \left(\frac{a + b}{2}\right) \times \frac{1 \text{ ac}}{43{,}560 \text{ ft}^2}$$

$$= 120.0 \text{ ft} \times \left(\frac{300.0 \text{ ft} + 450.0 \text{ ft}}{2}\right) \times \frac{1 \text{ ac}}{43{,}560 \text{ ft}^2}$$

$$= 120.0 \text{ ft} \times 375 \text{ ft} \times \frac{1 \text{ ac}}{43{,}560 \text{ ft}^2}$$

$$= 45{,}000 \times \frac{1 \text{ ac}}{43{,}560 \text{ ft}^2}$$

$$= 1.03 \text{ ac}$$

DETERMINING AREAS OF IRREGULAR-SHAPED FIELDS USING STANDARD GEOMETRIC SHAPES

Figure 13.7 shows the usefulness of knowing the areas of standard geometric shapes. We will illustrate this further by determining the area of the field illustrated in Figure 13.13. The approach we use solves for the area of each shape (A through F) and then adds the areas together for the total area. (All distances are in feet.)

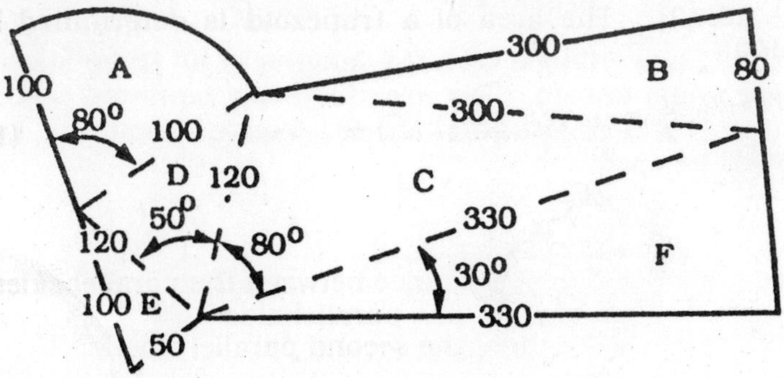

Figure 13.13. Determining the area of a field using standard geometric shapes.

Shape A is a sector of a circle with a known radius and angle. The area of this shape (A_A) can be found by using Equation (13-9):

$$A_A = \frac{\pi r^2 \times \varnothing}{360}$$

$$= \frac{3.14 \times 100^2 \times 80^\circ}{360}$$

$$= 6980 \text{ ft}^2$$

Shape B is a triangle with the length of the sides known. For this area (A_B) Equation (13-5) is used:

$$A_B = \sqrt{S(S-a)(S-b)(S-c)} \quad \text{and} \quad S = \frac{a+b+c}{2}$$

$$S = \frac{300 + 80 + 300}{2}$$

$$= 340$$

$$A_B = \sqrt{340 \times (340 - 300) \times (340 - 80) \times (340 - 300)}$$

$$= \sqrt{340 \times 40 \times 220 \times 40}$$

$$= 11{,}000 \text{ ft}^2$$

Shape C is a triangle with the lengths of all three sides known and one angle known. The area (A_C) can be found using either Equation (13-5) or Equation (13-6). For this example, Equation (13-6) will be used:

$$A_C = \frac{1}{2} \times (a \times b \times \sin \phi)$$

$$= \frac{1}{2} \times 120 \times 330 \times 0.985$$

$$= 19{,}500 \text{ ft}^2$$

The same situation exists for shape D. For this example Equation (13-6) will be used again. The area (A_D) is:

$$A_D = \frac{1}{2} \times (a \times b \times \sin \phi)$$

$$= \frac{1}{2} \times 120 \times 120 \times 0.766$$

$$= 5520 \text{ ft}^2$$

Shape E is a triangle with the lengths of the three sides known. This area (A_E) is found by using Equation (13-5):

$$A_E = \sqrt{S(S-a)(S-b)(S-c)} \quad \text{and} \quad S = \frac{a + b + c}{2}$$

$$S = \frac{100 + 120 + 50}{2}$$

$$= 135$$

$$A_E = \sqrt{135 \times (135 - 100) \times (135 - 120) \times (135 - 50)}$$

$$= \sqrt{135 \times 35 \times 15 \times 85}$$

$$= 2450 \text{ ft}^2$$

Shape F is triangle with an angle and the adjacent two sides known. This area (A_F) is found by sing Equation (13-6):

$$A_F = \frac{1}{2} \times (a \times b \times \sin \varnothing)$$

$$= \frac{1}{2} \times 330 \times 330 \times 0.500$$

$$= 27{,}200 \text{ ft}^2$$

Now that the area for each shape is known, the total area (A_T) is calculated by combining the areas for the individual shapes:

$$A_T = A_A + A_B + A_C + A_D + A_E + A_F$$

$$= 6980 \text{ ft}^2 + 11{,}000^2 + 19{,}500 \text{ ft}^2 + 5520 \text{ ft}^2 + 2450 \text{ ft}^2 + 27{,}200 \text{ ft}^2$$

$$= 72{,}650 \text{ ft}^2$$

DETERMINING AREAS OF IRREGULAR-SHAPED FIELDS USING TRAPEZOIDAL EQUATIONS

Occasionally it becomes necessary to determine the area of a field or other property that has one irregular-shaped boundary. This is a very common problem when one of the boundaries is formed by surface water. In this situation, the area can be determined by dividing the shape into a series of trapezoids. The total area can be determined by summing the area of each trapezoid, or, if the trapezoids can be laid out so the heights are the same, a trapezoidal summation equation can be used. We will illustrate both of these situations.

Problem: What is the area (acres) for the field illustrated in Figure 13.14?

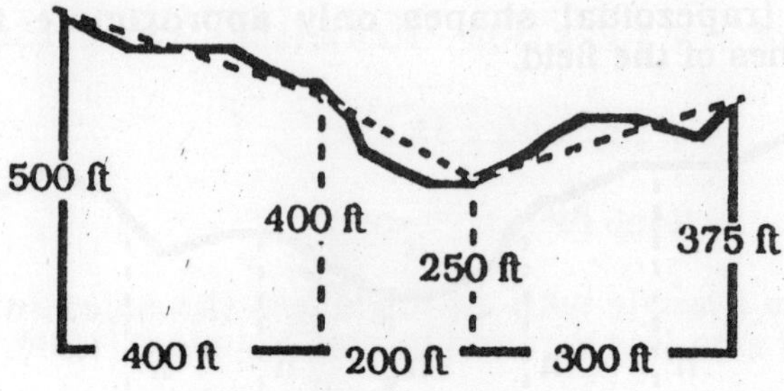

Figure 13.14. Area of irregular-shaped field using trapezoidal equation.

Solution: The total area (A_T) is the sum of each trapezoidal shape (dashed lines). We will determine the total area in square feet and then convert it to acres.

$$A = h \times \frac{a+b}{2}$$

$$A_T = \left(h \times \left(\frac{a+b}{2}\right)\right) + \left(h \times \left(\frac{a+b}{2}\right)\right) + \left(h \times \left(\frac{a+b}{2}\right)\right)$$

$$= \left(400\text{ ft} \times \left(\frac{500\text{ ft} + 400\text{ ft}}{2}\right)\right) + \left(200\text{ ft} \times \left(\frac{400\text{ ft} + 250\text{ ft}}{2}\right)\right) + \left(300\text{ ft} \times \left(\frac{250\text{ ft} + 375\text{ ft}}{2}\right)\right)$$

$$= (400\text{ ft} \times 450\text{ ft}) + (200\text{ ft} \times 325\text{ ft}) + (300\text{ ft} \times 312.5\text{ ft})$$

$$= 180{,}000\text{ ft}^2 + 65{,}000\text{ ft}^2 + 93{,}750\text{ ft}^2$$

$$= 338{,}750\text{ ft}^2$$

$$A\text{ (ac)} = 338{,}750\text{ ft}^2 \times \frac{1\text{ ac}}{43{,}560\text{ ft}^2}$$

$$= 7.78\text{ ac}$$

The field illustrated in Figure 13.14 contains approximately 7.78 acres. We say approximately because the dashed lines used to define the trapezoidal shapes only approximate the actual boundary lines of the field.

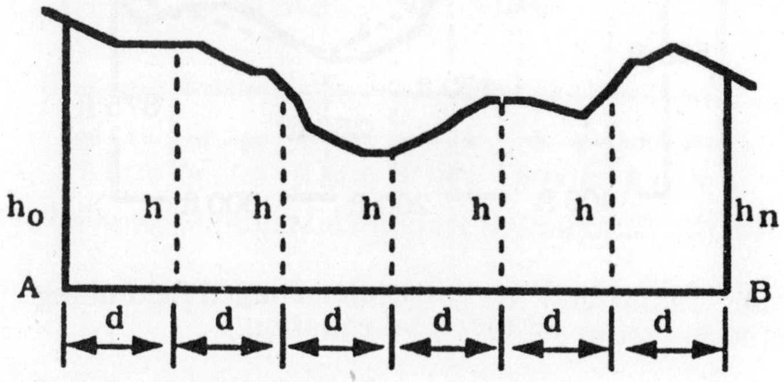

Figure 13.15. Sketch for summation trapezodial equation.

If the irregular boundary is uniform enough to allow a series of equal distances (d) along the base line to be established, the summation trapezoidal equation can be used. Study Figure 13.15 and the following equation for an illustration of this method.

$$A = d \times \left(\frac{h_o}{2} + \sum h + \frac{h_n}{2}\right) \qquad (13\text{-}12)$$

where:

A = Area

d = Distance between offsets (must be equal)

h_o and h_n = End offsets measured from base line AB

$\sum h$ = Summation of all interior offsets (excluding the two end offsets)

To use the summation equation, the field length, AB, is divided into a number of equal distances (d) and the offsets (perpendicular distances from line AB to the curved edge of the field), h, are measured and recorded.

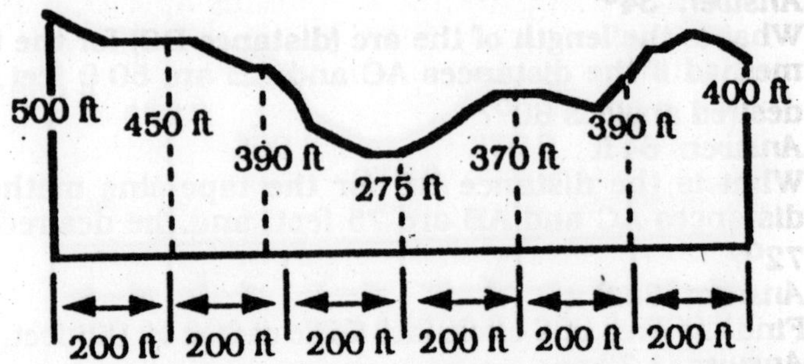

Figure 13.16. Summation trapezoidal equation applied to a field.

Problem: Determine the area (ac) of the irregular-shaped field illustrated in Figure 13.16.

Solution: By using Equation (13-12) to solve for the area in square feet and then converting square feet to acres, we obtain:

$$A\ (ft^2) = d \times \left(\frac{h_o}{2} + \sum h + \frac{h_n}{2}\right)$$

$$= 200\ ft \times \left(\frac{500\ ft}{2} + (450 + 390 + 275 + 370 + 390)\ ft + \frac{400\ ft}{2}\right)$$

$$= 200\ ft \times (250 + 450 + 390 + 275 + 370 + 390 + 200)\ ft$$

$$= 200\ ft \times 2325\ ft$$

$$= 465{,}000\ ft^2$$

$$A\ (ac) = 465{,}000\ ft^2 \times \frac{1\ ac}{43{,}560\ ft^2}$$

$$= 10.7\ ac$$

PRACTICE PROBLEMS

1. Make a sketch of the 3-4-5 method using a 9-12-15 triangle, and show what tape marks should be held together if 5 foot loops are used.
   Answer: 0 and 46, 9 and 14, 26 and 31
2. Using the tape-sine method, find the angle between two intersecting lines when distances AC and AB equal 79 feet, and distance BC equals 46 feet.

Answer: 34°

3. What is the length of the arc (distance BC) for the tape-sine method if the distances AC and AB are 50.0 feet, and the desired angle is 80°?
   Answer: 64 ft
4. What is the distance BC for the tape-sine method if the distances AC and AB are 75 feet, and the desired angle is 72°?
   Answer: 88.2 ft
5. Find the area of a circle (ac) if the radius is 155 feet.
   Answer: 1.73 ac
6. Find the area of a sector (ac) if the radius is 900 feet and the angle is 40°.
   Answer: 6.5 ac
7. What is the area of a sector (ac) if the radius is 210 feet, and the arc length is 460 feet?
   Answer: 1.11 ac

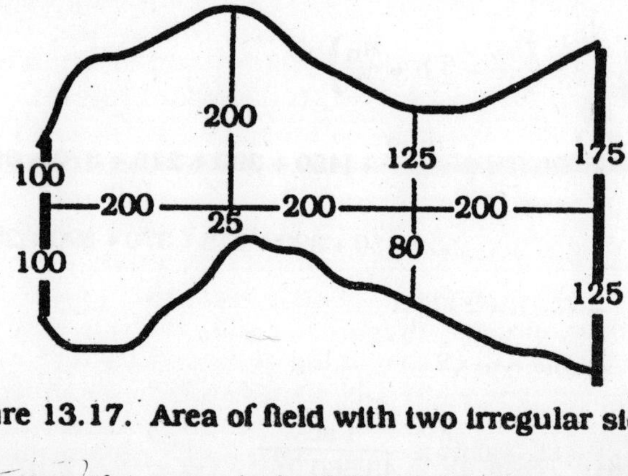

Figure 13.17. Area of field with two irregular sides.

8. Determine the area (ac) of the field illustrated in Figure 13.17.
   Answer: 3.1 ac
9. Explain how one individual with two tapes can lay out a 90° corner using the 3-4-5 method.
   Answer: Set a pin or stake at the turning point. Lay out a 3 or a 4 distance along the base line and set another pin. Hook a tape at each pin, and when both tapes are tight with a 5 and a 4 or a 3 held together, a line through that point and the turning point will be at 90° to the base line.

14
Land Description

OBJECTIVES

1. Understand the three common methods of describing land.
2. Be able to use the rectangular system to read and write legal descriptions.
3. Be able to use the rectangular system to determine the number of acres from a written description.

INTRODUCTION

From earliest times there was a need to mark and describe the boundaries of parcels of land. It is recorded that in about 1400 B.C. Egypt developed a system to reestablish land boundaries after each flood. The need to accurately establish and describe land boundaries has persisted to this day. To transfer ownership one must be able to describe what land is being considered, and where it is located. In the United States the three primary systems used to define land boundaries and location are the metes and bounds, block and lot, and rectangular systems.

METES AND BOUNDS

The metes and bounds system consists of a point of beginning (POB), such as a rock, tree, stake, or post, and lengths and bearings (angles) of successive lines from this point. Lengths may be in units of chains, poles, or rods, but as new surveys are conducted, these units are being replaced by feet and inches or metric measurements. The bearings may be assumed, magnetic, true, or grid. True or grid bearings are the preferred type. To read or write land descriptions with the metes and bounds system, the units used and the type of bearing used must be known.

A typical description might read as follows: "beginning at the rock about 2 minutes walk from the creek, thence easterly to the oak tree, thence southerly to the rock, thence northerly to the point of beginning." The dilemma that anyone faces trying to trace the boundaries many years later is obvious.

BLOCK AND LOT

This system is very common in cities where land has been arranged into small lots. City or county recorders' offices have map books giving the location and dimensions of all the blocks and lots. In most areas developers are required to provide such plans and have them approved before construction begins. A typical description might read: "Country Club plat, block 4, lot 23, book 543, page 201."

RECTANGULAR SYSTEM

The rectangular system of public land survey is used in 30 states. The system was adopted in 1785 by the Continental Congress to subdivide new lands west of the Ohio River in a logical and systematic manner. In general, the system divides the land by north and south lines following a true meridian, with other lines crossing at right angles to form townships 6 miles square. A few surveys laid out the lines 30 miles apart instead of 24. In this discussion we will consider only the 24-mile rectangular surveys. The townships are further divided into sections of approximately 640 acres each, and each section is still further subdivided into fractional parts. Because meridians converge, it is evident that the requirements that all lines follow true meridians and that townships be 6 miles square are mathematically impossible. A system of subdivisions was used as a practical solution. A description of the divisions is as follows:

1. *Quadrangles*: These square tracts are approximately 24 miles on each side.
2. *Townships*: Each quadrangle contains 16 townships, each approximately 6 miles on a side.
3. *Sections*: Each township is divided into 36 sections, each approximately one mile on a side and containing 640 acres.
4. *Quarter-sections*: Each section is divided into quarter-sections approximately one-half mile on a side and containing 160 acres. Quarter-sections may be divided into fractional areas, the individual tracts containing 80, 40, 20, 10, or 5 acres or combinations of these sizes.

The intent was to produce sections of land one mile to a side. Any variation because of convergence is placed in the western column and the top row of each township.

To begin an original survey, an initial point was established in each new area of land by astronomical observations. Thirty-seven initial points eventually were established. A base line, a true parallel of latitude that extends in an east-west direction, and a principal meridian, a true north-south line, passes through each initial point. The principal meridian may be designated by name or by number. The Oklahoma Territory was surveyed from two different meridians, the Indian Meridian and the Cimarron Meridian. The territory that became the states of Kansas, Colorado, and Nebraska was also surveyed from the Indian Meridian, but in these states it was called the 6th Prime Meridian. Figure 14.1 illustrates the rectangular system.

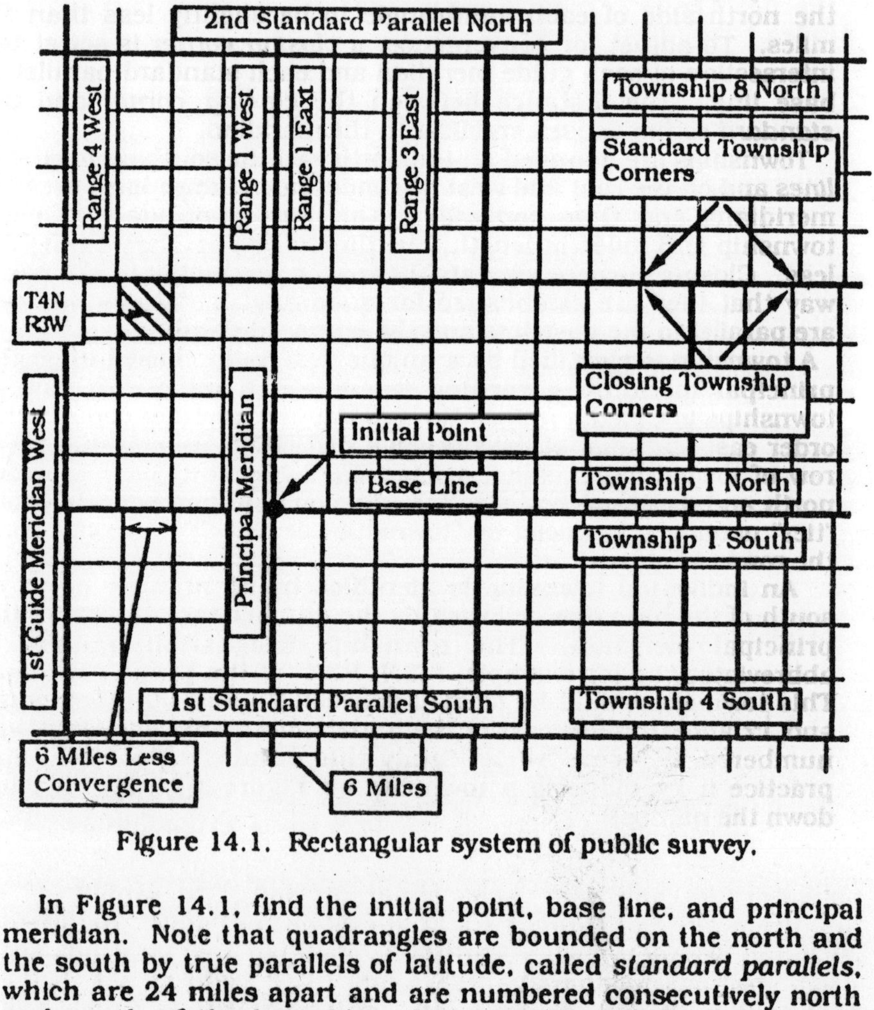

Figure 14.1. Rectangular system of public survey.

In Figure 14.1, find the initial point, base line, and principal meridian. Note that quadrangles are bounded on the north and the south by true parallels of latitude, called *standard parallels*, which are 24 miles apart and are numbered consecutively north and south of the base line. For example, the First Standard

Parallel North is 24 miles north of the base line, and the Fourth Standard Parallel North is 96 miles north of the base line. The east and west boundaries of quadrangles are true meridians known as *guide meridians.* They are 24 miles apart and are numbered consecutively east and west of the principal meridian. Thus, the First Guide Meridian West is 24 miles west of the principal meridian, and the Third Guide Meridian West is 72 miles east of the principal meridian.

Because the guide meridians are true meridians, they converge as they approach the North Pole and the South Pole. This causes the north side of each quadrangle to be slightly less than 24 miles. To adjust for convergence, a *closing corner* is set at the intersection of each guide meridian and each standard parallel or base line. The distance between the *closing corner* and the *standard corner* causes an offset in the meridian.

Townships are bounded on the north and the south by *township lines* and on the east and west by *range lines.* Range lines are true meridians and thus converge. The south boundary of each township is 6 miles in length, but the north boundary is slightly less. Closing corners are established for townships in the same way that they are established for quadrangles. Township lines are parallel to the base line and the standard parallel.

A township is identified by a unique description based upon the principal meridian governing it. A north-and-south row of townships is called a *range.* Ranges are numbered in consecutive order east and west of the principal meridian. An east-and-west row of townships is called a *tier.* Tiers are numbered in order north and south of the base line. By common practice, the word "tier" usually is replaced by "township" or just "T" in designating the rows.

An individual township is identified by its number north or south of the base line, followed by the number east or west of the principal meridian. The township designation usually is abbreviated, as for example, "T5N, R3E" of the prime meridian. This township would be located between 24 and 30 miles north and 12 and 18 miles east of the initial point. One township was numbered in Figure 14.1. Study this numbering system, and practice it by marking a township on Figure 14.1 and writing down the number.

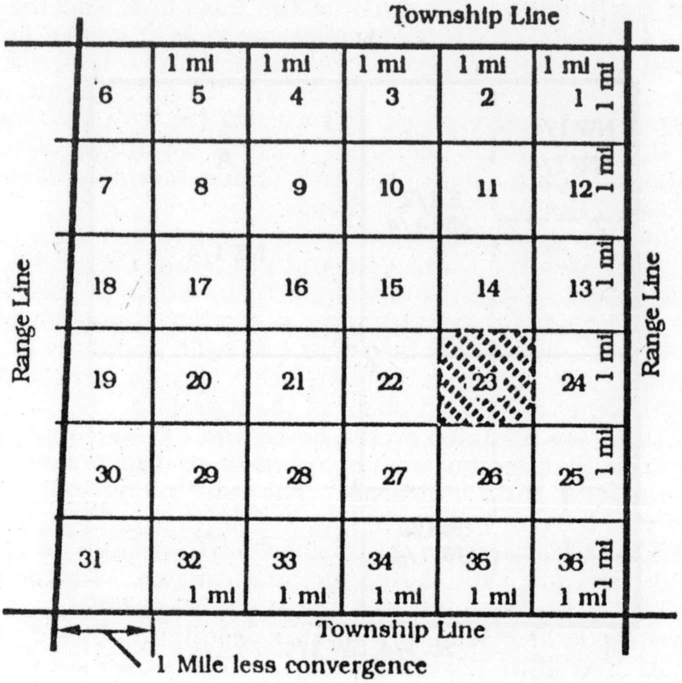

Figure 14.2. Subdivision of a township.

Figure 14.2 shows the method of subdividing a township into *sections* one mile square (640 acres). Sections are numbered by starting in the northeast corner and continuing west and east across the township as shown. If the survey is error-free, which is extremely improbable, all sections are one mile square except those along the west boundary of the township. These fractional sections are less than one mile in width because of convergence of the range lines.

The description of a property must include the section number. The description of the highlighted section in Figure 14.2 is "S23," and the township might be "T4N, R7E, Principal Meridian (or PM)."

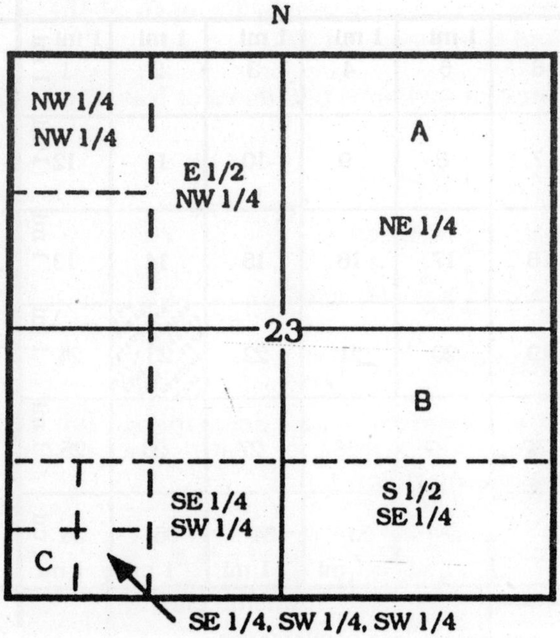

Figure 14.3. Subdivision of a section in Figure 14.2.

As shown in Figure 14.3, each section may be further subdivided into smaller tracts, with north being to the top of the page and east to the right. The fractions refer to the fraction of the section subdivision being considered. The legal description of the section subdivisions begins with the smallest unit of area.

Problem: What are the descriptions of the subdivisions labeled A, B, and C in Figure 14.3?

Solution: A = NE 1/4, S23, T4N, R7E, Principal Meridian; B = N 1/2, SE 1/4, S23, T4N, R7E, Principal Meridian; C = SW 1/4, SW 1/4, SW 1/4, S23, T4N, R7E, Principal Meridian.

The description for subdivision A is read as: "the northeast one quarter of section 23, located in township 4 north and range seven east of the Principal Meridian."

Land descriptions also can be used to determine the acres contained in each subdivision.

Problem: What is the area (acres) for each of the subdivisions labeled A, B, and C in Figure 14.3?

Solution: Because a section is 640 acres or less, the areas are:

$$A = 640 \times \frac{1}{4} = 160 \text{ acres}$$

$$B = 640 \times \frac{1}{2} \times \frac{1}{4} = 80 \text{ acres}$$

$$C = 640 \times \frac{1}{4} \times \frac{1}{4} \times \frac{1}{4} = 10 \text{ acres}$$

PRACTICE PROBLEMS

1. Write the complete legal description for each of the subdivisions in Figure 14.4. (Note: use section 17 and the 6th principle meridian.)

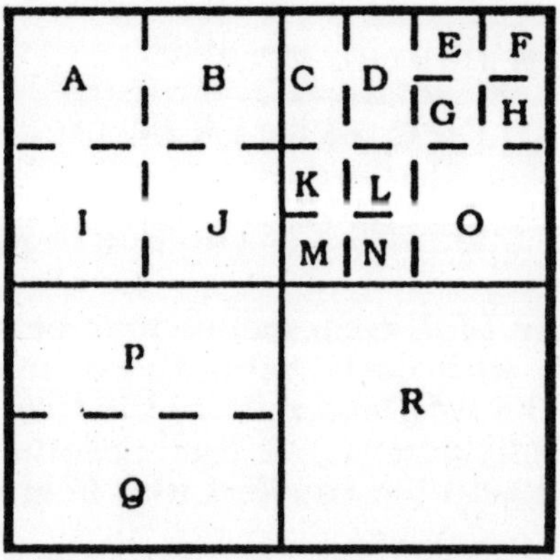

Figure 14.4. Subdivided section for practice problem.

Answers:
A. NW 1/4, NW 1/4, S 17, 6 PM
B. NE 1/4, NW 1/4, S 17, 6 PM
C. W 1/2, NW 1/4, NE 1/4, S 17, 6 PM
D. E 1/2, NW 1/4, NE 1/4, S 17, 6 PM
E. NW 1/4, NE 1/4, NE 1/4, S 17, 6 PM
F. NE 1/4, NE 1/4, NE 1/4, S 17, 6 PM
G. SW 1/4, NE 1/4, NE 1/4, S 17, 6 PM
H. SE 1/4, NE 1/4, NE 1/4, S 17, 6 PM
I. SW 1/4, NW 1/4, S 17, 6 PM

J. SE 1/4, NW 1/4, S 17, 6 PM
K. NW 1/4, SW 1/4, NE 1/4, S 17, 6 PM
L. NE 1/4, SW 1/4, NE 1/4, S 17, 6 PM
M. SW 1/4, SW 1/4, NE 1/4, S 17, 6 PM
N. SE 1/4, SW 1/4, NE 1/4, S 17, 6 PM
O. SE 1/4, NE 1/4, S 17, 6 PM
P. N 1/2, SW 1/4, S 17, 6 PM
Q. S 1/2, SW 1/4, S 17, 6 PM
R. SE 1/4, S 17, 6 PM

2. What is the area (ac) for each of the subdivisions in Figure 14.4?

Answers:

A. 40 ac	G. 10 ac	M. 10 ac
B. 40 ac	H. 10 ac	N. 10 ac
C. 20 ac	I. 40 ac	O. 40 ac
D. 20 ac	J. 40 ac	P. 80 ac
E. 10 ac	K. 10 ac	Q. 80 ac
F. 10 ac	L. 10 ac	R. 160 ac

15
Differential and Profile Leveling

OBJECTIVES

1. Be able to describe the equipment used in surveying.
2. Understand the terms used in differential and profile leveling.
3. Be able to read a surveying rod.
4. Be able to identify and control the common sources of error during leveling.
5. Be able to describe the processes of differential and profile leveling.
6. Be able to record a set of notes for differential and profile leveling.

INTRODUCTION

Surveying is used for two specific purposes: (1) *planning*, in which a site is surveyed to provide the information needed to develop the maps, charts, and drawings necessary to lay out buildings, roads, drains, etc.; and (2) *layout*, where surveying is used to establish the boundaries, lines, and elevation for the construction of those structures. Leveling, one of several procedures of surveying, is the process of determining the elevation of points such as the ground, the tops of stakes, or parts of a building. It ranks next to the measurement of distance in importance as a surveying technique. In this chapter we will discuss the terms, equipment, and procedures for two types of leveling.

LEVELING TERMS

BENCH MARK:

A bench mark (BM) is a permanent object whose elevation above sea level is known or assumed to be known. It is the reference point for all of the elevations for a survey. It is important to select an object for a bench mark that will not be disturbed. If the bench mark elevation is accidentally changed, all surveys that used it must be redone. Bench marks allow a survey to be repeated at a later date and permit a surveyor to tie elevations from the current survey to elevations established in previous surveys. A network of bench marks can thus be established over a large area, to the same reference elevation. Bench marks may vary in character and permanency according to the survey for which they were established. The U.S. Geological Survey (USGS) has established a nationwide network of bench marks, all referenced to mean sea level. These marks consist of bronze disks set in concrete monuments, similar to right-of-way markers, that have been firmly set in the ground. The date of the survey and the elevation and bench mark number usually are stamped in each bronze disk.

In many situations it is not necessary to know the exact elevation above sea level. For such surveys a local bench mark is used. Frequently this bench mark is given the elevation of 100.00 feet. If the terrain is hilly, the surveyor should choose a larger number, as it is not standard practice to use negative numbers in surveying.

When using a local bench mark, the survey crew must select and establish its location. Two rules should be followed. The object selected should: (1) be reasonably permanent for as long as it will be needed, and not easily moved or otherwise destroyed; and (2) be capable of being described in such a way that it can be easily relocated. A typical local bench mark might be an "X" chipped in a concrete curb or a bridge abutment, an iron pin driven firmly into the ground, or the rim of an electrical or sewer manhole. It is the job of the note keeper to describe accurately the name, number, type, elevation, and location of each bench mark, and to record this information on the right-hand page in the surveying notebook.

BACKSIGHT

A backsight (BS) is a rod reading taken on a point of known elevation, and is the vertical distance between the line of sight and the point of known elevation on which the rod is held. The reading is used to establish a new height of instrument (see below). A backsight will always be taken on a bench mark or a turning point; a backsight on a bench mark is used to start a survey, and a backsight on a turning point is used to continue a survey beyond the starting instrument position. The word "backsight" has nothing to do with the direction in which the instrument is pointed. It is important to remember that there is only one backsight for each setup of the instrument.

HEIGHT OF INSTRUMENT

The height of instrument (HI) is the elevation of the line of sight when the instrument is level. It is found by adding a backsight rod reading to the elevation of the point on which the backsight was taken.

FORESIGHT

A foresight (FS) is a rod reading taken on any point of *unknown* elevation. In differential leveling, there is only one foresight for each instrument setup, whereas profile leveling may have several foresights per instrument setup. The FS is subtracted from the HI to find the elevation of an unknown point.

TURNING POINT

A turning point (TP) is a temporary bench mark upon which foresight and backsight rod readings are taken for the purpose of continuing the line of the survey. In long lines several turning points may be needed. They should be selected with care and must not be moved until the instrument is moved forward and the new HI determined. A solid object such as a stake or a large solid rock should be used. *Do not* set the rod on the ground when making a turning point; doing so could result in a serious error.

SURVEYING EQUIPMENT

The equipment used in leveling consists of a leveling instrument and a leveling rod. The most common type of level is called an engineer's or a dumpy level. The leveling instrument is a telescope containing both vertical and horizontal cross-hairs and one or more spirit levels (bubble in a liquid-filled tube) to indicate when the instrument base is horizontal. The entire assembly, consisting of the frame, telescope and spirit level, can be "leveled" by turning the three or four leveling screws that hold the frame in position above the tripod head.

Another common level is the hand level. It usually has a spirit level for holding it horizontal and one set of cross-hairs. More sophisticated models may also have stadia hairs and direct reading angle scales.

The leveling rod is a wooden scale about 1 inch by 2 inches in cross section and about 14 feet long, graduated in feet and tenths and hundredths of feet. It is used to measure the vertical distance between the line of sight through the telescope and the object on which the leveling rod is resting.

READING A ROD

A rod is used to measure the vertical distance between the line of sight, established by the instrument, and the object on which the rod is resting. To provide an accurate reading it must be held in an upright position. Failure to hold the rod in a vertical position is a common error in surveying. The easiest way to ensure that the rod is vertical is to use a rod level. If a rod level is not available, the instrument person (person on the instrument) can determine if the rod is vertical to the left or the right by having the rod person (person holding the rod) align the rod with the vertical cross-hair of the telescope. The fore and aft alignment must be controlled by the rod person.

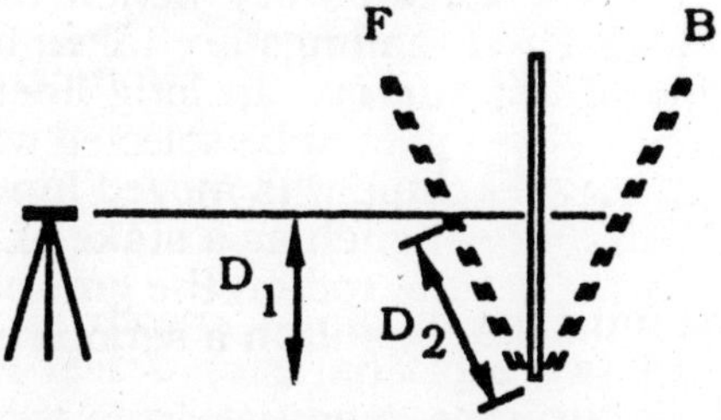

Figure 15.1. Reading a rod.

One method is for the rod person to slowly rock the rod forward (F) and backward (B). The instrument person records the shortest reading. This is illustrated in Figure 15.1. The shortest reading will occur when the rod is vertical. D_1 will always be less than distance D_2.

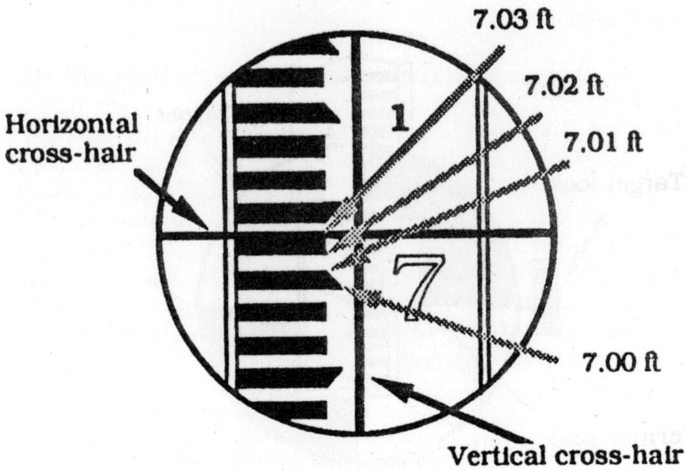

Figure 15.2. Reading the Philadelphia rod.

The most common type of rod is known as the Philadelphia type. This rod has two sections, each 7 feet long, that can be extended to give continuous readings from zero at the base to 13.00 feet at the top. The graduations consist of black marks painted on a white background. The black graduations are 0.01 foot thick and are spaced 0.01 foot apart. The size of the graduations allows the rod to be read, to the nearest 0.01 foot, directly for distances up to 250 feet. The tenths of a foot are indicated by black numerals, and each foot is indicated by a larger red numeral (see Figure 15.2). The foot interval usually is also indicated by a small red numeral between the whole foot marks. Figure 15.2 is read as 7.03 feet.

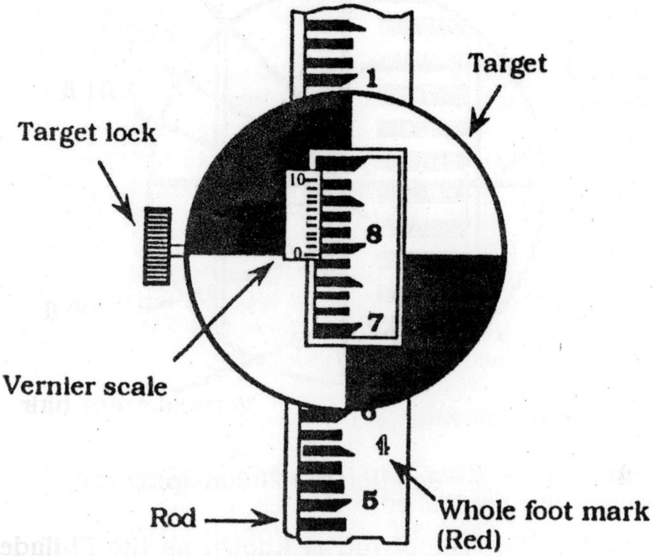

Figure 15.3. Reading a rod with a target.

If the sight distance is greater than 250 feet, or if the rod cannot be read directly for any reason, the target is used. The target (Figure 15.3) is an oval disk divided into quadrants, which are alternately red or white. When the rod cannot be read directly, the instrument person can signal the rod person to raise and lower the target until it is aligned with the horizontal cross hair. The note taker then can record the reading from the rod. The target also has a vernier scale that allows readings to be made to 0.001 foot.

SETTING UP A SURVEYING LEVEL

Many different types and variations of levels are used for surveying. The following procedure for setting up an engineer's level will also work with most other types. When not in use, the instrument is housed in a case for protection. To be used, it must be removed from this case and carefully threaded on the tripod head. The tripod legs are set about 4 feet apart and pushed firmly into the ground, thereby providing a stable base for the instrument and helping to ensure an accurate survey. If the tripod is set up with the head nearly horizontal, leveling of the instrument will be much easier and faster than it otherwise would be.

To level a four-legged instrument, the telescope is lined up over one pair of leveling screws, and the bubble is centered. Then the telescope is lined up over the other pair of leveling screws and centered again. The procedure is repeated until the bubble remains centered for any position of the telescope. The leveling screws should not over tightened, or they will bind and put excessive strain on the instrument frame.

To level a three-legged instrument, the position of the telescope is not critical. The instrument is leveled with the adjusting screws and the spirit level, and then the telescope is slowly rotated to check the accuracy of the leveling.

COMMON SOURCES OF ERROR

The accuracy of leveling can be greatly improved if several common errors are controlled:

1. *Instrument out of adjustment*: Anytime that the instrument is "bumped" or otherwise moved, it must be reset. It is a good practice to check the leveling bubble both before and after reading the rod.
2. *Rod not plumb*: The rod must always be held plumb using a rod level, or rocked back and forth as explained in the section on reading the rod. A good method of plumbing the rod is to stand behind the rod and balance it carefully on the stake by holding your hands lightly on each side.
3. *Parallax*: If the cross-hairs appear to move over the object as the eye is shifted slightly, parallax exists. If parallax exists, the line of sight of the eye may not be parallel to the line of sight of the instrument. This source of error is eliminated by adjusting the eyepiece until the cross-hairs are the darkest. Because this adjustment may be different for each person, one person should take all the readings for a survey.
4. *Sights not equal*: If field conditions permit, the length of backsights and foresights should be as nearly equal as possible. Thus, any errors due to the instrument's being out of adjustment are minimized because they tend to cancel out.
5. *Reading the rod incorrectly*: The person reading the rod must be very careful to ensure that the correct foot mark is used, and that the target is used correctly.

LEVELING FIELD NOTES

Standard note keeping procedures have been developed to simplify and systematize record keeping for leveling. The note book is divided into right- and left-hand pages. The left-hand page contains the title, the location, and the data. The right-hand page of the notes is used to describe the location of the bench marks, turning points, creeks, fence or property lines, or other conditions that might influence the design of the structure for which the survey is being made. The location of the starting stake also is described in the notes so that it can be relocated if it is pulled out or otherwise lost. A sketch of the general area, showing the location of the beginning and ending stations of the survey, bench marks, ditches, roads, and other landmarks, also is helpful. In addition, the right-hand side of the page should contain information about the weather, the names of the survey party, and the serial numbers of the instruments used.

Leveling notes are a simple form of bookkeeping with the following simple rules: (1) each point where a rod reading is made is identified by its station name, and whether it is a foresight or a backsight; (2) all pertinent information about a point is shown on the same horizontal line; (3) the height of instrument is recorded on the next line below the backsight reading and the foresight reading from this setup.

DIFFERENTIAL LEVELING

Differential leveling is the process of finding the difference in elevation between two points. If the two points are within the limits of the instrument, two readings are taken. The difference in rod readings represents the difference in elevation between the two points. If one of the points is beyond the range of the telescope, temporary stations, called turning points, must be established to allow the instrument to be moved.

One of the most common applications of differential leveling is to run a circuit of sights to determine the elevations of one or more bench marks relative to a previously established bench mark. The procedure for differential leveling will be described using this type of circuit, illustrated schematically in Figure 15.4. The diagram shows that three instrument setups were made in traveling from BM1 to BM2. Also note that a "return check" was made between BM2 and BM1, and that three more setups were made in this phase of the survey.

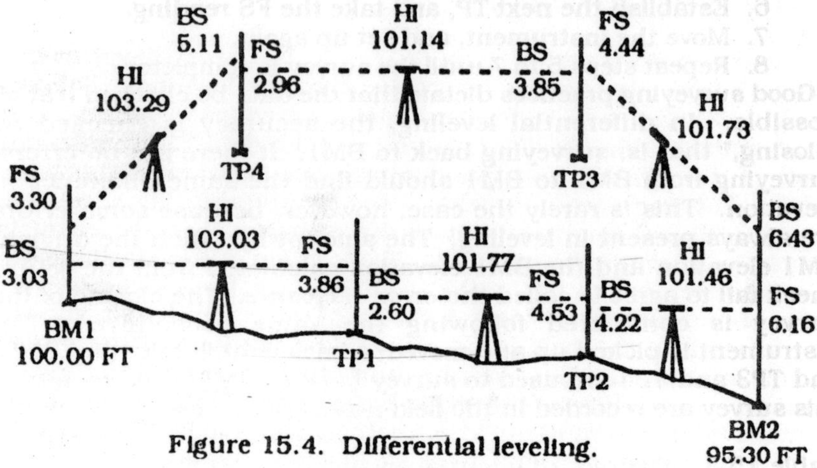

Figure 15.4. Differential leveling.

The survey begins with the instrument person going forward a convenient distance (not over 400 feet) and setting up the level, following the procedure previously described. The instrument person sights on the rod while it is held on the top of BM1 by the rod person, and notes a center cross hair reading of 3.03 feet. This is a backsight, so the 3.03 feet rod reading is added to the BM1 elevation (assumed 100.00 ft), resulting in a height of instrument (HI) of 103.03 feet. The rod person then goes forward past the instrument and selects a turning point, TP1. The rod reading of this TP, 3.86 feet, is a foresight (elevation of an unknown point). The foresight is subtracted from the HI, and the elevation of TP1 is found to be 99.17 feet. The instrument can now be moved forward and set up at a new position. A backsight rod reading of 2.60 feet is observed on TP1 and added to the TP1 elevation of 99.17 feet, and the HI for the second setup is found to be 101.77 feet. Again a new turning point, TP2, is selected, and a rod reading of 4.53 feet is recorded. This rod reading is subtracted from the HI of 101.77 feet, and an elevation of 97.24 feet is obtained for TP2. This process is repeated a third time, and the elevation of BM2 is found to be 95.30 feet. We now know that the difference in elevation between BM1 and BM2 is 100.00 feet minus 95.30 feet, or 4.7 feet.

In summary, the procedure for differential leveling is:

1. Set up the instrument.
2. Establish BM1, and take the BS reading.
3. Establish the TP, and take the FS reading.
4. Move the instrument, and set up again.
5. Take the BS on the TP.

6. Establish the next TP, and take the FS reading.
7. Move the instrument, and set up again.
8. Repeat steps 5 to 7 until the survey is complete.

Good surveying practices dictate that the data be checked if at all possible. In differential leveling, the accuracy is checked by "closing," that is, surveying back to BM1. If there are no errors, surveying from BM2 to BM1 should find the same difference in elevation. This is rarely the case, however, because some errors are always present in leveling. The amount by which the original BM1 elevation and the BM1 elevation calculated from the return check fail to agree is called the *error of closure*. The closing of the survey is conducted following the same procedure. The instrument is picked up and moved, a backsight is taken on BM2, and TP3 and TP4 are used to survey back to BM1. The results of this survey are recorded in the field notes (Table 15-1).

Table 15-1. Data for differential leveling.

STA	BS	HI	FS	ELEV
BM1	3.03			100.00
		103.03		
TP1	2.60		3.86	99.17
		101.77		
TP2	4.22		4.53	97.24
		101.46		
BM2	6.43		6.16	95.30
		101.73		
TP3	3.85		4.44	97.29
		101.14		
TP4	5.11		2.96	98.18
		103.29		
BM1			3.30	99.99

The left-hand page of surveying field notebooks contain six columns. Five columns are needed for differential leveling; from left to right the column headings are station (STA), backsight (BS), height of instrument (HI), foresight (FS), and elevation (ELEV). The sixth column is used to record additional information, for example, the distance for each sight.

ERROR CONTROL

In surveying, it is important to eliminate as many errors as possible. For differential leveling surveys two error checks should be conducted, the note check and calculation of the allowable error of closure. The note check is conducted to catch any mathematical errors in the notes. For checking notes, the absolute value of the sum of the foresights minus the sum of the backsights, should equal the absolute value of the difference (Δ) in elevation for BM1 (beginning and closure elevation). Expressed mathematically:

$$|\Sigma FS - \Sigma BS| = |\Delta Elevation| \quad (15\text{-}1)$$

Problem: Are the field notes in Table 15-1 accurate?

Solution: Using Equation (15-1):

ΣFS		ΣBS		
3.86		3.03		
4.53		2.60		
6.16		4.22		
4.44		6.13		
2.96		3.85		
3.30		5.11		
25.25	minus	25.24	equals	0.01 ft

$$|\Delta Elevation| = BM1_{beginning} - BM1_{ending}$$

$$= 100.00 - 99.99$$

$$= 0.01 \text{ ft}$$

The difference in the summation of the foresights minus the summation of the backsights equals the difference in beginning and ending elevations for BM1; therefore, the notes have no math errors.

The second check is for the error of closure. The allowable error of closure for differential leveling depends on the accuracy required for the survey. For most agricultural surveys the allowable error can be determined by:

$$AE = K\sqrt{M} \quad (15\text{-}2)$$

where:

AE = Allowable error
K = A constant ranging from 0.01 to 0.10
M = Distanced traveled (mi)

A value of 0.01 should be used if a high level of accuracy is required, 0.10 or 0.05 is acceptable for most agricultural surveys.

Problem: Is the closure error of 0.01 feet for the differential leveling survey in Figure (15-1) acceptable if the total distance surveyed, out and back, was 3600 feet?

Solution: Using Equation (15-2):

$$AE = 0.10\sqrt{M}$$

$$= 0.10\sqrt{3600 \text{ ft} \times \frac{1 \text{ mi}}{5280 \text{ ft}}}$$

$$= 0.10\sqrt{0.682 \text{ mi}}$$

$$= 0.082 \text{ ft}$$

The closure error is acceptable (0.01 < 0.082).

PROFILE LEVELING

Profile leveling is the process of determining the elevation of points at measured distances along a selected line. When this information is plotted on a graph, it will give a profile of the line and will enable one to establish grades, find high or low spots, and make estimates of cuts and fills. We will illustrate the procedure for profile leveling and the way to record the data.

Before a profile can be made, the surveying crew establishes the stations by setting a stake where the rod readings are to be taken. The stakes are usually set a fixed distance apart (25, 50, or 100 feet), depending upon the irregularity of the ground and the amount of detail required. Because the purpose of the profile is to show the true slope of the ground, the irregularity of the terrain will largely determine where the stations should be established. If there is a definite change in the slope of the ground, the crew should set a stake and determine the elevation, even if it does not fall on the preselected distance.

Once the centerline of the ditch, terrace outlet, channel, road, or other line to be profiled is established, the distance from the starting point to each station is accurately measured. For higher level surveys, 2 x 2-inch stakes may be driven flush with the ground surface, and rod readings taken on the tops of the stakes. On less important surveys, the foresights may be taken with the rod set directly on the ground.

Next, the level is set up, readings are taken, and elevations are established for each staked point along the line. A turning point is established when it becomes necessary to move the instrument to make another series of measurements.

Finally, a closing circuit of readings must be made to check the accuracy of the survey. This is done by running a line of differential levels back to the bench mark where the survey began. If no turning points are used, a sight is taken at the benchmark used to establish the height of instrument, and compared with the original backsight. Figure 15.5 and Table 15-2 illustrate the procedures for conducting a profile leveling survey.

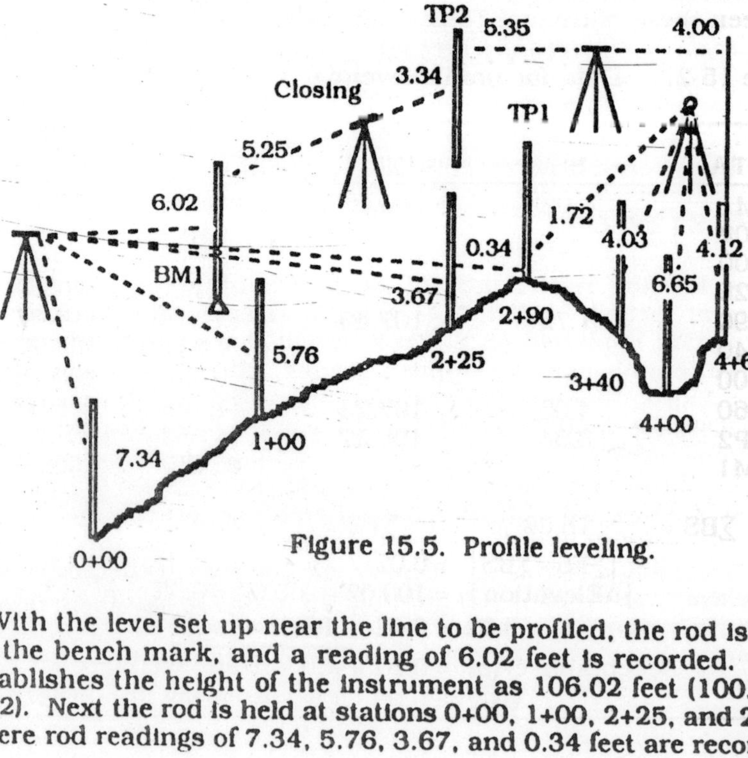

Figure 15.5. Profile leveling.

With the level set up near the line to be profiled, the rod is held on the bench mark, and a reading of 6.02 feet is recorded. This establishes the height of the instrument as 106.02 feet (100.00 + 6.02). Next the rod is held at stations 0+00, 1+00, 2+25, and 2+90, where rod readings of 7.34, 5.76, 3.67, and 0.34 feet are recorded.

At station 2+90 a stake is set flush with the surface so it can be used to record the elevation and also be used as a turning point. The elevation of each point is calculated by subtracting the rod reading from the height of instrument. Notice that the same HI is used for all stations up to and including 2+90, as all readings are made from the same instrument setup.

Because the surveying crew anticipated in advance the need for a turning point, the profile leveling exercise is continued by moving the instrument to a new location to provide a view of the remaining stations. A backsight of 1.72 feet is observed, establishing the new height of instrument as 107.40 feet. The survey continues by recording the rod readings for stations 3+40, 4+00, and 4+60. These readings are 4.03, 6.65, and 4.12 feet.

The profile leveling survey is completed by closing the circuit. The instrument is moved, and a backsight of 4.00 feet is observed on station 4+60. A stake is set at TP2, and a foresight of 5.35 feet is observed. The procedure is repeated to complete the survey from TP2 to BM1.

At the completion of the survey it is noted that an error of 0.02 foot has accumulated during the survey. Table 15-2 contains a set of notes for this survey. Note the similarities and differences between these notes and Table 15-1 (data for differential leveling).

Table 15-2. Data for profile leveling.

STA	BS	HI	FS	ELEV
BM1	6.02	106.02		100.00
0+00			7.34	98.68
1+00			5.76	100.26
2+25			3.67	102.35
2+90	1.72	107.40	(0.34)	105.68
3+40			4.03	103.37
4+00			6.65	100.75
4+60	4.00	107.28	(4.12)	103.28
TP2	3.34	105.27	(5.35)	101.93
BM1			(5.25)	100.02

$\sum BS =$ 15.08 $\qquad \sum FS =$ 15.06

$$|\sum FS - \sum BS| = 0.02$$

$$|\Delta \text{Elevation}| = 100.02 - 100.00 = 0.02$$

$$0.02 = 0.02 \quad \textit{Notes check}$$

$$\text{Acceptable error} = 0.10\sqrt{460 \div 5280} = 0.03$$

$$0.02 < 0.03 \quad \textit{Closure error acceptable}$$

ERROR CONTROL

Because profile leveling notes usually have more foresights than backsights, the method of checking for arithmetic mistakes is slightly different from that for differential leveling. The only foresights to be included when calculating the sum of the foresights (ΣFS) are those taken on turning points, including bench marks if they were used as TP's. In the sample notes (Table 15-2) the foresight readings that are to be used for checking are shown in parentheses. The data in Table 15-2 indicate there were no arithmetic errors in the survey, and the closure error was acceptable. *Note*: This procedure provides a check on the turning points only--not the intermediate foresights. There is *no* way to check those foresights not used for TP's except to rerun the entire profile. *Extreme care* must be used to prevent mistakes in reading and recording the rod readings and in calculating the elevations at all stations.

The results of profile leveling surveys are most useful when they are plotted on graph paper. The principal purposes for plotting a profile are: (1) to aid in the selection of the most economical grade, location, and depth of irrigation canals, drainage ditches, drain tile lines, sewer lines, roads, etc.; and (2) to determine the amount of cut or fill required for these installations. The graph is plotted with the elevation on the ordinate (vertical scale) and the stations on the abscissa (horizontal scale).

PRACTICE PROBLEMS

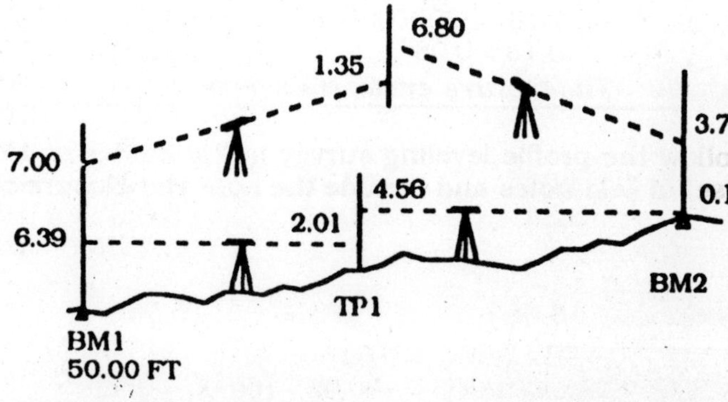

Figure 15.6. Differential leveling practice problem.

Answers:

Table 15-3. Data for differential leveling practice problem.

STA	BS	HI	FS	ELEV
BM1	6.39			50.00
		56.39		
TP1	4.56		2.01	54.38
		58.94		
BM2	3.78		0.14	58.80
		62.58		
TP2	1.35		6.80	55.78
		57.13		
BM1			7.00	50.13

Note check:

$$\begin{aligned}\Sigma FS &= (2.01 + 0.14 + 6.80 + 7.00) = 15.95\\ \Sigma BS &= (6.39 + 4.56 + 3.78 + 1.35) = 16.08\\ |\Delta \text{Elevation}| &= 50.13 - 50.00 = 0.13\\ |\Sigma FS - \Sigma BS| &= 15.95 - 16.08 = 0.13\end{aligned}$$

$0.13 = 0.13$ *Notes check*

Closure error:

$$0.10\sqrt{3200 \div 5280} = 0.08$$
$$0.13 > 0.08$$

The closure error is excessive.

. Follow the profile leveling survey in Figure 15.7. Complete a set of field notes and include the note and closure check.

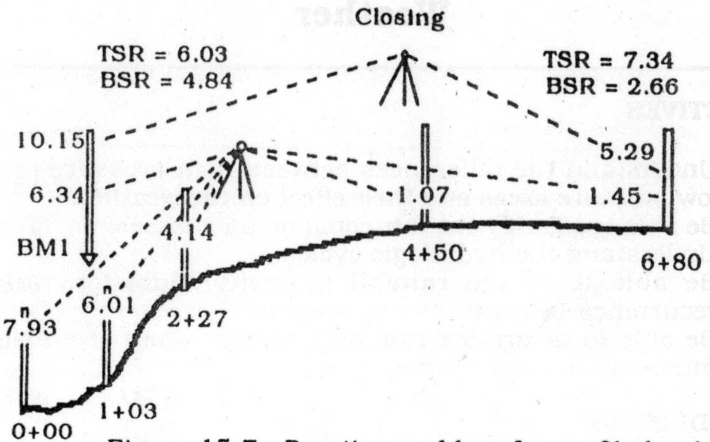

Figure 15.7. Practice problem for profile leveling.

Answers:

Table 15-4. Data for profile leveling practice problem.

STA	BS	HI	FS	ELEV
BM1	6.34	106.34		100.00
0+00			7.93	98.40
1+03			6.01	100.33
2+27			4.14	102.02
4+50			1.07	105.27
6+80	5.29	110.18	1.45	104.89
BM1			10.15	100.03
$\sum BS =$	11.63	$\sum FS =$	11.60	

$|\sum FS - \sum BS| = 11.60 - 11.63 = 0.03$
$|\Delta \text{Elevation}| = 100.03 - 100.00 = 0.03$
$0.03 = 0.03$ *Notes check*

Allowable closure $= 0.10\sqrt{1267 \div 5250} = 0.05$
$0.03 < 0.05$ *Closure error is acceptable.*

16
Weather

OBJECTIVES

1. Understand the differences between high pressure and low pressure areas and their effect on the weather.
2. Be able to identify the five common air masses.
3. Understand the hydrologic cycle.
4. Be able to define rainfall intensity, duration, and recurrence interval.
5. Be able to determine rainfall intensity when given the intensity-duration curve.

INTRODUCTION

The weather is the largest uncontrolled variable, as well as the most unpredictable variable, in the production of agricultural products. Agricultural production is based on the growth of plants, and those plants require an optimum environment for maximum production. However, maximum production is seldom realized in the natural environment because the weather seldom matches the needs of plants. Anytime that the real environment is significantly different from the optimum, plants are stressed, and production is decreased. The major limiting factor is water. An understanding of the mechanisms of the weather will improve the decision-making process for activities such as cutting hay, irrigating, harvesting, and tillage. Better decisions mean increased productivity for any agricultural enterprise. In this chapter we will discuss the pressure systems that influence the weather, the hydrologic cycle, and a few of the characteristics of rainfall and runoff.

AREAS OF HIGH AND LOW PRESSURE

Weather is greatly influenced by atmospheric pressure systems. High pressure and low pressure centers are indicators of the type of weather to be expected. Winds blow in a counterclockwise direction around a low pressure center and in a clockwise direction around a high pressure center. Closely spaced systems indicate a steep pressure gradient and high wind speeds; when the systems are farther apart, the wind speeds are lower. A trough line may develop between two low pressure areas, and a ridge line may develop between two high pressure areas. In general, cloudy or rainy weather is associated with a low pressure center, and clear, sunny weather accompanies areas of high pressure.

AIR MASSES

Differences in pressure are caused by air masses moving across the country. An air mass is a body of air that has a more or less uniform temperature and moisture content throughout the mass. Air masses that have been over water for a period of time contain large amounts of moisture, whereas those originating over land areas usually are dry.

The weather in the United States is influenced by five air masses. The following section lists and briefly describes these air masses:

1. *Tropical maritime*: This air mass forms off the Gulf of Mexico where it is subject to tremendous heating by the sun. This heating causes evaporation from the ocean, resulting in a warm, moist air mass. This mass contributes the largest amount of moisture to the central and eastern regions of the United States.
2. *Tropical continental*: The tropical continental forms over the Mexico countryside. It too is subject to tremendous heating by the sun; but because it forms over land, it is dry.
3. *Polar maritime*: This air mass forms over the polar regions of the ocean. It is very cool but dry because as air cools, the amount of water vapor that it can hold decreases.
4. *Polar continental*: This mass forms over the central plains of Canada. When the ground is snow-covered, significant amounts of negative radiation (the snow absorbs heat from the air) occur, cooling the air. This air mass also tends to move very slowly, and consequently usually is very cold.
5. *Superior*: The superior air mass is unique because it forms at high altitudes over the southwestern desert and then descends to the surface. It is usually very hot and dry.

Storms are the result of conflict between warm air masses and cold air masses. The zone of contact between the contrasting air masses is called a *front*. Fronts are classified as cold fronts or warm fronts depending on which air mass is the more dominant. If the cold air mass is dominant, it will move faster and overtake the warm air mass. Cold air is heavier than warm air; therefore, the warm air is forced upward, as shown in the cross section in Figure 16.1.

Figure 16.1. Cross section of a cold front.

As it rises, warm air cools rapidly. Extreme turbulence and heavy rainfall may occur over small areas. From a soil and water conservation standpoint, cold fronts may cause local rainstorms of high intensity that may result in serious soil erosion and local flooding.

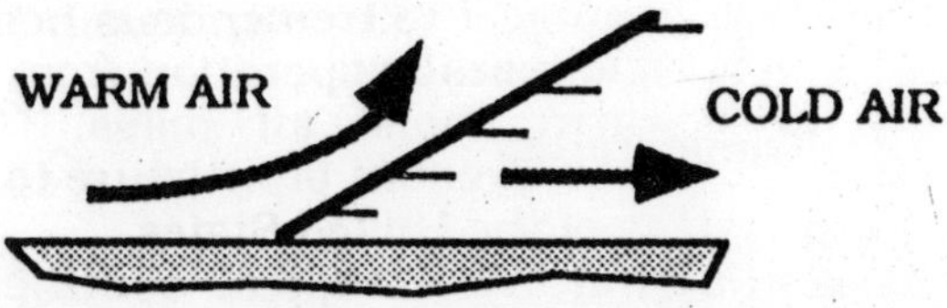

Figure 16.2. Cross section of a warm front.

A cross-sectional view of a warm front is shown in Figure 16.2. A warm front occurs when the warm air mass is dominant and overtakes cooler air. The rate of cooling is much less than for a cold front, and resulting rains are more gentle. The rains usually cover very large areas. Thus the potential for erosion is reduced, but the rains may cause widespread flooding if they persist for a long period of time.

HYDROLOGIC CYCLE

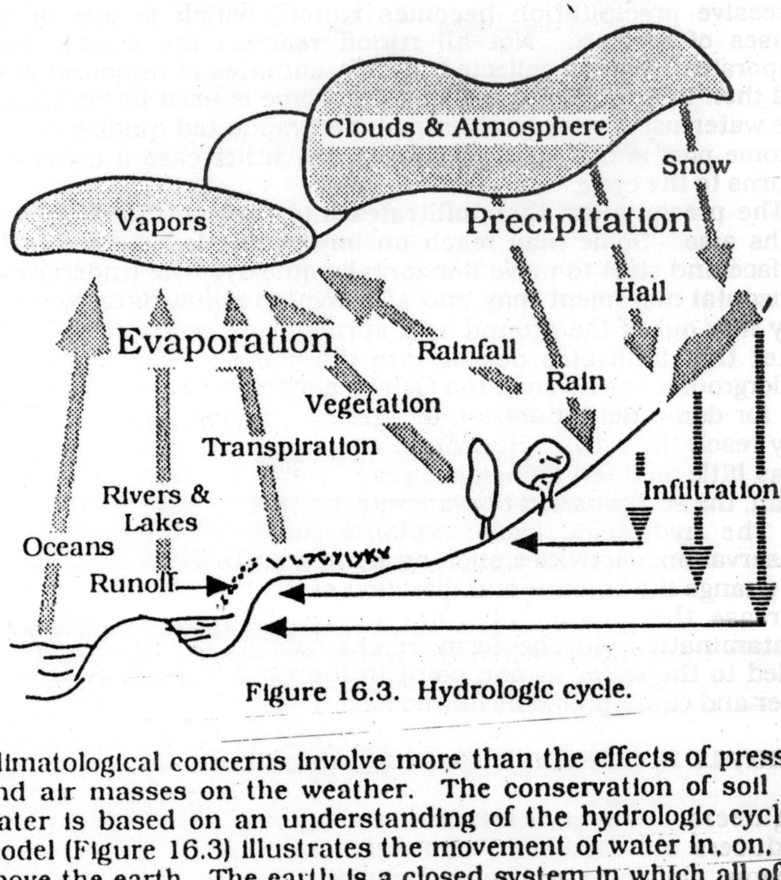

Figure 16.3. Hydrologic cycle.

Climatological concerns involve more than the effects of pressure and air masses on the weather. The conservation of soil and water is based on an understanding of the hydrologic cycle; a model (Figure 16.3) illustrates the movement of water in, on, and above the earth. The earth is a closed system in which all of the water circulates from one form to another. A study of the cycle can begin at any point, but we will start with precipitation.

Precipitation is caused by the condensation of water vapor in the atmosphere. Water vapor collects in the atmosphere as the sun evaporates water from the oceans, rivers, lakes, and plants. It falls to earth in the form of rain, hail, or snow, or forms on the surfaces of objects as dew or frost. Not all precipitation reaches the earth's surface; some evaporates as it falls, and some reaches the surface but does not move through the cycle because it is held for a long period of time in glaciers and the polar ice caps. Precipitation can follow several different paths before it eventually returns to the atmosphere in the form of vapor.

A portion of the precipitation will infiltrate the soil. It is not unusual for the infiltration rate (inches/hour) of the soil to be less than the rainfall intensity (inches/hour). In this case, the excessive precipitation becomes runoff, which is one of two causes of erosion. Not all runoff reaches the ocean; some evaporates, some is collected in different sizes of impoundments and then infiltrates into the soil, and some is used by vegetation. The water used by vegetation may be evaporated quickly or may become part of the plant processes. In either case it eventually returns to the cycle.

The precipitation that infiltrates into the soil takes different paths also. Some may reach an impervious layer close to the surface and start to move horizontally quickly. The underground horizontal movement may end at some type of surface water, or may flow out of the ground as a spring or an artesian well. The water that infiltrates deeper into the soil may collect in large underground basins such the Oglalla aquifer, and may be pumped out for domestic, industrial, or agricultural use, or it eventually may reach the ocean. Horizontal movement through the soil may be as little as a few inches per year. Once the water reaches the ocean, the sun causes it to evaporate, and the cycle begins again.

The hydrologic cycle explains the importance of water conservation. Activities such as pumping, dam building, and so on, change the amount and direction of the flow of water, and can decrease the amount of water for a later user in the cycle. Contamination, in the form of chemicals, silt, and so forth, added to the water at one point in the cycle may remain in the water and cause problems for the next user.

RAINFALL INTENSITY, DURATION, AND RECURRENCE

Engineers, conservationists, ecologists, and agricultural producers are interested in rainfall because of its impact on erosion, floods, and water available for crops. The most important characteristics of rainfall are the intensity, duration, total amount, and recurrence interval (for storms), all discussed in this section.

INTENSITY

Rainfall intensity is expressed as the rate of rainfall in inches per hour. The intensity is an important characteristic of rainfall because, other things being equal, more erosion is caused by one rainstorm of high intensity than by several storms of low intensity.

DURATION

Duration is the period of time that rain falls at a particular rate or intensity. It does not mean the total time, from beginning to end, of rainfall. During any storm the rainfall intensity many vary from quite high to very low; so it is necessary to think in terms of how long a time a rainfall intensity lasts (minutes or hours) at a certain rate (inches/minute). The total amount of rain (inches) for a rainfall event is the product of the rate of rainfall times the duration.

The average rainfall intensity for the entire duration of a storm is between the highest and the lowest rainfall intensity. As a general rule, the high-intensity portion of a storm has a shorter duration than the low-intensity portions. A typical relationship between rainfall intensity and duration is illustrated in Figure 16.4.

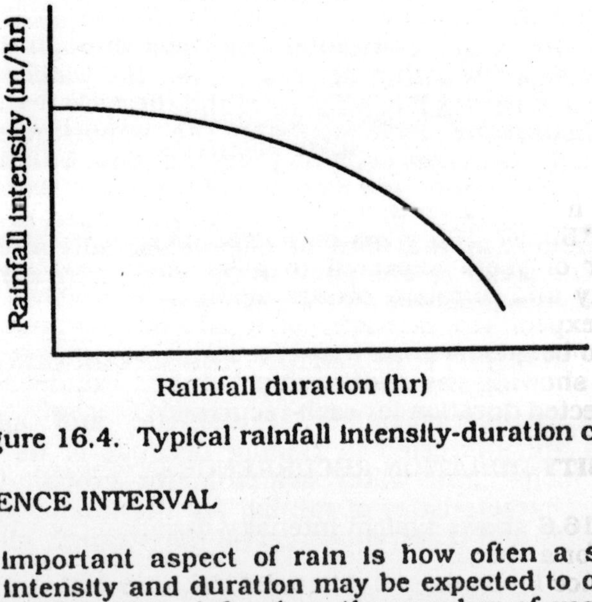

Figure 16.4. Typical rainfall intensity-duration curve.

RECURRENCE INTERVAL

Another important aspect of rain is how often a storm of a specified intensity and duration may be expected to occur. The recurrence interval is defined as the number of years (on the average) before a storm of a given intensity and duration can be expected to recur. A storm that would be expected on an average of once in 25 years is said to have a 25-year recurrence interval, or is called a 25-year storm. It is important to remember that this is all based on the laws of probability, or chance, and that *these estimates are based on averages only.* There is nothing to prevent a 25-year storm from happening in two successive years, or even more than twice in one year, although the odds against such frequent occurrence are great.

The National Weather Service has studied the rainfall records of major storms for many years. The results of these studies have been published in the form of Rainfall Intensity Recurrence Interval Charts. Such a chart would look like Figure 16.5.

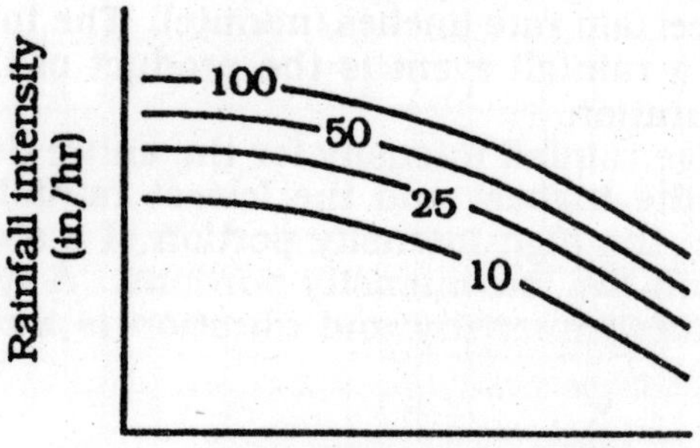

Figure 16.5. Typical rainfall intensity-duration-recurrence interval curves.

Thus, a storm is considered to have a recurrence interval of 2, 5, 10, 25, 50, or 100 year, or longer, depending on the average number of years expected to pass before a storm of similar intensity and duration occurs again. For a given duration we would expect the intensity of a 100-year recurrence interval storm to be greater than that of a 10-year storm. A curve can be plotted showing the relationship between rainfall intensity and the expected duration for each recurrence interval.

INTENSITY-DURATION-RECURRENCE INTERVAL

Figure 16.6 shows typical intensity-duration-recurrence interval curves for a specific location. The lines in the chart represent the recurrence intervals of 2, 5, 10, 25, 50, and 100 years. Note that both axes in the graph are logarithmic scales and must be carefully read. To design conservation structures, a graph appropriate for the area under study should be used.

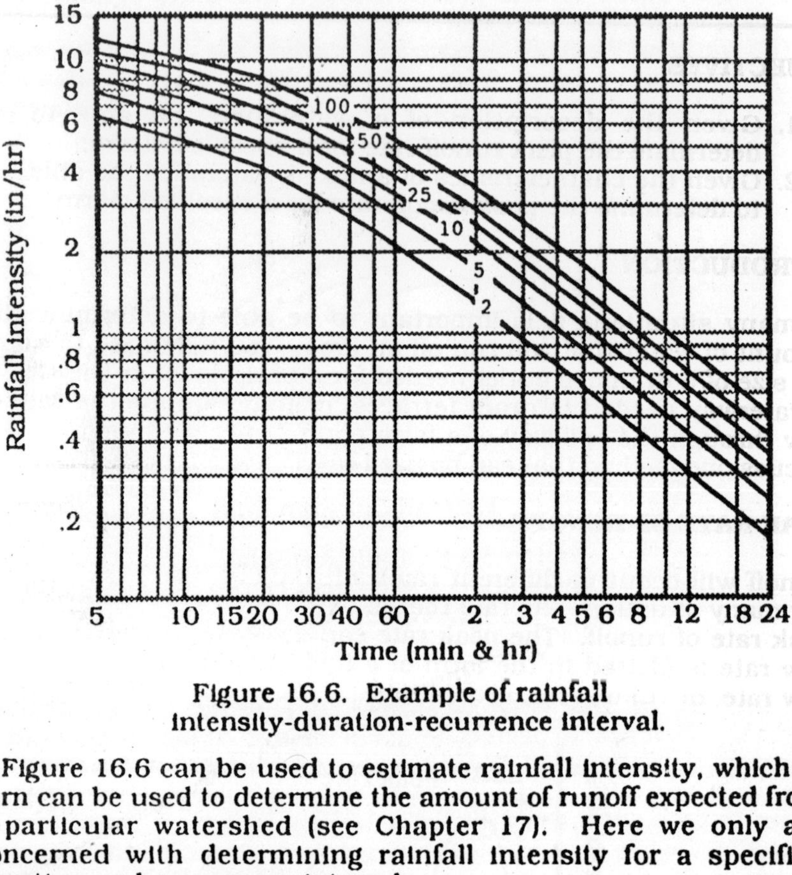

Figure 16.6. Example of rainfall intensity-duration-recurrence interval.

Figure 16.6 can be used to estimate rainfall intensity, which in turn can be used to determine the amount of runoff expected from a particular watershed (see Chapter 17). Here we only are concerned with determining rainfall intensity for a specified duration and recurrence interval.

PRACTICE PROBLEMS

1. Determine the rainfall intensity for a 10-year storm of 33 minutes' duration.
   Answer: Enter Figure 16.6 at the bottom, at 33 minutes, and move vertically to the 10-year line. Then move horizontally to the left, where you should read 4.5 in/hr intensity.
2. Find the rainfall intensity for a 2-year storm of 2.5 hours' duration.
   Answer: 1.1 in/hr
3. Find the rainfall intensity for a 50-year storm of 25 minutes' duration.
   Answer: 7.0 in/hr

17
Water Runoff

OBJECTIVES

1. Given the description of a watershed, be able to determine the peak runoff rate for a specified storm.
2. Given the characteristics of a mixed watershed, be able to determine the peak runoff rate for a specified storm.

INTRODUCTION

In many situations it is important to be able to determine the amount of water that will run off an area. You may need to know the size of a drainage outlet needed for a parking lot or the size of a waterway needed to drain terraces, or to determine the rate of flow through the spillway of a farm pond. In this chapter we will discuss one method that can be used to calculate the rate of runoff.

PEAK RATE OF RUNOFF

Runoff will occur at different rates within a storm (Figure 17.1). For many situations the rate that is of the greatest concern is the peak rate of runoff. The peak rate can easily be visualized if the flow rate is plotted in the form of a hydrograph, which plots the flow rate, or runoff rate, versus time.

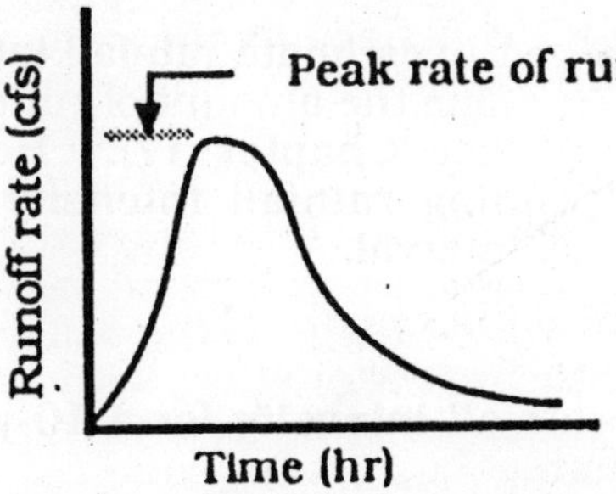

Figure 17.1. Typical runoff hydrograph.

Notice that after a storm begins, the runoff rate rapidly increases from zero until a maximum or peak rate is reached, and then slowly decreases until runoff ceases at some later time. The flow rate on a hydrograph usually is expressed in cubic feet per second (ft^3/sec or cfs). The peak rate is used to determine the capacity of water-conveying structures.

RATIONAL METHOD OF CALCULATING PEAK RATE OF RUNOFF

The rational method is one of the oldest methods of calculating the peak rate of runoff. The equation is:

$$Q = CIA \tag{17-1}$$

where:

Q = Peak rate of runoff (ft^3/sec)
C = Runoff coefficient
I = Rainfall intensity (in/hr)
A = Drainage area, watershed (ac)

The accuracy of this equation as a predictor of the peak runoff rate is only as good as the numbers used for each of the variables. The following tables contain generalized values and should be used only as examples. If the calculations are critical, the actual values for a particular watershed should be obtained from the Soil Conservation Service.

RUNOFF COEFFICIENT (C)

The runoff coefficient (C) is defined as the ratio of the peak runoff rate to the rainfall intensity. The runoff coefficient mathematically indicates for a watershed whether the runoff is likely to be high or low. The value of C depends on the type and characteristics of the watershed. If the watershed is composed of very tight soil, steep slopes, or cultivated land (or all three of these), the runoff rate will be high. If the soil is sandy, with flat slopes, and covered with good vegetation, the runoff will be low.

The runoff coefficient for watersheds with various topographic, soil, and cover conditions can be estimated by using the values given in Table 17-1.

Table 17-1. Table of runoff coefficients (C).

Topography, vegetation and slope	Soil Texture: Open sandy loam	Clay and silt loam	Tight clay
Woodland			
Flat 0-5%	0.10	0.30	0.40
Rolling 5-10%	0.25	0.35	0.50
Hilly 10-13%	0.30	0.50	0.60
Pasture			
Flat 0-5%	0.10	0.30	0.40
Rolling 5-10%	0.16	0.36	0.55
Hilly 10-13%	0.22	0.42	0.60
Cultivated			
Flat 0-5%	0.30	0.50	0.60
Rolling 5-10%	0.40	0.60	0.70
Hilly 10-13%	0.52	0.72	0.82

RAINFALL INTENSITY (I)

The rainfall intensity used in the rational method is based on a very special *rainfall duration and recurrence interval.* The recurrence used depends on the importance of the project. Terraces and waterways are designed for a 10-year recurrence, whereas spillways for dams may require a design based on a recurrence interval of 100 years or more. The duration of rainfall used in the rational method is determined by the time of concentration of the watershed.

TIME OF CONCENTRATION

The time of concentration for a watershed is defined as the time required for water to flow from the most remote point of the watershed to the outlet. If the duration of the rainstorm is long enough that it continues to rain throughout the entire time required for a drop of water to flow from the most remote point to the outlet, then the entire watershed will be contributing runoff at its maximum rate. The slope of the principal drainageway, called the drainageway gradient, and the maximum length of the principal drainageway are the most important factors affecting the time of concentration. Obviously, if the drainageway is short and steep, the water will arrive at the outlet quickly and the time of concentration will be short. A low, meandering, flat drainageway gradient has the opposite effect. The time of concentration for small watersheds with various lengths and drainageway gradients is shown in Table 17-2.

Table 17-2. Time of concentration for small watersheds (min).

Maximum length of flow (ft)	Drainageway gradient (slope), %					
	0.05	0.10	0.50	1.00	2.00	5.00
500	18	13	7	6	4	3
1,000	30	23	11	9	7	5
2,000	51	39	20	16	12	9
4,000	86	66	33	27	21	15
6,000	119	91	46	37	29	20
8,000	149	114	57	47	36	25
10,000	175	134	67	55	42	30

Using the value of the time of concentration determined from Table 17-2 and selecting an appropriate recurrence interval, one can obtain a value for rainfall intensity from a rainfall intensity duration curve (Figure 16.6).

Problem: Determine the peak runoff for a watershed consisting of 90 acres of pasture with tight clay soil and an average slope of 4%. The drainageway for the watershed is approximately 4000 feet with a gradient of 0.5%. Assume a recurrence interval of 10 years.

Solution: Using Equation (17-1):

$$Q = CIA$$

where:

C = (using Table 17-1) 0.40
I = (using Table 17-2 for time of concentration and Figure 16.6 for intensity) 4.9 in/hr
A = 90 ac

so that:

$$Q = 0.40 \times 4.9 \times 90$$

$$= 176 \frac{ft^3}{sec} \quad \text{or } 180 \frac{ft^3}{sec}$$

EFFECT OF VARYING RECURRENCE INTERVAL

The choice of recurrence interval will have a great influence on the peak rate of runoff to be expected from a watershed. This is illustrated by the following example:

Problem: Given the same watershed as the previous example, calculate the peak runoff rate for recurrence intervals of 2, 5, 10, 25, 50, and 100 years.

Solution: Using Equation (17-1) and Table 16.6 for each recurrence interval, we get the values listed in Table 17.3.

Table 17-3. Effect of varying recurrence interval.

Recurrence interval (yr)	Time of concentration (min)	Rainfall intensity (in/hr)	Runoff coefficient (C)	Watershed area (ac)	Peak runoff rate (cfs)
2	33	2.8	0.40	90	100.8
5	33	3.7	0.40	90	133.2
10	33	4.5	0.40	90	162.0
25	33	5.2	0.40	90	187.2
50	33	5.8	0.40	90	208.8
100	33	6.5	0.40	90	234.0

Note: If you observe the peak runoff rates for various recurrence intervals, you can find several interesting relationships. For example, the runoff rate from a 50-year storm is approximately twice as great as that from a 2-year storm and approximately 1.3 times as great as that from a 10-year storm.

MIXED WATERSHEDS

The previous examples were the simplest kind because they had the same slope, vegetation, and soil conditions throughout the watershed. In nature, this only occurs for very small areas. Watersheds usually contain different slopes, vegetation, soil types, and farming practices. All of these variables affect the amount of runoff that will occur. To cope with this type of situation it is necessary to calculate the weighted *runoff coefficient* (C_W) for the watershed.

The weighted runoff coefficient is determined by finding the appropriate value of C for each field or portion of the watershed that is different, multiplying that value of C by the appropriate area (ac), adding up these products for all of the different areas in the watershed, and then dividing their sum by the total watershed area.

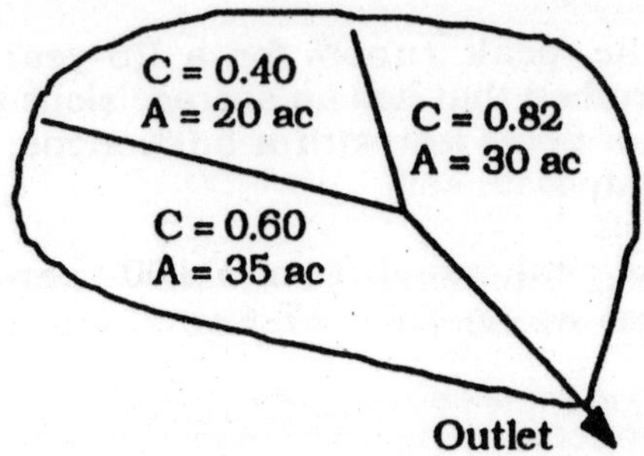

Figure 17.2. Example of a mixed watershed.

Study Figure 17.2 and the following equation:

$$(C_W) = \frac{(A_1C_1) + (A_2C_2) + (A_3C_3)}{A_T} \quad (17\text{-}2)$$

Problem: Determine the weighted C for the watershed in Figure 17.2.

Solution: Using Equation (17-2):

$$Cw = \frac{(A_1C_1) + (A_2C_2) + (A_3C_3)}{A_T}$$

$$= \frac{(20 \times 0.40) + (36 \times 0.60) + (30 \times 0.82)}{20 + 35 + 30}$$

$$= \frac{8.00 + 21.6 + 24.6}{85}$$

$$= \frac{54.2}{85}$$

$$= 0.64$$

PRACTICE PROBLEMS

1. Determine the peak runoff for a 25-year storm on a 120-acre watershed that has an average slope of 2.0%, and a drainageway of 6000 feet with a 5.0% slope, is cultivated, and has a sandy loam soil.
   Answer: 252 cfs
2. Determine the peak runoff from a 100-year storm for the watershed described by Table 17-4.

Table 17-4. Example of a mixed watershed.

	Field 1	Field 2	Field 3
Area (ac)	120 ac	40	56
Average slope	2%	8%	11%
Vegetation	Cultivated	Pasture	Woodland
Soil texture	Sandy loam	Tight clay	Silt loam
Gradient = 4000 ft and 0.1 % slope			

Answer: $C_W = 0.40$ and runoff = 432 cfs

18
Erosion and Erosion Control

OBJECTIVES

1. Understand the development of soil.
2. Understand the causes of erosion.
3. Be able to identify the two types of erosion.
4. Determine the rate of erosion using the Universal Soil Loss Equation.
5. Be able to explain common erosion control practices.

INTRODUCTION

Soil is a complex, constantly changing resource. It affects the life of plants and thereby all animals, and is affected by plants and animals. Soil is the primary medium of growth for plants. It supplies nutrients, water, and a place to anchor roots. Soil has an economic value, that with the most value being topsoil because it is the primary source of nutrients, water-holding capacity, and organic matter. Soil is formed and destroyed by erosion. In this chapter we will discuss soil development, destruction, and conservation.

SOIL DEVELOPMENT

Soil develops from the breakdown, or geological erosion, of sedimentary or volcanic parent material, which is a beneficial process. As the forces of nature, wind, water, heat, and cold erode the parent material, the particle size gradually decreases, and nutrients, water, and organic matter are mixed in. The exact rate of breakdown is debatable, but one estimate is that it takes 100 to 500 years to develop one inch of top soil.

CAUSES OF EROSION

The erosion we commonly refer to is man-made or man-accelerated erosion. Many activities accelerate the erosion process. Land with permanent vegetation is very stable, but as soon as the natural vegetation is removed, erosion accelerates. Activities such as the construction of roads and buildings, cultivation of fields, and timber harvesting all remove the natural protective cover. The two agents of erosion, water and wind, will be discussed in the next section, and then a method for estimating the amount of soil that is lost by water erosion will be illustrated.

TYPES OF EROSION

WATER

The amount of erosion caused by water is dependent on four factors: climate, soil, vegetation, and topography. The impact of *climate* is related to the amount and the intensity of rain. There is a correlation between the amount of soil loss and storm intensity. The greater the annual rainfall is, the greater the potential for water erosion; and the greater the frequency of intense storms is, the greater the potential for water erosion.

The contribution of *soil* to erosion relates to the size of the soil particles and the moisture content of the soil. Sandy and organic soils have the greatest potential for water erosion. These soils are not bound together, especially when wet, and the soil particles are easily moved.

Vegetation plays an important role in water erosion; it reduces the energy of the raindrops, in turn reducing the displacement of the soil. In cultivated fields, crop residues in and on the soil provide the same function as natural vegetation. Residues can be measured by randomly laying out a 100-foot tape across a field and counting the number of one foot marks that are over or touching any residue. This number is the residue cover as a percent. If four foot marks are over a piece of residue, then the percent is 4%.

The influence of *topography* is associated with the slope of the land. The greater the slope is, the greater the potential for water erosion.

These four water erosion factors predict what type of erosion occurs and how much there is. Water erosion usually is divided into three stages: raindrop, sheet and rill, and gully. *Raindrop* erosion is the soil splash resulting from the impact of water on soil particles. If the soil is covered with vegetation, raindrop erosion is almost zero. If the soil is a bare cultivated field, raindrop erosion can be significant. It is estimated that raindrops can displace soil particles 2 feet vertically and 5 feet horizontally. The effect of raindrop erosion increases as the slope increases.

Sheet and *rill* erosion are the next two stages. They are combined because many experts believe sheet erosion only exists in theory. As the rainfall intensity exceeds the infiltration rate of the soil, water starts to move across the soil's surface in a thin sheet. Almost as soon as the movement begins, small but well-defined channels develop, which are called rills. Rills can be farmed over and are easy to overlook, but they account for most of the water erosion.

Gully erosion is the next stage. Gullies are an advanced stage of rills. Small ones may still be farmed over, but if they are not checked, they become too large and then must be farmed around.

WIND

Movement of the soil due to wind erosion is not down the slope as in water; instead the direction is determined by the wind. If the soil is completely covered with vegetation, very little wind erosion occurs because the vegetation reduces the velocity of the wind at the surface of the soil. If the wind has access to the surface, the amount of erosion is determined by the velocity of the wind, the characteristics of the soil and the amount of moisture in the soil. The greater the velocity is, the greater the volume and size of particle that the wind can pick up. Fine sandy soils are affected by wind more than clay soils. Dry soils are easier to erode than moist soils.

Wind erosion cannot be divided into types; it only varies by degree (stages). There are three stages of movement, all of them usually occurring simultaneously. The first stage, *suspension*, occurs when soil particles are fine enough and the velocity is high enough to keep the particles in the air. Very fine particles can be transported for hundreds of miles. The second stage is skipping and bouncing, or *saltation*, which accounts for the largest volume of soil movement. In saltation the wind is strong enough to pick up the soil particle, but not strong enough to hold it in suspension. The third stage is rolling or *creep*. In the creep stage the wind can move the soil particles across the surface of the soil, but cannot pick them up.

The five factors used to estimate wind erosion are soil erodibility, climate, soil roughness, field length, and vegetation. To estimate the amount of wind erosion for a specific location, contact the Soil Conservation Service.

UNIVERSAL SOIL LOSS EQUATION

A Universal Soil Loss Equation has been developed to estimate the impact of the water and wind erosion factors. The equation for water erosion is:

$$A = RKLSCP \tag{18-1}$$

where:

A = Predicted average annual soil loss (T/ac/yr)
R = Rainfall factor
K = Soil erodibility factor
L = Slope length factor
S = Slope gradient factor
C = Cropping management factor
P = Erosion control practice factor

For this discussion, several of these factors will be combined to give the following equation:

$$A = R \times K \times LS \times CP \qquad (18\text{-}2)$$

The Universal Soil Loss Equation assigns numerical values to all of the factors that influence water erosion. Therefore, the accuracy of the calculated soil loss is only as good as the numerical values representing these factors. The tables and graph included here are used to show typical values. More accurate values for specific areas can be obtained from the Soil Conservation Service.

RAINFALL FACTOR (R)

The rainfall factor is a measure of the erosion force of a specific rainfall. Common values for R can range from 100 to 350.

SOIL ERODIBILITY (K)

Table 18-1. Soil erodibility factor (K) (ton/ac).

	Organic Matter Content %		
Textural Class	0.50	2.00	4.00
Fine sand	0.16	0.14	0.10
Very fine sand	0.42	0.36	0.28
Loamy sand	0.12	0.10	0.08
Loamy very fine sand	0.44	0.38	0.30
Sandy loam	0.27	0.24	0.19
Very fine sandy loam	0.47	0.41	0.33
Silt loam	0.48	0.42	0.33
Clay loam	0.28	0.25	0.21
Silty clay loam	0.37	0.32	0.26
Silty clay	0.25	0.23	0.19

The K value is a measure of the erosion rate for a soil type. Typical values for some soils can be found in Table 18-1.

TOPOGRAPHIC FACTOR (LS)

The topographic factor is a combination of the slope length and the percent of slope. An estimate for LS can be found in Figure 18.1.

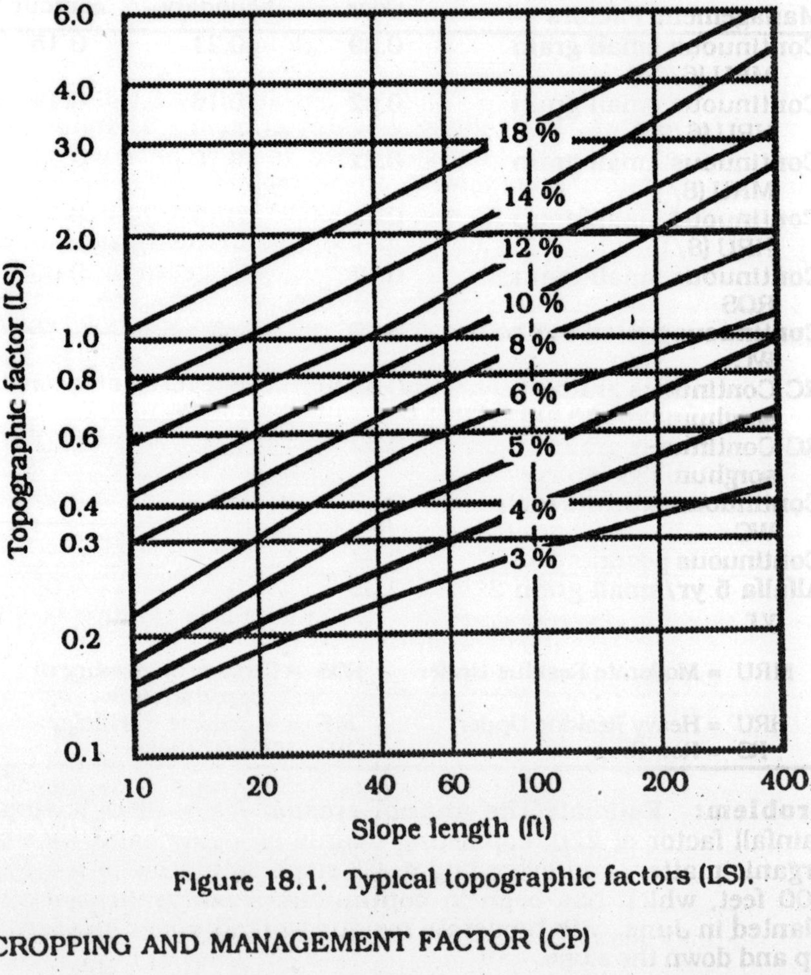

Figure 18.1. Typical topographic factors (LS).

CROPPING AND MANAGEMENT FACTOR (CP)

This factor is a function of the crop raised, the management practice, the planting date, the amount of residue on the surface, and the tillage practice. Values representing these factors can be found in Table 18-2.

Table 18-2. Typical cropping and management factors (CP).

	Cropping practices		
Management Factors	Up and down the slope	Terraces and field boundary	On the contour
Continuous small grain MRU (6/20)	0.29	0.21	0.15
Continuous small grain HRU (6/20)	0.22	0.16	0.11
Continuous small grain MRU (8/1)	0.22	0.16	0.11
Continuous small grain HRU (8/1)	0.18	0.13	0.09
Continuous small grain ROS	0.12	0.09	0.06
Continuous cotton MF no WC	0.59	0.42	0.30
RC Continuous grain sorghum (25--30 bu)	0.48	0.34	0.24
RC Continuous grain sorghum (35--45 bu)	0.42	0.30	0.21
Continuous peanuts with WC	0.43	0.30	0.22
Continuous peanuts no WC	0.54	0.38	0.27
Alfalfa 5 yr/small grain 2 yr	0.05	0.05	0.05

MRU = Moderate Residue Under
HRU = Heavy Residue Under
RC = Row Crop
ROS = Residue on Surface at Seeding Time
MF = Moderate Fertilizer
WC = Winter Cover

Problem: Estimate the annual erosion for a field having a rainfall factor of 220, consisting mainly of loamy sand with 2% organic matter, and averaging a 4% slope with a slope length of 400 feet, which has been in continuous small grain, normally planted in June, with moderate residue worked under and farmed up and down the slope.

Solution: Using Equation (18-2) and the appropriate tables and figure:

$$A = R \times K \times LS \times CP$$

where:

R = 220
K = 0.10 (Table 18-1)
LS = 0.65 (Figure 18.1)
CP = 0.29 (Table 18-2)

Thus:

$$A = 220 \times 0.10 \times 0.65 \times 0.29$$

$$= 4.1 \text{ T/ac/yr}$$

EROSION CONTROL

The best philosophy for erosion control is that it is better to prevent erosion than to try to correct it. The "best" method for erosion control is influenced by the situation; for example, appropriate control methods for a construction site may not be appropriate for cultivated land.

On cultivated land, the best methods to use are those activities that will reduce the effect of wind and water on the soil particles. For the prevention of water erosion it is important to provide as much protection as possible for the surface of the soil. This includes management of tillage practices to leave residue on the surface and the use of cover crops in nonproductive seasons. Additional protection is provided by reducing the length of the continuous slope by installing terraces. To illustrate the effect of these practices, we will rework the sample problem with the appropriate values for terraces and residue.

Problem: Estimate the annual erosion for a field that has a rainfall factor of 220, consists mainly of loamy sand with 2% organic matter, averages a 4% slope with a slope length of 200 feet, and has been in continuous small grain with heavy residue, normally planted in June, and farmed with terraces.

Solution: Using Equation (18-2) and the appropriate values:

$$A = R \times K \times LS \times CP$$

where:

$$R = 220$$
$$K = 0.10$$
$$LS = 0.52$$
$$CP = 0.16$$

Thus:

$$A = 220 \times 0.10 \times 0.52 \times 0.16$$

$$= 1.8 \text{ T/ac/yr}$$

In the original problem the soil loss was 4.1 T/ac/yr. This example shows that by changing the tillage practices to increase the residue on the soil and by terracing the field, the soil loss is reduced by more than half.

Residues on the surface also help prevent wind erosion, but reducing the length of the slope does not. The critical factors for preventing wind erosion, other than residue, are the roughness of the surface and the unobstructed distance that the wind can blow. Reducing the unobstructed distance is an effective control. This explains the prevalent use of shelterbelts in the Great Plains region. A shelterbelt will provide protection downwind for up to ten times its height.

Other methods are appropriate for the control of both water and wind on small areas for a short duration, such as construction sites. At these sites temporary terraces can be constructed from small bales of hay or straw or the entire surface may be covered by netting to reduce the effects of water erosion. Wind erosion can be controlled by installing temporary wind barriers and keeping the ground covered.

PRACTICE PROBLEMS

1. Estimate the soil loss for a clay loam soil with 2% organic matter and a rainfall factor of 200 that has been in an alfalfa-small grain rotation and farmed on the contour. The slope length is 600 feet, and the slope averages 6%.
   Answer: 3.4 T/ac/yr (R = 200, K = 0.28, LS = 1.2, and CP = .05)
2. What will be the expected soil loss for the field in the previous problem if it is taken out of alfalfa-small grain rotation and put into continuous small grain with residue on the surface at seeding time?
   Answer: 4.0 T/ac/yr

19
Irrigation

OBJECTIVES

1. Understand the purpose and use of irrigation.
2. Be able to describe the common irrigation systems.
3. Be able to calculate the required system capacity.
4. Be able to determine the irrigation interval and the depth of water to apply.

INTRODUCTION

The most limiting and most variable environmental factor affecting the productivity of plants is water. Throughout history the universal solution to this problem has been irrigation. For effective and efficient use of irrigation one must know its effect on plant production, the best system for a given field and water supply, how much water to apply and when to apply it, and the quality of the water. This chapter will discuss some of these aspects of irrigation.

IRRIGATION SYSTEMS

Once the decision has been made to irrigate, the next consideration is what type of system to use. Water is applied in one of three ways: from above the ground, on the ground surface, or from below the surface. The choice usually is based on cost and topography. This section will review the basic types of irrigation systems.

SPRINKLER

In sprinkler systems water is sprayed into the air by either a rotating sprinkler or a perforated pipe. Sprinkler systems can be used on any land that can be cultivated. Sprinklers may be solid set (in a permanent position) or movable. The common means of movement are: (1) manual--lawn sprinkler or pipe system; (2) tractor-moved--skid or wheel-mounted system; (3) self-moved--side wheel roll or big gun system; and (4) self-propelled--center pivot and lateral move system. The best system depends on the amount and cost of labor for movement and the value added for the crop. For sprinkler systems it is important that the application rate not exceed the infiltration rate of the soil.

SURFACE

In surface irrigation, water is applied by allowing it to flow over the surface by gravity or through drip valves (a process called trickle or drip irrigation). In trickle irrigation, drip valves or emitters are located along a line at uniform distances or at each large plant. Gravity systems require relatively flat land, where the water may be distributed in level borders, contoured levees, or level furrows. For level borders and contoured levees, the water usually is delivered by surface ditch. Water for level furrows may be delivered by ditches, but a gated pipe or a siphon tube also may be used to supply the water at the head of the furrows. As a general rule, gravity systems require more labor than sprinkler systems to maintain the ditches and the dikes, move the gated pipe, and control the flow of the water.

SUBSURFACE

Two different technologies exist: in one system a porous pipe is buried in the root zone, whereas in the second system water is applied by ditch or pipe in a region that has an impermeable layer close to the surface. A water table develops close to the surface, from the applied water, which can be tapped by the plants.

DEPTH OF WATER TO APPLY

Seasonal water demand and peak daily use vary considerably from crop to crop and from one field to the next. Deciding when to irrigate and deciding how much water to apply are the two most difficult decisions to make in managing irrigation systems. The following discussion will explore some of the factors influencing these decisions.

The amount of water used by plants depends on five factors:

1. The length of the growing season
2. The amount of daylight per day
3. The daily temperature
4. The speed and direction of the wind
5. The crop's stage of growth

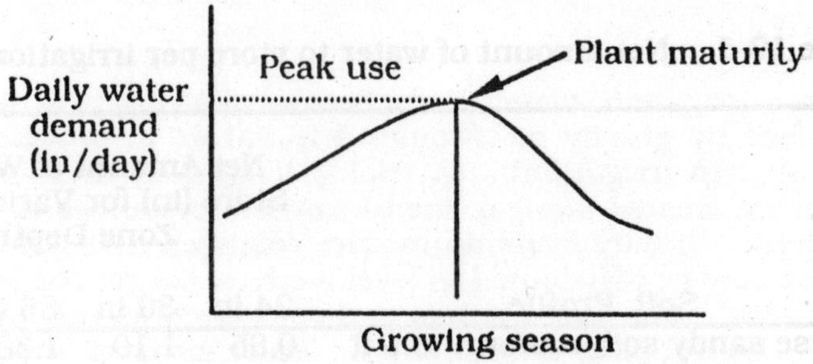

Figure 19.1. Typical daily water demand.

For any given plant, the daily rate of use will increase until the plant reaches maturity, and then it will decrease (see Figure 19.1). The peak water use rate occurs at the height of the growing season.

Table 19-1. Root zone depth and peak water use rate.

Crop	Root zone depth of principle moisture extraction (in)	Length of Growing Season: 180-210 days Peak use (in/day)	Length of Growing Season: 210-250 days Peak use (in/day)
Alfalfa	48	0.29	0.32
Beans	24	0.20	0.20
Corn	36	0.30	0.35
Cotton	36	---	0.28
Grain sorghum	30	0.20	0.20
Melons	30	0.20	0.22
Other truck	24	0.20	0.22
Pasture	24	0.28	0.30
Peas	36	0.19	---
Potatoes	24	0.38	0.20
Small grain	30	0.20	0.22
Sugar beets	36	0.28	0.30
Tomatoes	48	0.20	0.22
Vineyards	48	0.22	0.25

Table 19-1 shows the peak use for a number of crops with both short and long growing seasons, and the root zone depth from which each crop extracts most of its moisture.

Table 19-2. Net amount of water to store per irrigation.

Soil Profile	Net Amount of Water to Store (in) for Various Root Zone Depths			
	24 in	30 in	36 in	48 in
Coarse sandy soil, uniform to 6 ft	0.85	1.10	1.30	1.75
Coarse sandy soil over compacted subsoil	1.50	1.75	2.00	2.50
Fine sandy loam uniform to 6 ft	1.75	2.20	2.60	3.00
Fine sandy loam over compacted subsoil	2.00	2.40	2.80	3.25
Silt loam uniform to 6 ft	2.25	2.75	3.00	4.00
Silt loam over compacted subsoil	2.50	3.00	3.25	4.25
Heavy clay or clay loam soil	2.00	2.40	2.85	3.85

Two characteristics of soil must be considered in determining how much water should be applied: (1) the rate at which soil can absorb (store) water, or the infiltration rate, is determined by the texture of the soil; and (2) the total amount of water that can be stored by the soil is a function of the soil texture and depth. Loams and clays can hold more water than sands, as shown in Table 19-2. Also note that the type and the depth of subsoil make a difference in the amount of water that can be stored per irrigation. For example, soils having a more compact subsoil can store a greater amount of water than the same soils having a uniform depth.

The rooting depth of the crop also influences the amount of water that should be stored. Any water that infiltrates the soil to a depth below the root zone is lost to the plant. These factors were taken into consideration during the development of Tables 19-1 and 19-2.

To use these tables first consult Table 19-1 for a particular crop and growing season length and obtain values for (1) the root zone depth of principal moisture extraction and (2) the peak daily water use. Then if you know the soil type or profile on which the irrigation is to take place and the root zone depth of principal moisture extraction of the crop, you can refer to Table 19-2 and obtain a value for the number of inches of water to store per irrigation.

a location where the season is greater than 210 days on a silt loam soil over compacted subsoil?

Solution: Using Tables 19-1 and 19-2:

Root zone depth = 36 in
Peak daily use = 0.35 in/day
Net amount to store per irrigation = 3.25 in

These figures show that the net amount of water to store per irrigation is 3.25 inches.

Next we must determine the amount of water to apply because not all of the water will reach the crop. Water that evaporates, runs off, and deep percolates (water which moves through the root zone) is lost to the crop.

The term *application efficiency* is used to describe the efficiency with which water is added to the soil, and is defined as the ratio of the depth of water stored to the depth of water applied, expressed as a percent. The application efficiency of a well-designed irrigation system will be between 60% and 80%. Application efficiency can be used to determine the amount of water to apply in the following manner:

$$\text{Depth of water to apply} = \frac{\text{Depth of water stored (in)}}{\text{Application efficiency}} \qquad (10\text{-}1)$$

or:

$$DWA = \frac{DWS}{AE}$$

where:

DWA = Depth of water to apply (in)
DWS = Depth of water to store (in)
AE = Application efficiency (as a decimal)

Problem: How much water should be applied for the corn crop in the previous problem if the application efficiency is 70%?

Solution: Using Equation (19-1):

$$DWA = \frac{DWS}{AE}$$

$$DWA = \frac{DWS}{AE}$$

$$= \frac{3.25 \text{ in}}{0.70}$$

$$= 4.65 \text{ in}$$

It is also necessary to determine an *irrigation interval*, which is the number of days it takes the crop to use up the water stored in the soil. The irrigation interval is determined by dividing the amount of water stored in the soil by the plants' daily use. For peak use the irrigation interval is:

$$IRI = \frac{DWS}{PDU} \qquad (19\text{-}2)$$

where:

IRI = Irrigation interval (days)
DWS = Depth of water to store (in)
PDU = Peak water use (in/day)

Problem: What is the irrigation interval for the corn crop in the previous problem?

Solution: Using Equation (19-2):

$$IRI = \frac{DWS}{PDU}$$

$$= \frac{3.25}{0.35}$$

$$= 9.3 \text{ days}$$

For this corn crop, if 3.25 inches of water is stored in the soil per irrigation, at the time of peak use it must be irrigated every 9.3 days.

If there is rainfall during the irrigation season, the irrigation interval should be adjusted accordingly. For example, if there were 1.25 inches of rain on the corn crop in the previous problem, then we would divide the amount of rain by the water needs of the crop and extend the interval the corresponding number of days. For the peak demand of the corn crop, 1.25 + 0.35 = 3.6 days.

Instead of irrigating again in 9.3 days, the irrigation interval could be extended to 12.9 days.

SYSTEM CAPACITY

System capacity is the maximum amount of water that an irrigation system can deliver on a continuous basis. Several different units are used to describe the size of irrigation systems. Common units are acre-feet (ac-ft, that is, the amount of water it will take to cover one acre, one foot deep), acre-inch (ac-in), gallons per minute (gal/min or gpm), and cubic feet per second (ft^3/sec or cfs). The required pumping capacity of an irrigation system depends on the area to be irrigated (ac), the depth of water to apply (in), and the length of time that the irrigation system is operated (hr).

The amount of time per day that an irrigation system can operate depends on the type of system and the amount of maintenance it requires. A self-propelled unit may be able to run several days without stopping, whereas manual-move, tractor-towed, and self-moved systems must be shut down at regular intervals. Only a portion of a field is irrigated at one time, and some time is required to move the system from one portion of the field "set" to another "set." The term *irrigation period* is used to designate the number of days that a system can apply the water for one irrigation to a given area. Note that it is necessary for the irrigation period to be equal to or less than the irrigation interval. The required capacity of a system, in gallons per minute, can be determined by the following equation:

$$RSC = \frac{450 \times A \times DWA}{IRP \times HPD} \qquad (19\text{-}3)$$

where:

RSC = Required system capacity (gal/min)
450 = Units conversion constant
A = Area irrigated (ac)
DWA = Depth of water to apply per irrigation (in)
IRP = Irrigation period (day)
HPD = Time operating (hr/day)

Problem: Determine the required system capacity (gal/min) for the corn crop in the previous problem if the field area is 200 acres, and the system can operate for 18 hours per day for 7.7 days.

$$RSC = \frac{450 \times A \times DWA}{IRP \times HPD}$$

$$= \frac{450 \times 200 \text{ ac} \times 4.65 \text{ in}}{7.7 \text{ day} \times \frac{18 \text{ hr}}{1 \text{ day}}}$$

$$= \frac{418{,}500}{138.6}$$

$$= 3{,}019.48 \frac{\text{gal}}{\text{min}} \text{ or } 3{,}000 \frac{\text{gal}}{\text{min}}$$

For 200 acres of long-season corn grown on silt loam soil over compacted subsoil, irrigated with a system that is 70% efficient and limited to operating 18 hours per day for 7.7 days, the system must be able to deliver 3,000 gallons of water per minute.

In some situations it might be necessary to use units of capacity other than gallons per minute. In these cases units cancellation and/or the appropriate conversion factors (Appendix I) can be used to convert the units.

Problem: What will the system capacity need to be in units of acre-feet/min?

Solution: Using units cancellation:

$$\frac{\text{ac-ft}}{\text{min}} = \frac{200 \text{ ac}}{1} \times \frac{1 \text{ hr}}{60 \text{ min}} \times \frac{1 \text{ day}}{18 \text{ hr}}$$

$$\times \frac{1}{7.7 \text{ day}} \times \frac{1 \text{ ft}}{12 \text{ in}} \times \frac{4.65 \text{ in}}{1}$$

$$= \frac{930}{99{,}792}$$

$$= 9.319 \text{ X } 10^{-3} \frac{\text{ac-ft}}{\text{min}} \text{ or } 9.32 \text{ X } 10^{-3} \frac{\text{ac-ft}}{\text{min}}$$

Solution: Converting from gal/min to ac-ft/min:

$$\frac{\text{ac-ft}}{\text{min}} = \frac{1\ \text{ac}}{43{,}560\ \text{ft}^2} \times \frac{0.13368\ \text{ft}^3}{1\ \text{gal}} \times \frac{3000\ \text{gal}}{1\ \text{min}}$$

$$= \frac{401.04}{43{,}560}$$

$$= 9.2066... \times 10^{-3}\,\frac{\text{ac-ft}}{\text{min}} \text{ or } 9.21 \times 10^{-3}\,\frac{\text{ac-ft}}{\text{min}}$$

The two solutions to this problem are a good example of one of the advantages of the units cancellation method. Because both 0.13368 and 3000 are rounded numbers, the answer 9.21×10^{-3} is not as accurate as 9.32×10^{-3}. Any differences due to rounding are increased when the numbers are multiplied.

As we noted earlier, system capacity is a function of four variables: area (ac); water flow rate (gal/min, ft^3/min, ac-ft/min, etc.); depth of water applied or peak use (in); and time (min, hr, or days). This relationship is expressed mathematically as:

$$D \times A = Q \times T \qquad (19\text{-}4)$$

where:

D = Depth of water, either applied or peak use (in)
A = Area irrigated (ac)
Q = Water flow rate (cfs)
T = Length of time water is applied (hr)

If any three of the variables are known, the other one can be calculated by rearranging the equation and substituting the values of the known variables. You must enter flow rate (Q) in cubic feet per second, depth in inches, and time in hours. The following discussion will illustrate several uses of this equation.

In the previous problem we determined the system capacity using units cancellation. If it is necessary to know how much water has been applied, the peak use does not accurately describe what we are solving for. When we want to know the depth of water that has been applied, D becomes the depth of water applied (DWA). This will work because the unit of measure is the same for both peak use and DWA (inches).

Problem: A producer spends 120 hours irrigating 90.0 acres. If the pump discharges 1350 gallons per minute, what average depth of water (in) is applied?

Solution: Because we want to know the amount of water applied, not the amount available to the plants, the efficiency factor is not used. Also, Q must be converted from gal/min to ft^3/sec. Rearranging Equation (19-4), substituting depth of water to apply (DWA) for the depth (D), and including the conversion factor 1 $ft^3/sec = 2.25 \times 10^{-3}$ gal/min[1]:

$$DWA \times A = Q \times T$$

$$DWA = \frac{Q \times T}{A}$$

$$= \frac{\left(1350 \frac{gal}{min} \times \frac{2.25 \times 10^{-3} \frac{ft^3}{sec}}{\frac{gal}{min}}\right) \times 120 \text{ hr}}{90 \text{ ac}}$$

$$= \frac{3.04 \frac{ft^3}{sec} \times 120 \text{ hr}}{90.0 \text{ ac}}$$

$$= \frac{365}{90.0}$$

$$= 4.01 \text{ in}$$

Solution: Using units cancellation the answer is:

$$\text{in} = \frac{231 \text{ in}^3}{\text{gal}} \times \frac{1350 \text{ gal}}{\text{min}} \times \frac{60.0 \text{ min}}{1 \text{ hr}} \times \frac{120.0 \text{ hr}}{1} \times \frac{1 \text{ ft}^2}{144.0 \text{ in}^2} \times \frac{1 \text{ ac}}{43{,}560 \text{ ft}^2} \times \frac{1}{90.0 \text{ ac}}$$

---

[1] If $\frac{ft^3}{sec} = \frac{1 \text{ gal}}{\text{min}} \times \frac{1 \text{ min}}{60.0 \text{ sec}} \times \frac{1 \text{ ft}^3}{7.40 \text{ gal}} = 2.25 \times 10^{-3} \frac{ft^3}{sec}$

then $\frac{1 \text{ gal}}{\text{min}} = \frac{2.25 \times 10^{-3} \text{ ft}^3}{1 \text{ sec}}$

$$= \frac{2.24 \times 10^9}{5.64 \times 10^8}$$

$$= 3.97 \text{ in}$$

Variations occur in the use of Equation (19-4) for different types of irrigation systems. In situations where the limiting factor is the availability of water, we need to determine the maximum area that can be irrigated with the available water supply.

Problem: What is the largest size of lawn (ft^2) that can be irrigated in 6 hours if a minimum of 0.5 inch of water is applied at each irrigation, the system is 90% efficient, and the water supply delivers 3.5 gal/min?

Solution: Rearranging Equation (19-4), adding the efficiency factor, and converting the area to square feet:

$$D \times A = Q \times T$$

$$A\ (ac) = \left(\frac{Q \times T}{D}\right) \times 0.90$$

$$A\ (ft^2) = \left(\frac{Q \times T}{D} \times \frac{43{,}560\ ft^2}{1\ ac}\right) \times 0.90$$

$$= \left(\frac{\left(\frac{3.5\ gal}{min} \times \frac{2.3 \times 10^{-3}\ \frac{ft^3}{sec}}{1\ \frac{gal}{min}}\right) \times 6\ hr}{0.5}\right) \times \frac{43{,}560\ ft^2}{1\ ac} \times 0.90$$

$$= \frac{8.05 \times 10^{-3} \times 6\ hr}{0.5} \times 43{,}560\ ft^2 \times 0.90$$

$$= 3900\ ft^2$$

If flood irrigation is used to water a field, assuming that the water flow rate is limited, it usually is necessary to determine the amount of time that the water should flow to cover the field at the desired depth.

Problem: How long will it take to apply 4 inches of water uniformly over 120 acres if the water is available at the rate of 20 cfs? (Assume 100% efficiency.)

Solution: Using Equation (19-4) to solve for time (T):

$$D \times A = Q \times T$$

$$T\ (hr) = \frac{D \times A}{Q}$$

$$= \frac{4\ in \times 120\ ac}{20\ \frac{ft^3}{sec}}$$

$$= 24\ hr$$

Solution: Using units cancellation:

$$hr = \frac{1\ hr}{60\ min} \times \frac{1\ min}{60\ sec} \times \frac{1\ sec}{20\ ft^3} \times \frac{43{,}560\ ft^2}{1\ ac} \times \frac{120\ ac}{1} \times \frac{1\ ft}{12\ in} \times \frac{4\ in}{1}$$

$$= \frac{2.1 \times 10^7}{8.6 \times 10^5}$$

$$= 24\ hr$$

During furrow irrigation it is important to know how long the water must run to apply the desired amount for each set of furrows. Three values are necessary to calculate time: the water flow rate for each furrow or for the entire set, the area of the furrow or the set, and the amount of water to be applied. The area is determined from the number of rows in the set, the row spacing, and the length of the row.

Problem: How much time is required to apply 3 inches of water to sixty 32-inch rows if the rows are one half mile long, and the system capacity is 30 gal/min/row?

Solution: Rearranging Equation (19-4):

$$T = \frac{D \times A}{Q}$$

The area is:

$$A = \frac{\text{No. of rows x row spacing (ft) x length (ft)}}{43{,}560 \frac{ft^2}{ac}}$$

$$= \frac{60 \times 32 \frac{in}{row} \times \frac{1\ ft}{12\ in} \times \frac{5280\ ft}{2}}{43{,}560 \frac{ft^2}{ac}}$$

$$= \frac{4.2 \times 10^5\ ft^2}{43{,}560 \frac{ft^2}{ac}}$$

$$= 9.6\ ac$$

and the flow rate must be in units of ft^3/sec:

$$Q\left(\frac{ft^3}{sec}\right) = \left(\frac{30 \frac{gal}{min}}{row} \times 60\ row\right) \times \frac{2.25 \times 10^{-3} \frac{ft^3}{sec}}{1 \frac{gal}{min}}$$

$$Q = 1800 \frac{gal}{min} \times \frac{2.25 \times 10^{-3} \frac{ft^3}{sec}}{1 \frac{gal}{min}}$$

$$= 4.0 \frac{ft^3}{sec}$$

so the time (hr) is:

$$T = \frac{D \times A}{Q}$$

$$= \frac{3.0 \times 9.6}{4}$$

$$= 7.2 \text{ hr}$$

It will take 7.2 hours to apply 3.0 inches of water to the field.

SEASONAL NEED

Seasonal water demand is the amount of water (in inches) that a crop must have during one growing season for maximum production. The seasonal water demand will vary from season to season, and for each crop and region. Table 19-3 contains some typical values for three regions of the United States.

Table 19-3. Typical seasonal water demand for some crops (in).

	Western region	Central region	Eastern region
Alfalfa	36.0	36.0	33.0
Corn	23.0	25.0	21.0
Cotton	31.0	20.0	19.0
Grain sorghum	20.0	22.0	21.0
Oranges	33.0	----	----
Hay	31.0	----	36.0
Sugar beets	36.0	29.0	----
Tomatoes	19.0	----	14.0

Source: *Planning for an Irrigation System*, American Association for Vocational Instructional Materials (AAVIM), Athens, Georgia.

Knowledge of the seasonal water demand for a crop in a given area is useful for determining the contribution of irrigation to the cost of production and the total amount of water that will be needed. If the cost of water is known (usually expressed as dollars per acre-feet), as well as the seasonal demand of the crop, the normal rainfall during the growing season, and the number of acres, it is possible to estimate the total amount of water that will be needed and what it will cost. To determine total seasonal use, the efficiency of the irrigation system also must be considered. Typical efficiency is 60 to 80%.

Problem: How much water (ac-ft/yr) is needed to supply 120 acres of cotton in the central region if the normal rainfall during the growing season is 5 inches, and the efficiency of the irrigation system is 70%?

Solution: Using units cancellation:

$$\frac{\text{ac-ft}}{\text{yr}} = \frac{120\ \text{ac}}{1} \times \frac{1\ \text{ft}}{12\ \text{in}} \times \frac{20\ \text{in} - 5\ \text{in}}{1\ \text{yr}} \times \frac{1}{0.70}$$

$$= 214 \frac{\text{ac-ft}}{\text{yr}}$$

Problem: What is the total water cost if the price is $25.00 per acre-foot?

Solution: Using units cancellation:

$$\frac{\$}{\text{yr}} = \frac{25.00\ \$}{\text{ac-ft}} \times 214 \frac{\text{ac-ft}}{\text{yr}}$$

$$= 5350 \frac{\$}{\text{yr}}$$

PRACTICE PROBLEMS

1. Find the depth of water to apply and the irrigation interval for a crop of sugar beets grown on a silt loam soil uniform to 6 feet. The length of the growing season is greater than 210 days, and the application efficiency is 75%.
Answer: DWA = 4 in, IRI = 13 days
2. Find the depth of water to apply and the irrigation interval for a crop of grain sorghum grown on a fine sandy loam soil over more compacted subsoil. The length of the growing season is less than 210 days, and the application efficiency is 70%.
Answer: DWA = 3.4 in, IRI ≐ 17 days
3. What system capacity (gal/min) is required to irrigate 120 acres of grain sorghum in problem 2 if the system can operate 21 hours per day?
Answer: 517 gpm

4. What quantity of water will be needed in problem 3 in units of ac-ft/hr?
   Answer: 0.10 ac-ft/hr
5. What size of lawn can be irrigated in 10 hours if a minimum of 0.75 inch of water needs to be applied, the system efficiency is 85%, and the water supply delivers 2.75 gallons per minute?
   Answer: 3000 ft^2
6. How much water will be needed to irrigate 250 acres of alfalfa in the western region (ac-ft/yr) if the normal rainfall is 25.0 inches and the system efficiency is 85.0%?
   Answer: 270 ac-ft/yr
7. What is the total cost ($/yr) of the water for the alfalfa in problem 6 if the pumping costs are $0.0002 per gallon?
   Answer: $17,600 per year

20
Handling, Moisture Management, and Storage of Biological Products

OBJECTIVES

1. Be able to describe the common methods of handling biological products.
2. Be able to determine the size and horsepower requirements of screw-type conveyors.
3. Be able to determine the size and horsepower requirements of pneumatic conveyors.
4. Be able to determine the amount of water to extract from or add to biological products.
5. Understand the requirements of biological product storage.

INTRODUCTION

The term biological products describes all of the food, feed, and fiber produced by agriculture. These products include everything from fruits and vegetables to grain, hay, and cotton. Although the diversity of agricultural production is too broad to be totally covered in this text, we will discuss some of the principles involved in the handling, drying, and storage of these products.

HANDLING

Because of differences in shape, size and consistency, each product must have a handling system capable of moving that specific product. The designer of a handling system also must consider product perishability and the desired form of the finished product. A harvester designed to harvest tomatoes for the fresh vegetable market will be different from one designed to harvest tomatoes used for catsup. Because of the prevalence of grains across the United States, they will be used to illustrate some of the basic principles of handling biological products.

Grains have several characteristics that enable mechanized systems to handle them easily. Grains flow by gravity, are small, and have a relatively hard outer coat. These characteristics allow them to be moved by several different mechanical devices. In this section we will discuss and illustrate some of the principles of moving grain with augers and pneumatic conveyors.

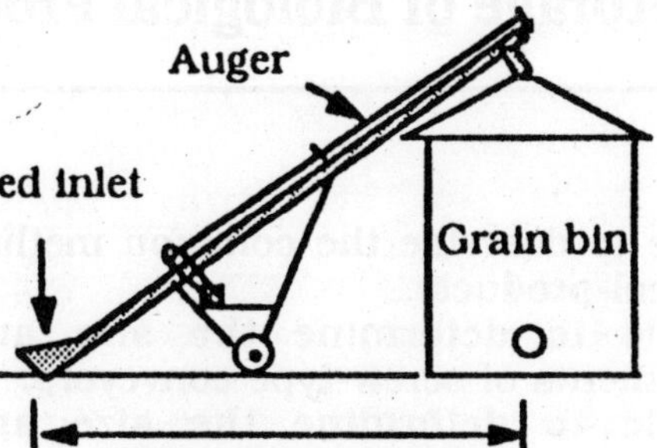

Figure 20.1. Auger conveyor.

AUGERS

Augers are available in several diameters and are capable of handling many different types of products. An auger is like a bolt, but instead of threads it uses flights that turn inside a tube. As the auger rotates, the flights move the product through the tube similarly to the way that threads move a nut on a bolt. Augers require less horsepower per bushel and have fewer mechanical parts than pneumatic systems; but there is the danger of the exposed auger at the inlet, and they require more space because the inlet is some distance from the outlet (see Figure 20.1). Augers are selected on the basis of the diameter of the tube and the flights, and the length needed to deliver the grain to the required location. The following discussion will illustrate how the capacity and energy requirements for augers can be determined.

Table 20-1. Screw auger capacity handling dry corn.

Auger		Auger Angle of Elevation					
		0°		45°		90°	
Size	RPM	bu/hr	hp/10 ft	bu/hr	hp/10 ft	bu/hr	hp/10 ft
4 in	200	150	0.12	120	0.15	60	0.11
	400	290	0.29	220	0.29	130	0.24
	600	420	0.38	310	0.45	190	0.36
6 in	200	590	0.38	500	0.44	280	0.32
	400	1090	0.56	850	0.88	520	0.70
	600	1510	0.84	1160	1.28	740	1.05

Note: For total horsepower, 10% must be added for drive train losses.

Source: *Structures and Environment Handbook, MWPS-1,* Midwest Plan Service, Iowa State University, Ames, Iowa, 1987, Section 534.

Table 20-2. Screw auger capacity handling dry soybeans.

Auger		Auger Angle of Elevation					
		0°		45°		90°	
Size	RPM	bu/hr	hp/10 ft	bu/hr	hp/10 ft	bu/hr	hp/10 ft
4 in	200	140	1.00	125	0.17	70	0.12
	400	270	0.21	215	0.35	130	0.26
	600	390	0.34	315	0.51	180	0.40
6 in	200	500	0.40	360	0.57	220	0.40
	400	990	0.84	690	1.20	390	0.79
	600	1350	1.20	930	1.71	500	1.10

Note: For total horsepower, 10% must be added for drive train losses.

Source: *Structures and Environment Handbook, MWPS-1,* Midwest Plan Service, Iowa State University, Ames, Iowa, 1987, Section 534.

Tables 20-1 and 20-2 contain typical values for two sizes of screw augers and two different crops. This type of information can be used to make decisions in managing a grain handling system, such as determining the size of auger required to convey grain at a given rate (bu/hr).

Problem: What is the minimum size of auger that can be used to convey dry corn at the rate of 500 bushels per hour if the auger is inclined 45°?

Solution: Using Table 20-1, the minimum size of auger is 6 inches.

Another use of Tables 20-1 and 20-2 is to determine the horsepower required to operate the auger.

Problem: How much horsepower (including drive train) is required to operate a 100-foot, 6-inch auger, installed at 45°, if it is conveying 690 bushels of soybeans per hour?

Solution: Using Table 20-2, the power requirement is 1.2 hp/10 ft. Therefore:

$$hp = \frac{1.2 \text{ hp} \times 1.10}{10 \text{ ft}} \times 100 \text{ ft}$$

$$= 13 \text{ hp}$$

The horsepower required by the auger, including the drive train, is 13 hp.

PNEUMATIC CONVEYORS

Pneumatic conveyors are used to move grain and other products using air. Pneumatic conveyors are more flexible than augers because the duct does not need to be in a straight line. They are self-cleaning, and do not have an exposed auger at the inlet. They do require more horsepower per bushel and are noisier than augers. Three types of pneumatic conveyors are used: positive pressure (push units), negative pressure (vacuum), and a combination of negative and positive pressure.

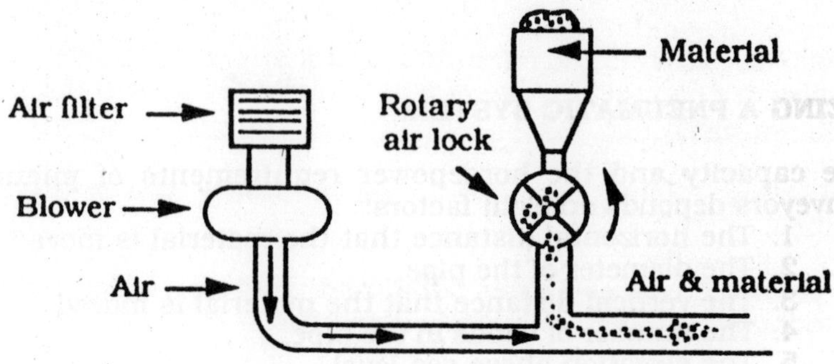

Figure 20.2. Positive pressure pneumatic system.

In a positive pressure unit, the pressure is supplied by a blower, and the product enters the air stream through a rotary air lock. The material then is blown through the duct (see Figure 20.2).

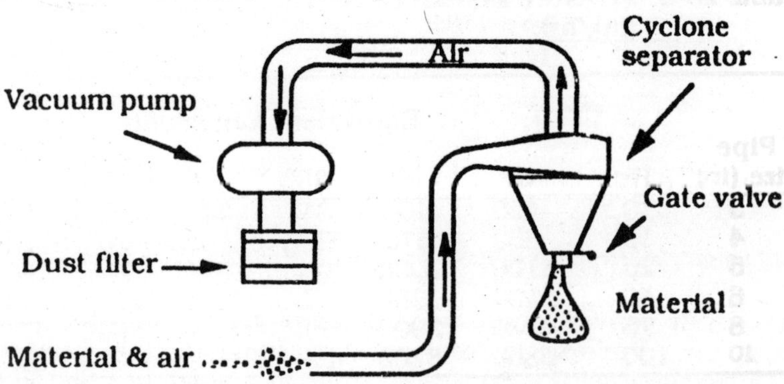

Figure 20.3. Negative pressure pneumatic system.

In a negative pressure unit, the material is vacuumed up by the inflow of air and then separated from the air in a cyclone separator. The material collects in the bottom of the separator where it can be released with a gate valve or a rotary lock. The air continues on to the pump and out through a filter into the atmosphere (see Figure 20.3).

In a combination system, the material is picked up by the inflow of a negative pressure system, and then it passes through a rotary air lock into the positive pressure air stream coming from the pump.

SIZING A PNEUMATIC SYSTEM

The capacity and the horsepower requirements of pneumatic conveyors depends on eight factors:

1. The horizontal distance that the material is moved.
2. The diameter of the pipe.
3. The vertical distance that the material is moved.
4. The number of bends in the pipe.
5. The elevation above sea level.
6. The temperature of the outside air.
7. The type of material being conveyed
8. The moisture content of the material.

To size a pneumatic system the effect of each of these factors must be accounted for.

Table 20-3. Pressure system conveyor capacities for dry corn (bu/hr).

Pipe size (in)	Hp	Equivalent Length (ft) 50	100	200	250	300	350
3	10	450	400	350	320	295	265
4	15	650	575	500	460	420	380
5	25	1100	1000	900	830	755	685
6	40	2100	1950	1800	1650	1510	1370
8	75	4300	3900	3500	3220	2940	2660
10	100	5800	5100	4500	4240	3980	3720

Modifications to Capacity:

1. Vertical pipe x 1.20 = Equivalent horizontal length.
2. Capacity in wheat = 90% of Corn.
3. Capacity in soybeans = 80% of Corn.
4. Add 20 ft of equivalent horizontal pipe for each 90° bend in pipe.
5. Reduce capacity by 4.0% for each 1000 ft above sea level.
6. Reduce capacity by 2.0% for each 10°F above 70°F.

Source: Beard Industries, Frankfort, Indiana 46041.

Table 20-3 is an example of the type of information that is available for sizing pneumatic systems. The data show that as the horizontal length (ft) of the pipe increases the capacity of the system (bu/hr) decreases and as the pipe diameter increases (in) the capacity increases.

To provide an easy way to estimate the amount of reduction caused by factors 3 and 4 the equivalent feet of pipe is determined. Equivalent feet of pipe is a procedure which uses constants to determine the amount of horizontal pipe that will cause the same reduction in capacity as the factor in question. For example, the fourth modification to capacity listed in Table 20-3 shows that each foot of vertical pipe causes the same reduction in capacity as 1.2 feet of horizontal pipe. Thus the equivalent feet for a vertical section of pipe is determined by multiplying the vertical length (ft) by 1.2.

Adjustments for factors 5 through 8 are handled differently. The capacity of the system is adjusted for the effect of factors 5, 6, and 7 by reducing the capacity an appropriate percentage. Factor 8 is accounted for by either assuming a standard moisture content, or developing a separate table for a range of moistures.

Expressed as an equation:

$$TEF = (F_H + F_B + F_V) \tag{20-1}$$

where:

TEF = Total equivalent feet
F_H = Horizontal distance (ft)
F_B = Equivalent feet for bends
F_V = Equivalent feet for vertical sections

Problem: What is the capacity of the system in Figure 20.4 if the material to be moved is dry soybeans?

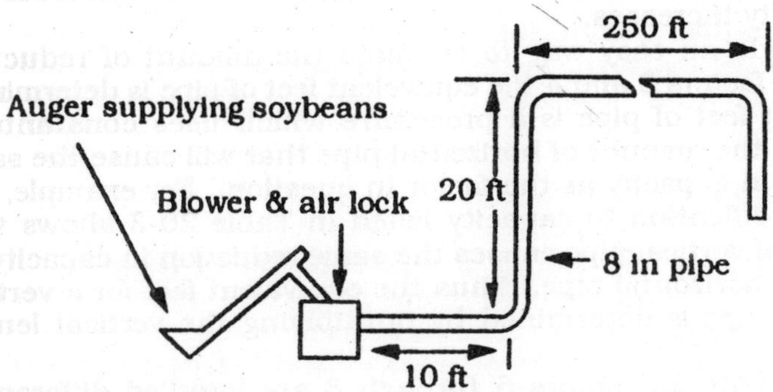

Figure 20.4. Pressurized conveyor for sample problem.

Solution: The first step is to determine the total equivalent feet for the pipe. In this example, factors 1, 2, 3, 4, and 7 are used. The first step is to determine the equivalent feet of pipe. Using the first part of Equation (20-1):

$$TEF = (F_H + F_B + F_V)$$

$$= (250\text{ ft} + 10\text{ ft}) + \left(3\text{ bends} \times \frac{20\text{ ft}}{\text{bend}}\right) + (20\text{ ft} \times 1.2)$$

$$= 260\text{ ft} + 60\text{ ft} + 24\text{ ft}$$

$$= 344\text{ ft}$$

Although the actual length of pipe in Figure 20.4 is 280 feet, because of the bends and the vertical sections the equivalent distance is 344 feet.

The next step is to use Table 20-3 to determine the capacity of an 8-inch duct with an equivalent distance of 344 feet. The closest value is 2660 bu/hr. Note that Table 20-3 gives values for corn. Because the capacity of a pressurized system for soybeans is 80% of the capacity for corn (modification 3), the system capacity in Figure 20.4 is:

$$\frac{\text{bu}}{\text{hr}} = 2660\,\frac{\text{bu}}{\text{hr}} \times 0.80$$

$$= 2100\,\frac{\text{bu}}{\text{hr}}$$

information to determine the capacities of auger, pneumatic, and bucket conveyor systems for other crops and situations are available from manufacturers and agricultural extension personnel.

MOISTURE MANAGEMENT

Water and its addition to or removal from agricultural products and materials is an extremely important topic in nearly all aspects of agriculture. The moisture contents of grain, feed, or hay to be bought or sold, of crops to be dried, or of meat and dairy products to be processed are but a few examples of products where moisture must be carefully managed. Moisture may be added to or removed from the product depending upon the desired final condition. Moisture is removed from products by drying. Drying usually is done to change the consistency or to extend the storage life of the product. For example, fruits and meats may be dried to change the way that they are handled, stored and eaten. Grains and forages are dried to extended their storage life.

Some agricultural products, such as grains and forages, will dry naturally to an *equilibrium moisture content* (the same as that of the environment) if left in the field. But with these and other products good management sometimes dictates that the crop be harvested at a wetter stage and dried artificially. Artificial drying is accomplished by causing air to flow around and/or through the product. Natural or artificially heated air is often used because heating reduces the relative humidity of the air, increasing the amount of moisture each pound of air can absorb.

The management of a drying system requires the ability to be able to predict the amount of moisture which must be removed from the product. For other products it is important to be able to predict the amount of water that must be added. The following discussion presents a method for determining the amount of moisture that must be added to or removed from biological products.

The moisture content of a given material is stated on either a wet-*weight* or a *dry-weight* basis as a percent. Because moisture content is expressed as a percent, we know that a ratio is involved. The difference between the wet-weight basis and the dry-weight basis is the value used in the denominator of the ratio. The wet-weight basis uses the weight of the product as it is received; the dry-weight basis uses the oven-dry weight (dry matter) of the product.

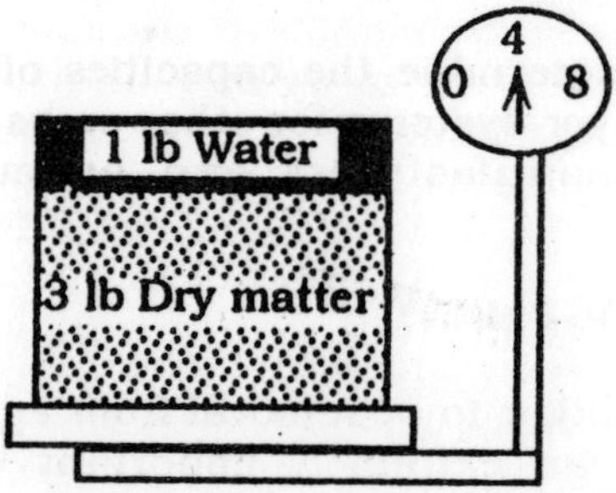

Figure 20.5. Dry-weight, wet-weight basis illustration.

Study Figure 20.5. The total weight of the product is 4 pounds. If the amount of water is expressed on the dry-weight basis, then it is $\frac{1\text{ lb}}{3\text{ lb}}$ x 100, or 33%. Expressed on the wet-weight basis, the amount of water is $\frac{1\text{ lb}}{4\text{ lb}}$ x 100, or 25%. This relationship is explained in the following equations:

Dry-weight basis:

$$\%MDB = \left(\frac{WW - DW}{DW}\right) \times 100 \qquad (20\text{-}1)$$

Wet-weight basis:

$$\%MWB = \left(\frac{WW - DW}{WW}\right) \times 100 \qquad (20\text{-}2)$$

where:

%MDB = Percent moisture, dry-weight basis
%MWB = Percent moisture, wet-weight basis
WW = Wet weight or weight of product before drying
DW = Oven-dry weight, or weight of product after drying
WW-DW = Weight of moisture removed

It is impractical to remove all of the moisture from grain as well as other products. Grain usually is considered to be dry when the moisture content is sufficiently low to discourage the growth of molds, enzymatic action, and insects. This is usually about ' moisture content, %MDB, depending upon the grain. Star have been established to determine the heating time required to obtain an official oven dry sample of grain.

Either moisture content basis may be used with agricultural products; so to avoid confusion or misunderstanding, one should always specify which basis is being used to express the moisture content. This can be accomplished by writing the numerical value of the moisture content followed by %MDB or %MWB.

Problem: Express the moisture content on the wet-weight basis and the dry-weight basis for a product that weighs 150 pounds when wet, and that after drying weighs 80 pounds.

Solution: Using Equation (20-1), the percent moisture on the dry weight basis is:

$$\%MDB = \left(\frac{WW - DW}{DW}\right) \times 100$$

$$= \left(\frac{150 \text{ lb} - 80 \text{ lb}}{80 \text{ lb}}\right) \times 100$$

$$= 88\%$$

On the dry-weight basis, the product is 88% moisture. Using Equation (20-2), the percent moisture on the wet-weight basis is:

$$\%MWB = \left(\frac{WW - DW}{WW}\right) \times 100$$

$$= \left(\frac{150 \text{ lb} - 80 \text{ lb}}{150.0 \text{ lb}}\right) \times 100$$

$$= 47\%$$

On the wet-weight basis, the product is 47% moisture.

Notice that the only difference in the values used in the two equations is in the denominator of the ratio. For the DW basis the dry weight is used, and for the WW basis the wet weight is used.

One of aspect of the DW basis is that the percentage of moisture can be greater than 100%. For example, if a product has a wet-weight of 100 ounces and a dry weight of 40 ounces, the MWB is 60% and the MDB is 150%. This is why the standard moisture of many products is given on the wet-weight basis.

ADDING OR REMOVING WATER

During the life of many products it may be necessary to remove and to add water. Grain must be dried for storage, and the same grain may have to be tempered (have water added). For processing, water may be added to or removed from products such as catsup to produce the desired consistency, and so on. Equations (20-1) and (20-2) also can be used to determine the amount of water to put into or take out of any biological product.

There are three steps in the procedure used to determine how much water to remove or add, and they must be completed in sequence:

1. Determine the dry weight of the material at its original state. The weight of the dry material does not change from one moisture content to another; moisture may be added or removed, but the amount of dry matter or the dry weight remains the same.
2. Using the dry weight that was determined, solve for the wet weight (the weight of the material at the new moisture content).
3. The amount of moisture to add or to remove is the difference between the weight of the product in the original state and at the calculated wet weight.

To solve for the dry weight or the wet weight, Equations (20-1) and (20-2) are rearranged, as follows:

Dry-weight basis:

$$DW = \frac{WW}{\left(1 + \frac{\%MDB}{100}\right)} \tag{20-3}$$

$$WW = DW \times \left(1 + \frac{\%MDB}{100}\right) \tag{20-4}$$

Wet-weight basis:

$$DW = WW \times \left(1 - \frac{\%MWB}{100}\right) \tag{20-5}$$

$$WW = \frac{DW}{\left(1 - \frac{\%MWB}{100}\right)} \tag{20-6}$$

The following problems illustrate the uses of these equations.

Problem: How much water needs to be removed (lb) to dry 1000 pounds of product at 70% MWB to 20% MWB?

Solution: Because the moisture has been measured by the wet-weight basis, Equations (20-5) and (20-6) will be used. First solve for the dry weight using Equation (20-5):

$$DW = WW \times \left(1 - \frac{\%MWB}{100}\right)$$

$$= 1000 \text{ lb} \times \left(1 - \frac{70\%}{100}\right)$$

$$= 300 \text{ lb}$$

Next solve for the wet-weight at the desired moisture content using Equation (20-6):

$$WW = \frac{DW}{\left(1 - \frac{\%MWB}{100}\right)}$$

$$= \frac{300 \text{ lb}}{\left(1 - \frac{20\%}{100}\right)}$$

$$= 375 \text{ lb}$$

The amount of water that needs to be removed is the difference between the original WW and the new WW. Thus the amount of water (lb) that must be removed is:

$$\text{lb} = WW_{70\%} - WW_{20\%}$$

$$= 1000 \text{ lb} - 375 \text{ lb}$$

$$= 625 \text{ lb (water)}$$

To change the product from the original 70% MWB to 20% MWB, 625 pounds of water must be removed.

Problem: A miller needs to raise the moisture content of 1000 bushels of wheat from the storage condition of 9.0% MDB to 16.0% MDB. How much water (lb) needs to be added?

Solution: Using Equations (20-3) and (20-4) and the conversion value of 1 bu = 60 lb:

$$DW = \frac{WW}{\left(1 + \frac{\%MDB}{100}\right)}$$

$$= \frac{1000 \text{ bu} \times \frac{60 \text{ lb}}{1 \text{ bu}}}{\left(1 + \frac{9.0\%}{100}\right)}$$

$$= \frac{60{,}000 \text{ lb}}{1.09}$$

$$= 55{,}000 \text{ lb (dry matter)}$$

and:

$$WW = DW \times \left(1 + \frac{\%MDB}{100}\right)$$

$$= 55{,}000 \times \left(1 + \frac{16.0\%}{100}\right)$$

$$= 55{,}000 \times 1.16$$

$$= 63{,}800 \text{ lb (dry matter and water at 16\% MDB)}$$

Water to add:

$$\text{lb} = WW_{16.0\%} - DW_{9.0\%}$$

$$= 63{,}800 \text{ lb} - 55{,}000 \text{ lb}$$

$$= 8800 \text{ lb (water)}$$

The miller should add 8800 pounds of water to the wheat to bring it up to 16% MDB.

On occasion it is useful to know how to convert from one moisture base to the other. This can be accomplished with the following equations:

$$\%MDB = \frac{100 \times \%MWB}{100 - \%MWB} \tag{20-7}$$

$$\%MWB = \frac{100 \times \%MDB}{100 + \%MDB} \tag{20-8}$$

Problem: Determine the %MDB of a product if the %MWB is 50%.

Solution: Using Equation (20-7):

$$\%MDB = \frac{100 \times \%MWB}{100 - \%MWB}$$

$$= \frac{100 \times 50\%}{100 - 50\%}$$

$$= 100\%$$

Problem: Determine the %MWB of a product that is 23.25% MDB.

Solution: Using Equation (20-8):

$$\%MWB = \frac{100 \times \%MDB}{100 + \%MDB}$$

$$= \frac{100 \times 23.25}{100 + 23.25}$$

$$= 18.864\% \text{ or } 18.9\%$$

STORAGE OF BIOLOGICAL PRODUCTS

The term biological products has been used throughout this chapter because products such as grains, fruits, and vegetables are living organisms. Because they are alive, there are minimum requirements for moisture, temperature, and air to maintain their viability; but the life of the product can be extended if the temperature or moisture or air is modified during storage. The challenge for managers of many such products is to extend the storage life of the product without damaging its viability, color, taste, or texture. Recommendations for optimum environments for the storage of biological products can be obtained from the extension service or any department of agricultural engineering.

PRACTICE PROBLEMS

1. What will the increase in capacity (bu/hr) be if a 4-inch horizontal grain auger, used with corn and operated at 400 rpm is replaced with a 6-inch auger operating at 600 rpm?
Answer: 1220 bu/hr
2. What is the capacity of a pneumatic conveyor moving wheat if it uses 6-inch pipe and has 100 feet of horizontal pipe, 25 feet of vertical pipe, and four 90^0 bends?
Answer: 1620 bu/hr
3. What size motor will be required to operate the conveyor in problem 2?
Answer: 40 hp
4. Find the WB and DB moisture content of a material weighting 250 pounds wet and 205 pounds after drying.
Answer: 22.0% MDB and 18.0% MWB
5. How much water must be removed to dry 6000 pounds of hay at 75% MWB down to 20% MWB?
Answer: 4125 lb
6. How much water must be added to 100 pounds of product at 5% MDB to bring the moisture content up to 18% MDB?
Answer: 12 lb

21
Animal Waste Management

OBJECTIVES

1. Understand the importance of animal waste management.
2. Be able to describe the methods of handling solid animal wastes.
3. Be able to determine the maximum amount of solid animal wastes that can be applied to the soil.
4. Be able to describe the methods of handling liquid animal wastes.
5. Be able to determine the capacity of storage units for animal waste.
6. Be able to describe animal waste treatment methods.

INTRODUCTION

Animal waste management is no longer an option in a livestock business; it is a requirement. Failure to provide adequate waste management facilities and equipment can lead to pollution problems with legal complications, animal health problems, increased production costs and a generally undesirable working situation.

There are three basic aspects of animal waste management:

1. Waste handling
2. Waste treatment
3. Waste disposal

If the decisions are made in the planning process for the facility, animal producers usually can choose from a variety of waste handling systems to manage the animal waste. The waste can be collected, transported, and disposed of in two forms: solid and liquid. In the following sections we will discuss the handling and disposal of animal wastes, and then will investigate some of the common methods of treating waste.

HANDLING SOLID ANIMAL WASTES

Waste containing 20% or more solids or with a moisture content of 50% MWB or less is considered to be solid waste. Proper handling of solid wastes inside buildings requires solid floors that can be bedded or drained. The wastes usually are collected with hand scrapers, power scrapers, or front loaders, and usually are not treated except by the natural processes that occur as they are stored. Usually they are disposed of by spreading them on the land. If not done correctly, disposal of solid animal wastes on the land can reduce plant production, produce offensive odors, and contribute to the contamination of ground and surface water. The Soil Conservation Service[1] has developed standards for the application of solid animal wastes on land. These standards are based on soil type, slope, and distance from surface and ground water. According to these standards, if any *one* of the following eight conditions exists, land application of solid animal wastes is not acceptable:

1. If a water table is within 2 feet of the surface.
2. The soil is less than 10 inches deep.
3. The soil is subject to frequent flooding.
4. Any area within 100 feet of a stream or a watercourse.
5. The soil is frozen or snow-covered.
6. There are active eroded areas.
7. Stones in the surface layer exceed 35% by volume.
8. The land slope exceeds 15%.

If none of these conditions exists, solid animal wastes can be applied within acceptable limits.

For accurate results, the first step in determining the amount of solid animal wastes that can be applied to the soil is to analyze both the solid wastes and the soil for the amounts of nitrogen and phosphorous they contain. If the waste has not been tested, Appendix IV may be used to estimate the nutritional content. These values are estimates because the animal's ration, the type and quantity of bedding used, the amount of liquid added, the type of housing and manure handling system, and the application system all affect the nutrient content of the animal wastes. If the nutritional content of the soil is unknown, one must estimate it before Appendixes V, VI, and VII can be used to determine the amount of waste that may be applied.

The object is to apply only the amount of nutrients that will be utilized by plants in one season. It is unlikely that the amount of each nutrient in the waste can be matched with the needs of the plants; so the nutrient with the most restrictive amount determines the amount of waste that can be applied. *Note*: This method assumes that more than one application per year will be used to distribute the total amount of waste.

---

[1] *State Standard and Specifications for Waste Utilization*, United States Department of Agriculture, Soil Conservation Service, 1988.

Problem: Determine the amount of solid wastes from 1000-pound dairy cows that can be applied to a coarse loamy soil with a pH of 6.5 that will be used to raise 40 bushels per acre of wheat. *Note:* In this example we will assume that there are no nutrients in the soil.

Solution: In this type of a problem a table is useful for determining the answer. First, we must determine the amount of nutrients in the waste and the maximum amounts of phosphorous and nitrogen that can be applied. This is accomplished by selecting the correct values from Appendixes IV, V, VI, and VII, and converting them to pounds of nutrient per pound of waste.

From Appendix IV the nutrients in the waste are:

$$\text{Nitrogen (N)} = 0.14\ \frac{\text{lb}}{\text{day}}$$

$$\text{Phosphorus (P)} = 0.27\ \frac{\text{lb}}{\text{day}}$$

Because each cow produces 82 pounds of waste per day (Appendix IV). Converting to pounds of nutrient per pound of waste can be accomplished using units cancellation:

$$\frac{\text{lb of nitrogen}}{\text{lb of waste}} = \frac{0.14\ \text{lb N}}{\text{day}} \times \frac{1\ \text{day}}{82\ \text{lb waste}}$$

$$= \frac{1.7 \times 10^{-3}\ \text{lb N}}{\text{lb waste}}$$

$$\frac{\text{lb of phosphorus}}{\text{lb of waste}} = \frac{0.27\ \text{lb P}}{\text{day}} \times \frac{1\ \text{day}}{82\ \text{lb waste}}$$

$$= \frac{3.3 \times 10^{-3}\ \text{lb P}}{\text{lb waste}}$$

The next step is to use Appendixes V and VII to determine the nutrients used by the crop:

$$\text{Nitrogen} = 80\ \text{lb/ac}$$

$$\text{Phosphorous} = 21.2\ \text{lb/ac}$$

The last information needed to find the solution is the maximum amount of phosphorous that can be applied to the soil. Consult Appendix VI for this information:

Phosphorous = 400 lb/ac

The solution is found by calculating the application rate (lb/ac/yr) of waste for each nutrient. The maximum amount of waste that can be applied is determined by the smallest of three values: the nitrogen used by the plant, the phosphorous used by the plant, and the phosphorous that can be applied to the soil. The results are shown in Table 21-1.

Table 21-1. Solution to problem.

Nutrient	Soil limits (lb/ac)	Net nutrients used by crop (lb/ac)	Pounds of nutrient per pound of waste (lb/lb)	Application rate of wastes (lb/ac/yr)
Nitrogen	---	80.0	1.7 X 10-3	47,000 *
Phosphorous	---	21.2	3.3 X 10-3	6400 **
Phosphorous	400	---	---	120,000 ***

$$\text{*Application Rate} = \frac{80 \text{ lb N}}{\text{ac}} \times \frac{1 \text{ lb waste}}{1.7 \times 10^{-3} \text{ lb N}} = 47{,}000$$

$$\text{**Application Rate} = \frac{21.2 \text{ lb P}}{\text{ac}} \times \frac{1 \text{ lb waste}}{3.3 \times 10^{-3} \text{ lb P}} = 6400$$

$$\text{***Application Rate} = \frac{400 \text{ lb P}}{\text{ac}} \times \frac{1 \text{ lb waste}}{3.3 \times 10^{-3} \text{ lb P}} = 120{,}000$$

Table 21-1 shows that phosphorous is the most restricted nutrient (6400 lb/ac/yr). Therefore, the maximum amount of waste from the dairy cows that can be annually applied is 6400 pounds per acre per year.

In the previous sample problem, the nutrients available in the soil were not considered. The actual amount of waste than can be applied is the difference between the nutrients used by the crop and the amount of nutrients already available in the soil.

Another aspect of solid waste management is determining how many acres are required to dispose of the waste being produced.

Problem: How many acres will be required to distribute all of the waste from a 50-cow dairy? Use the cows in the previous problem.

Solution: The answer to this question can be found by using the 6400 pounds of waste per acre per year from the previous problem, additional information from Appendix IV, and units cancellation. Appendix IV shows that each 1000-pound dairy cow produces 82.0 pounds of waste per day. Then:

$$\text{ac} = \frac{1 \text{ ac}}{6400 \text{ lb waste}} \times \frac{82.0 \text{ lb waste}}{\text{cow-day}} \times 50 \text{ cows} \times 365 \text{ days}$$

$$= \frac{1.50 \times 10^6}{6400}$$

$$= 234 \text{ ac}$$

For the 50-cow dairy herd, a minimum of 234 acres is required to dispose of the animal wastes each year. It is important to remember that in the original problem we assumed that the soil contained no nitrogen or phosphorous. Any nitrogen or phosphorous in the soil *reduces* the amount of waste that may be applied and *increases* the number of acres required.

HANDLING LIQUID WASTES

The handling of liquid or slurry waste from buildings involves scraping or flushing the waste from where it is dropped by the animal to a pit or a storage tank. Once collected, the waste is treated and/or disposed of. Open feedlot waste is handled as runoff-carried waste, with natural precipitation carrying the liquid or the slurry, flowing from the pens into a drainage and collection system for subsequent removal or treatment and disposal. Liquid wastes usually are handled by pumping, and are disposed of by being spread on the surface of or injected into the soil. The maximum amount of waste that can be spread in liquid form is determined by using the same procedure as that used for solid waste.

Liquid wastes are more difficult to manage than the solid because they must be stored in tanks or pits and must be pumped. In addition, because animal wastes should not be spread on frozen ground, the storage unit must have the capacity to store all of the waste while the ground is frozen.

Problem: What size of above-ground tank (gal) is required to store all of the waste from a 100-sow farrowing barn if the pigs are with the sows, and the waste must be stored for 6 weeks?

Solution: Using Appendix IV and units cancellation (*note*: weights can be converted to volumes if the density is known):

$$\text{gal} = \frac{1\ \text{gal}}{0.13368\ \text{ft}^3} \times \frac{1\ \text{ft}^3}{60\ \text{lb}} \times \frac{33.0\ \text{lb}}{\text{day-sow}} \times \frac{7.0\ \text{day}}{1\ \text{week}} \times \frac{6\ \text{weeks}}{1} \times 100\ \text{sows}$$

$$= \frac{140{,}000}{8.0}$$

$$= 18{,}000\ \text{gal}$$

WASTE TREATMENT

Waste treatment is an operation performed on waste that makes it more amenable to ultimate disposal. Two basic methods of biological treatment are used: aerobic and anaerobic.

AEROBIC TREATMENT

Aerobic treatment occurs when there is sufficient dissolved oxygen available in the waste to allow aerobic bacteria (oxygen-using) to break down the organic matter in the waste. It is essentially an odorless process. Three methods of treatment that use aerobic bacteria are: *composting, aerobic lagoons* and *spray-runoff.*

Composting is accomplished by piling the waste and turning it frequently to provide aeration for aerobic bacterial decomposition while maintaining a high-enough temperature in the pile to destroy pathogenic organisms and weed seeds. The volume of composed waste may be reduced to between 30% and 60% of the volume of the original waste.

An aerobic lagoon is a relatively shallow basin (3 to 5 feet deep) into which a slurry is added. The decomposition of the organic matter is accomplished by aerobic bacteria. Oxygen for the bacteria is provided by beating or blowing air into the liquid.

In the spray-runoff treatment, an area is leveled and sloped so that water flows evenly, and then is planted to grass. Decomposition of the waste is accomplished by the bacteria that live on the wet surface of the grass and soil.

ANAEROBIC TREATMENT

Anaerobic treatment is accomplished by anaerobic bacteria that consume the oxygen in the organic matter itself as the organic matter decomposes. In this process, odorous gases are produced. The most common method using this treatment is the *anaerobic lagoon*.

The anaerobic lagoon is a relatively deep (12- to 14-foot) basin that contains liquid wastes and provides a climate for decomposition by anaerobic bacteria. Thus, no attempt is made to introduce oxygen into the liquid. The anaerobic lagoon is able to decompose more organic matter per unit of volume than the aerobic lagoon. However, the odor it produces may determine where it can be located.

PRACTICE PROBLEMS

1. Determine the amount (lb/ac) of layer wastes that can be applied to a soil with a clay content of 40% and a pH of 5.5, if the crop is Bermudagrass averaging 3 tons of hay per acre. A soil test indicates there are 120 pounds per acre of nitrogen and 50 pounds of phosphorous in the soil.
   Answer: None may be applied.
2. What size storage unit (ft^3) is required to store all of the waste from 20 horses, if the waste is usually only removed once a month?
   Answer: 450 ft^3
3. If the stalls for the horses in problem 2 are bedded with 1 ft^3 of sawdust per day, what size storage unit will be needed for all of the waste?
   Answer: 1050 ft^3
4. What size (gal) storage unit is needed to store the waste from 150 finishing pigs, each weighing 200 pounds, if the waste must be stored for 4 months?
   Answer: 2900 gal
5. If a round storage unit is used in problem 4 and it is limited to a 14-foot diameter, how tall must it be?
   Answer: 26 ft

22
Insulation and Heat Flow

OBJECTIVES

1. Understand the principles of insulation and heat flow.
2. Understand the function of insulation.
3. Understand R-values and U-values.
4. Be able to calculate the total thermal resistance of a building component.
5. Be able to determine the amount of heat flowing through a building component.

INTRODUCTION

Heat is transmitted in three different ways: by radiation--the exchange of thermal energy between objects by electromagnetic waves; by convection--the transfer of heat from or to an object by a gas or a liquid; and by conduction--the exchange of heat between contacting bodies that are at different temperatures. In this chapter we will discuss and illustrate the principles of conduction as heat is moved into and out of buildings.

The amount of heat transferred by conduction is determined by the area, the difference in temperature, and the thermal resistance of the materials. The type of construction and the type and amount of insulating material used will determine the rate of heat flow (BTU/hr) for a particular building or building component. Buildings have walls, doors, windows, floors, ceilings and roofs. Knowledge of the relative insulating values of different construction materials and of how to put them together to estimate the overall insulating value of a building or a building component is a great help in selecting appropriate insulation materials for a particular application.

INSULATION

Insulation is any material reducing the rate that heat moves by conduction. All building materials have some resistance to the movement of heat, but some are more resistant than others. Any material with a high resistance to heat flow (thermal resistance) is called insulation. A common characteristic of insulation materials is low density. If the density of a material is increased, for example, by compressing the material or adding water, its thermal resistance is reduced.

Some materials, such as wood, concrete, and certain insulation materials, are *homogeneous*; that is, they have a uniform consistency throughout. The construction of other building materials, such as concrete blocks or insulation backed siding, is not uniformly consistent; they may have holes in them, or they may be composed of more than one type of material. These building materials are called *nonhomogeneous*.

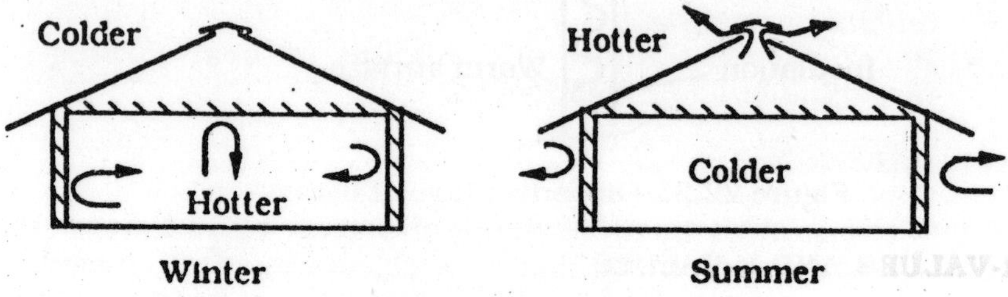

Figure 22.1. Advantages of insulation.

There are three common reasons for insulating houses and other structures (see Figures 22.1 and 22.2): (1) insulation conserves the heat inside any type of enclosure during the winter months, reducing the amount of supplemental heat required to maintain the temperature of the enclosure; (2) insulation helps reduce heat gain during the summer months, reducing the load on cooling equipment; and (3) insulation increases the inside surface temperature, thus reducing condensation on interior surfaces when they are cooler than the air. Condensation is the transformation of water vapor to a liquid, which occurs when warm moist air is cooled or comes in contact with a cool surface. This may occur on the outside surface of a wall (see Figure 22.2) or on any surface inside the wall if no vapor barrier is used.

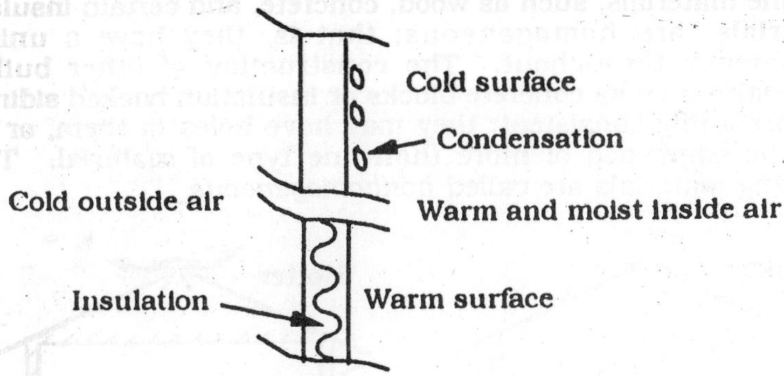

Figure 22.2. One advantage of insulation.

R-VALUES AND U-VALUES

Two different numbers are used to describe the insulating properties of construction materials: R-values and U-values. The R-value is a number that represents the thermal resistance of a material. The U-value is a measurement of the thermal conductivity of a material. A U-value of 1 means that 1 BTU/hr of heat will flow per square foot of area per degree difference in temperature on each side of the material. (The term BTU stands for British Thermal Unit, and represents the amount of heat required to raise the temperature of one pound of water one degree Fahrenheit.) R-values are the inverse of the U-value ($R = 1/U$). Therefore, the insulating ability of a material increases as the R-value increases and as the U-value decreases. The R-value of a nonhomogeneous building component is the sum of the R-values of the materials that make up the component. Appendix VIII contains R-values for some common building materials.

To determine the total thermal resistance of a wall, simply list and add together the thermal resistance of the individual parts. For homogeneous materials, the total thermal resistance value is determined by the thickness (in) of the material used times the R-value per inch of thickness. For nonhomogeneous materials, select the thermal resistance value for the thickness of material specified.

Two additional factors are important in determining the total thermal resistance of a wall. The first is the thermal resistance associated with the layer of still air next to any surface, as well as any air space within the wall, floor, or ceiling. Still air is a good insulating material, and a thin air film clings to exterior and interior surfaces providing a measurable thermal resistance. Typical R-values for the inside and outside air film are found in

Appendix VIII. The second factor is an understanding of common construction methods. In wood frame construction, the walls usually will be made from 2 x 4 or 2 x 6 inch lumber. Lumber is sold using nominal sizes; the actual size is less. A 2 x 4 is actually 1 and 1/2 inches by 3 and 1/2 inches, and a 2 x 6 is actually 1 and 1/2 inches by 5 and 1/2 inches. Frame walls usually are constructed with the long dimension of the board perpendicular to the wall, with different materials attached to both sides to form the wall. The cavity between the surfaces may be filled or partially filled with insulation (see Figure 22.3).

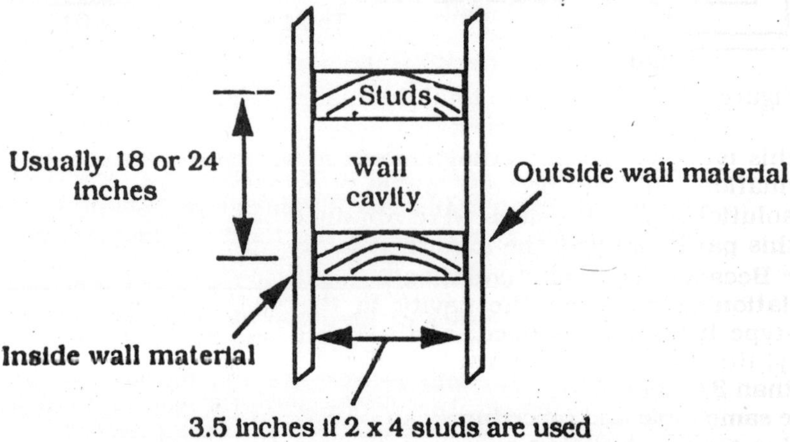

Figure 22.3. Typical wood frame construction.

Problem: Determine the total thermal resistance (R_T)of a 2 x 4 wood frame wall. The outside is covered with medium-density particle board and insulation-backed metal siding. The inside surface is 1/2-inch plasterboard. The wall is filled with high-density, loose-fill cellulose.

Solution:

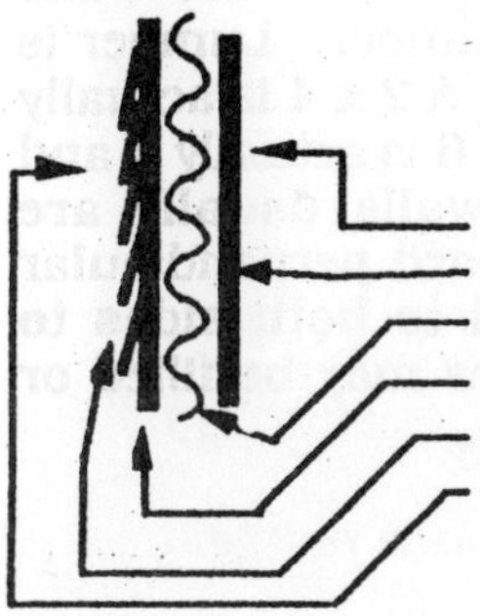

Inside air film =	0.68
Plasterboard (1/2 in) =	0.45
Cellulose (3.5 in x 3.13 R/in) =	10.96
Particleboard (1/2 in) =	0.53
Insulated siding =	1.82
Outside air film =	0.17
Total =	14.61

Figure 22.4. Solution to total thermal resistance problem.

For this type of problem, a diagram of the wall and a table of the information will help prevent mistakes. Study Figure 22.4 for the solution. The R-values were obtained from Appendix VIII. For this particular wall the total thermal resistance (R_T) is 14.61. *Note*: Because loose-fill insulation is used, the thickness of the insulation is equal to the cavity in the wall, 3.5 inches. If batt-type insulation is used, and it is not as thick as the wall cavity, the R-value for two inside surfaces is used if the air gap is less than 3/4 inch.

The same table and procedures can be used to determine the total R-value for any building component. Simply sum the R-values for each type of material and the inside and outside air films.

Problem: What is the total R-value (R_T) for a ceiling constructed of 1/2-inch plywood for the inside surface with 8.0 inches of low-density batt insulation on top of the plywood?

Solution: This problem presents a different situation. If the velocity of air moving in the attic is very low, then the R-value for inside air film should be used on both sides of the ceiling. Using Appendix VIII:

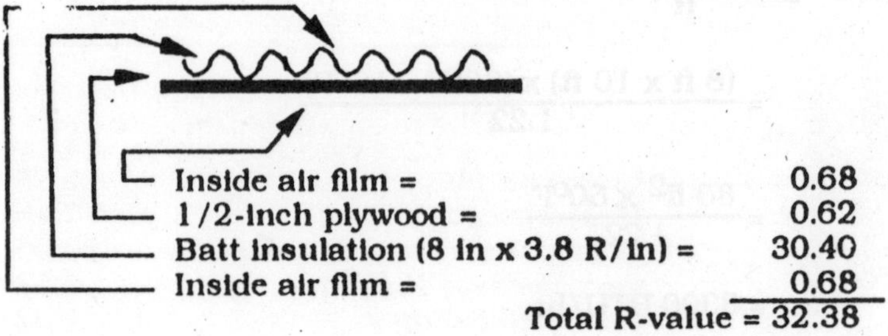

Figure 22.5. Solution to total thermal resistance problem.

In this example the total R-value of the ceiling is 32.38.

HEAT FLOW

The rate of heat flow (BTU/hr) through a building component depends upon the thermal resistance of the wall, the temperature difference on both sides of the wall, and the area of the component. Expressed as an equation:

$$Q = \frac{A \times \Delta T}{R} \tag{22-1}$$

where:

Q = Heat flow rate (BTU/hr)
A = Area of building component (ft^2)
ΔT = Temperature difference between wall surfaces (^oF)
R = Total thermal resistance of the building component

Heat flows from the area of higher temperature to the area of lower temperature. With the inside temperature greater than the outside temperature, the heat flow will be from inside to outside.

Problem: Determine the heat flow for an 8.0 x 10.0 foot wall that has a total R-value of 1.22 and is subject to an inside temperature of 60^oF and an outside temperature of 10^oF.

Solution: Using Equation (22-1):

$$Q = \frac{A \times \Delta T}{R}$$

$$= \frac{(8 \text{ ft} \times 10 \text{ ft}) \times (60^{o}\text{F} - 10^{o}\text{F})}{1.22}$$

$$= \frac{80 \text{ ft}^2 \times 50^{o}\text{F}}{1.22}$$

$$= 3300 \text{ BTU/hr}$$

Heat will move through this wall at the rate of 3300 BTU/hr.

The heat flow rate for all building components except floors can be calculated by using this method. If the floor is a concrete slab, the difference in temperature (ΔT) across the floor will change as one moves in from the outside edge of the building. The effective R-values for this type of floor or a concrete slab floor with insulation beneath it can be found in Appendix VIII. If either of these two values are used, the perimeter of the building (ft) is substituted for the area (ft^2) in Equation (22-1). If a floor has a crawl space underneath it, the total R-value can be calculated by using the same procedures used for a ceiling. Floors over basements will not be discussed.

PRACTICE PROBLEMS

1. Determine the total R-value for a wall constructed of 8-inch concrete block.
   Answer: 1.96
2. Determine the total R-value for a wall constructed of 4-inch common brick and 8-inch lightweight concrete block with a one-inch air space between the block and the brick.
   Answer: 4.55
3. What is the U-value for the wall in problem 2?
   Answer: 0.27
4. Determine the total R-value for a 2 x 6 wood frame wall if the inside surface is 5/8-inch medium density particleboard and 1/2-inch solid wood paneling. The outside is 25/32-inch insulating sheathing and hollow metal siding. The wall contains 4 inches of high-density blanket insulation.
   Answer: 17.0

23
Heating, Ventilation, and Air-conditioning

OBJECTIVES

1. Understand the principles of heating.
2. Be able to determine a heat balance for a building.
3. Be able to list and define the seven physical properties of air.
4. Given two properties of air, be able to find the other properties on a psychrometric chart.
5. Be able to calculate the required ventilation rate.
6. Understand the principles of air-conditioning.

INTRODUCTION

Air is a complex mixture of gases, water vapor, and heat. All living organisms require these three components, but not necessarily in the same proportions. Each organism has an optimum range of all three conditions, and any time the conditions are less than optimum, the organism is stressed. Management of these components may be critical within agricultural structures. Heating, ventilation, and air-conditioning are used to modify the natural environment to reduce the environmental stress of animals and biological products.

The ability to manage building environments is based on an understanding of the psychrometric chart. The following sections explain the psychrometric chart and provide examples of how it is used for heating, and ventilation.

PSYCHROMETRIC CHART

A psychrometric chart is a graphical representation of the seven physical properties of air. These physical properties are defined and described as follows:

1. *Dry-bulb temperature (dbt)*: The dry-bulb temperature is the temperature of air measured with a standard thermometer. Dry-bulb temperatures usually are expressed in degrees Fahrenheit (^{O}F).
2. *Wet-bulb temperature (wbt)*: The wet-bulb temperature is determined with a standard thermometer having the bulb surrounded by gauze or a sock and a means for keeping the sock wet. As air passes over the wet sock it

will absorb (through evaporation) some of the water from the sock, cooling the bulb of the thermometer. The drier the air is, the greater the evaporation and the greater the cooling effect. The difference between the dry-bulb temperature and the wet-bulb temperature sometimes is called *wet-bulb depression*. Dry-bulb and wet-bulb temperatures are measured with an instrument called a psychrometer. Two general types are used: to use a sling psychrometer one must rotate a dry-bulb and a wet-bulb thermometer rapidly through air; the second type uses a fan to blow air across stationary thermometers.

3. *Relative humidity (r.h.)*: Relative humidity is a ratio of the amount of water in the air relative to the maximum amount of water the air could hold (if it were fully saturated). Relative humidity is expressed as a percent and the values can range from 0% (dry air) to 100% (fully saturated).
4. *Moisture content*: The moisture content is a measure of the actual amount of water held in the air in the form of vapor. Moisture content is measured in terms of pounds of water per pound of air (lb water/lb air) or grains of water per pound of air (gr of water/lb air). (*Note*: 7000 grains of water equals one pound.)
5. *Dew point*: Dew point is the temperature at which, as air is cooled, the moisture in the air begins to condense or form droplets that are too large to remain suspended in the air. Condensation occurs on any object with a surface temperature equal to or less than the dew point. The dew point temperature is measured in degrees Fahrenheit.
6. *Total heat content*: The total heat is the total heat energy in the air. It includes heat due to the temperature of the air, heat required to change water vapor present in the air from liquid to vapor, and heat energy in the water vapor itself. The total heat content of air is expressed as BTU per pound of dry air.
7. *Specific volume:* Specific volume is the volume of space occupied by a pound of dry air at standard atmospheric pressure (14.7 psi), expressed in cubic feet per pound of dry air (ft^3/lb air).

READING A PSYCHROMETRIC CHART

A psychrometric chart is designed so that if any two properties of the air are known, values for the other properties can be found on the chart. Several different charts are used. It is common to see high temperature, normal temperature, and low temperature charts. In addition, charts are produced for special purposes. To complete the activities of this section you should obtain a normal temperature psychrometric chart[1].

A psychrometric chart has a scale and lines for each property. To find the values for the properties of air, you must be able to locate what is called the *state point*. The state point is the junction of any two property lines. To help in finding a state point on a psychrometric chart, we will first illustrate the different lines representing the physical properties of the air.

DRY-BULB TEMPERATURE

The dry-bulb temperature scale is located along the bottom of the chart. Because this is a basic measurement, it usually is given or known. Locate it first, and then move vertically into the chart along the dry-bulb temperature line (Figure 23.1).

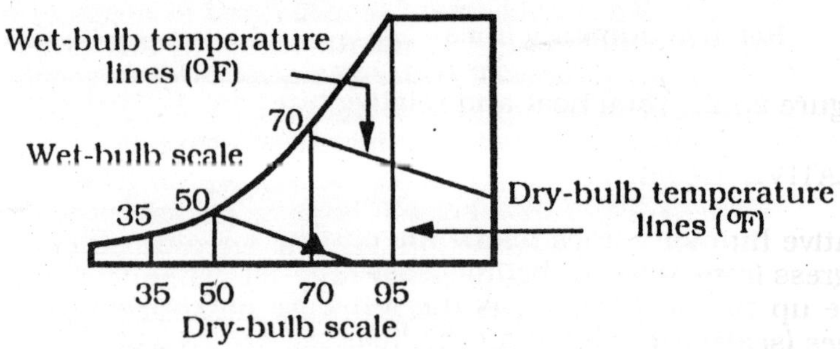

Figure 23.1. Dry-bulb and wet-bulb temperature lines and scales.

WET-BULB TEMPERATURE

The wet-bulb scale is found along the curved side of the chart with the lines leading down and to the right. Locate the wet-bulb temperature, and then follow the line down and to the right into the chart until it meets the line of another known property of the air, for example the vertical dry-bulb temperature line (Figure 23.1). If the temperatures of 70°Fdb and 50°Fwb are known, then

[1]Psychrometric charts can be obtained from ASHRAE (American Society of Heating, Refrigerating and Air-conditioning Engineers, Inc. 1791 Tullie Circle, NE, Atlanta, Georgia, 30329. (404-636-8400)

the state point is located at the junction of these two lines, the "▲" shown in Figure 23.1.

TOTAL HEAT

The total heat scale is found by following the wet-bulb lines up and to the left of the wet-bulb scale. The total heat lines and wet-bulb lines coincide but use different scales (Figure 23.2).

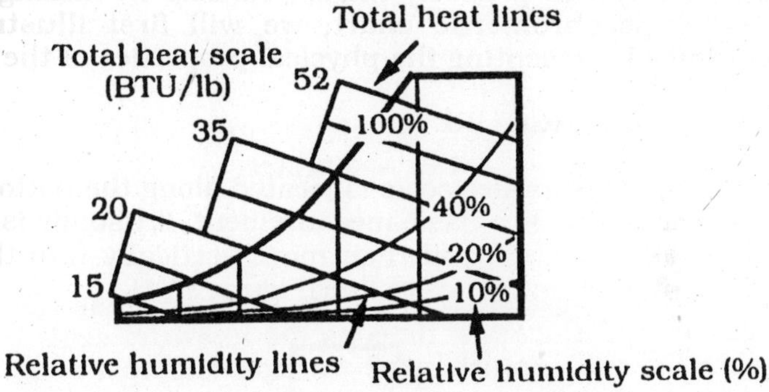

Figure 23.2. Total heat and relative humidity lines and scales.

RELATIVE HUMIDITY

Relative humidity lines follow the curved side of the chart. They progress from 10% on the line closest to the dry-bulb temperature scale up to 100%, which is the wet-bulb scale. Notice that the values (scale) are located on the lines, not at the edge of the chart (Figure 23.2).

MOISTURE CONTENT

The moisture content scales are located on either the left, the right, or both sides of the chart. To locate a value for moisture, move to either the left or to the right from the state point (Figure 23.3).

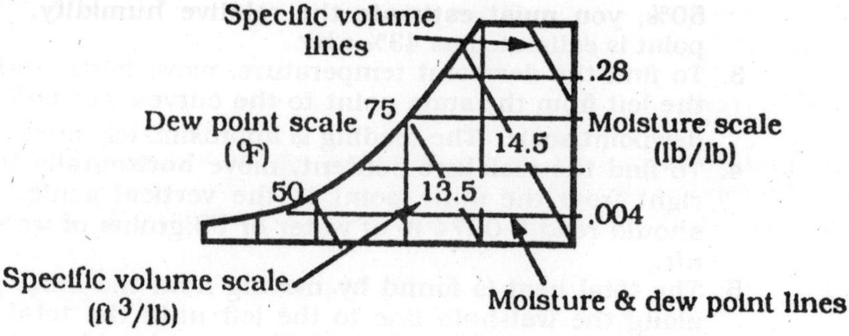

Figure 23.3. Moisture, specific volume, and dew point lines and scales.

DEW POINT

The dew point temperature uses the same scale as the wet-bulb temperature and the same lines as the moisture scale. To locate the value for dew point, move horizontally to the left (Figure 23.3).

SPECIFIC VOLUME

The specific volume scale is located on vertical lines angling up and to the left from the dry-bulb temperature scale. They start at less than 12.5 ft^3/lb in the lower left corner and progress to greater than 15.0 ft^3/lb in the upper right corner of the chart (Figure 23.3). The values (scale) are contained on the lines.

Problem: What are the physical properties of air if the dry-bulb temperature is 75°F, and the wet-bulb temperature is 60°F?

Solution: Using a psychrometric chart:

1. The first step is to find the state point. Locate the vertical line that represents the 75°F dry-bulb temperature. Then, locate the slanting wet-bulb line that represents 60°F wet-bulb. The intersection of these two lines is the state point.
2. The state point is just above the 40% r.h. line. Therefore the value of the relative humidity is between 40% and 50%. Because there are no other lines between 40% and

50%, you must estimate the relative humidity. This point is estimated as 43% r.h.

3. To find the dewpoint temperature, move horizontally to the left from the state point to the curved wet-bulb and dewpoint scale. The reading is approximately 50°F.
4. To find the moisture content, move horizontally to the right from the state point to the vertical scale. You should read 0.0074 lb of water or 53 grains of water/lb air.
5. The total heat is found by moving from the state point along the wet-bulb line to the left until the total heat (BTU/lb) scale of air is reached. You should read 26.6 BTU/lb of air.
6. Finally, the specific volume is determined by locating and identifying the specific volume lines (ft^3/lb of dry air) that fall on either side of the state point, which in this case are 13.6 and 13.7. Estimating the state point distance between these lines gives an approximate value of 13.64 ft^3/lb.

Many other relationships can be illustrated using a psychrometric chart--for example, what happens to air as it is heated or cooled.

Problem: What are the values for the physical properties of the air in the previous problem (75°Fdb and 60°Fwb) if the air is heated to 90°Fdb?

Solution: To solve this problem you must determine the direction and the distance to move from the first state point to the second state point. In this problem, because heat is added, the second state point is located to the right of the first along the horizontal moisture line. Move right until this line intersects with the vertical 90°Fdb line, and then read the values for the characteristics at the second state point. Values are:

Heat =	30.5 BTU/lb	Dew point =	50°F
Specific volume =	14.0 ft^3/lb	Moisture =	0.008 lb/lb
Relative humidity =	26%	Wet-bulb =	65°F

Compare these results with those for the previous problem. If you understand the principles of air illustrated by a psychrometric chart, you should be able to explain why the values for some of the characteristics changed, and why some did not.

HEATING

Heating is used to modify an environment by raising the dry-bulb temperature, or to offset the effects of heat loss from a building. The amount of heat required depends upon the use of the building (animal housing, product storage, etc.), the heat flow out of the building, the ventilation needed, and the sources of heat within the building. In buildings used for product storage, a minimum amount of or no ventilation may be needed, but buildings used for livestock housing must be ventilated to remove the moisture given off by the animals as they breathe.

VENTILATION RATE

Ventilation is the movement of air through a building. Air is used to remove moisture, reduce the temperature if the outside air is cooler than the inside, and replace gases inside the building with outside air. The amount of ventilation needed depends upon which of the these uses is the most critical. For livestock buildings, if the ventilation rate is sufficient to remove excess moisture, it usually will be more than enough for the other needs.

In this section, a procedure involving the use of a psychrometric chart is used to make estimates of the amount of ventilation required to remove the excess moisture from a livestock building. For buildings used for other purposes, you must determine which aspect of the environment is critical, and base your calculations on that factor. Table 23-4 contains values for moisture and heat released by several different animals.

When outside air is introduced into a building, it must be uniformly distributed within the building and mixed with the building air to prevent drafts. One method commonly used is to introduce the air through small openings distributed around or throughout the building. Another method is to use heat exchangers. A heat exchanger uses the heat of the exhaust air to preheat incoming air, thus reducing the chilling effects of drafts and reducing the amount of heat that must be added. Actual air flow rates required for animal buildings will vary with the type and size of animal, management system, type of floor and floor drainage, and the number of animals in the building.

As moisture evaporates, the physical properties of the air change. The amount of change can be determined by locating the state points, using dry-bulb and wet-bulb temperatures, for both conditions. The numerical differences in the moisture content and the total heat of both conditions provide the information used to determine the amount of air and the heat required to evaporate the moisture.

Problem: How much air and heat will be needed to evaporate 2 pounds of water per hour from within a building if the inside air dry-bulb (db) temperature is 55°F and 48°F wet-bulb (wb), and the outside air conditions are 40°Fdb and 35°Fwb?

Solution: In this problem we will use values for five of the properties of air for two different air conditions. Constructing a table (see Table 23-1) is very helpful and is recommended for solving problems of this type.

The first step is to use the psychrometric chart to find the values for moisture content, total heat, and specific volume for both the inside and outside air. These values are recorded in the columns "Inside" and "Outside".

Table 23-1 Psychrometric data for ventilation problem.

Properties	Inside	Outside	Difference
Dry-bulb (°F)	55	40	
Wet-Bulb (°F)	48	35	
Moisture (lb H_2O/lb of air)	0.0056	0.003	0.0026
Total heat (BTU/lb)	19.20	12.90	6.3
Specific volume (ft³/lb)	13.08	12.66	

The next step is to determine the differences in moisture content and in total heat between the inside and the outside air. These values are recorded in the column labeled "Difference." Values for the differences in temperature and in specific volume are not needed in this problem.

The third step is to determine the amount of air (lb) required to remove the moisture. The amount of air required to evaporate the moisture is determined from the difference in the moisture content of the inside and the outside air. A difference of 0.0026 pound of water per pound of air means that every pound of outside air brought in and raised to inside conditions is capable of evaporating 0.0026 pound of moisture. If each pound of air absorbs the maximum amount of water, 0.0026 pound, and the amount of water that must be removed is 2 pounds per hour, then the required amount of air (lb) is:

$$\text{lb air} = \frac{1 \text{ lb air}}{0.0026 \text{ lb water}} \times \frac{2.0 \text{ lb water}}{1 \text{ hr}}$$

$$= 770 \frac{\text{lb air}}{\text{hr}}$$

For these inside and outside conditions, 770 pounds of air per hour moving through the building will be needed to remove 2 pounds of water per hour, assuming that the air absorbs the maximum amount of water.

Before air can absorb water in liquid form it must be vaporized, and this requires heat. In addition, if the inside of the building is warmer than the outside, ventilation causes a loss of heat from the building. The total amount of heat lost is determined by using the difference in the heat of the incoming and the outgoing air. The amount of heat in the inside air is 19.20 BTU/lb, and that of the outside air is 12.90 BTU/lb; so a difference of 6.3 BTU/lb is the amount of heat lost with each pound of air ventilated. We have already determined that 770 pounds of air per hour will be needed to evaporate the water produced in the building; so the heat loss due to ventilation is:

$$\frac{\text{BTU}}{\text{hr}} = 770 \frac{\text{lb air}}{\text{hr}} \times 6.3 \frac{\text{BTU}}{\text{lb air}}$$

$$= 4900 \frac{\text{BTU}}{\text{hr}}$$

For these conditions, 4900 BTU per hour of heat will be transported outside the building with the ventilation air.

Ventilation fans usually are sized in units of cubic feet per hour. This will require a units conversion from weight to volume. This conversion is made using the specific volume values from the psychrometric chart. If the ventilation fan is exhausting building air (the most common situation), then the inside specific volume is used. If the fan is blowing in outside air, the outside specific volume is used. Because it takes 770 pounds of air per hour to evaporate the water produced in the building, the volume of air (ft^3/hr) that is required is determined by multiplying the pounds of air per hour by the specific volume. The size of fan required is:

$$\frac{\text{ft}^3}{\text{hr}} = 770 \frac{\text{lb}}{\text{hr}} \times 13.08 \frac{\text{ft}^3}{\text{lb}}$$

$$= 10{,}100 \frac{ft^3}{hr}$$

A fan, or several fans with a combined capacity of 10,100 cubic feet per hour is required to provide enough ventilation to remove the excess moisture from the building.

The values calculated in the previous problem are accurate only as long as the inside and the outside environments do not change. This only occurs for short periods of time. Heating, ventilating, and cooling systems must be able to react to change, and if they are required to maintain a constant inside environment, they must have the capacity for the most extreme inside and outside situations.

BUILDING HEAT BALANCE

The principles of heating, ventilation, and air-conditioning are all used to determine the amount of ventilation, heat, or air-conditioning needed to maintain the temperature inside a building. The process of determining what changes are occurring in the environment inside a structure is call a *heat balance*. Expressed mathematically a heat balance is:

$$\pm \text{Heat} \left(\frac{\text{BTU}}{\text{hr}}\right) = \text{Total heat gain } (H_G) - \text{Total heat loss } (H_L) \qquad (23\text{-}1)$$

Three possible answers can result from using Equation (23-1). If the amount of heat gain is larger than the heat loss, the answer will be positive (+). In this situation the temperature of the building will increase. The second possibility is that heat gain and heat loss will be the same. If this is true, the answer for Equation (23-1) is zero, and the temperature within the building is stable. The third possibility is that heat loss is greater than heat gain. If this is true, the answer for the equation is negative (–) and the temperature inside the building is decreasing.

The four factors needed to determine heat gain and loss are: mechanical equipment heat, animal heat, heat flow, and ventilation. Mechanical equipment, such as electric motors and heat lamps, and animals put heat into the building. Heat flows from areas of high temperature to areas of low temperature. The term *heat flow* is used to describe the movement of heat through the components of a building. Ventilation and its effect on the environment was discussed in a previous section.

These factors usually result in either a heat gain or a heat loss, depending on the season of the year and the temperatures. For a winter heat balance, the heat gain is the sum of the animal heat and the mechanical equipment heat, and the heat losses are due to heat flow and ventilation. For a summer heat balance, the heat gain is the sum of the animal heat, mechanical equipment heat, and heat flow. Ventilation results in a heat loss as long as the outside temperature is less than inside.

The following problem illustrates the procedure for calculating a winter heat balance for a building.

Problem: Determine the daytime heat balance (BTU/hr) for a 30 foot by 60 foot structure with 8 foot walls, which houses two hundred 150.0-pound feeder pigs. The building has two, 3.0-foot by 6.6-foot pine doors, 1.0 inch thick. In addition, it has ten 24-in by 42-inch single-pane windows. The walls are 8.0-inch lightweight concrete block with the cores filled. The ceiling is 3/8-inch plywood with 6 inches of low-density batt insulation between the joists. Mechanical equipment adds 3000 BTU/hr. The attic space is well ventilated and is at the same temperature as the outdoors. The building is on an insulated concrete slab. The temperatures are 70°Fdb and 60°Fwb inside and 40°Fdb and 34°Fwb outside.

Solution: Two values are required to determine a heat balance--the total heat loss and the total heat gain. Begin by determining total heat loss. For winter conditions, total heat losses are heat flow and ventilation.

Heat Losses: Equation (22-1) is used to determine the total heat flow into or out of a building. The total heat flow is found by calculating and summing the heat flow for each component of the building having a unique R-value. The different R-values in this problem include those of the walls, windows, door, ceiling, and floor. Errors can be reduced by setting up a table of the required information. Because heat flow is a function of area, temperature difference, and thermal resistance, table columns are included for this information. Study Table 23-2. In addition, it may be helpful to sketch components, as in the example in Chapter 22. A sketch was not used in this example because each building component has only a few parts.

Table 23-2. Solution for building heat flow problem.

Component	Total R Value	Area (ft^2)	ΔT (^oF)	Q (BTU/hr)
Walls (less openings)	5.88	1330	30	6790
Windows	0.91	70	30	2310
Doors	2.10	40	30	571
Ceiling	24.63	1800	30	2190
Floor	2.22	180 *	30	2430
		Total Heat Flow (Q_T) =		14,300

* The perimeter (ft) is used for slab floors, not the area (ft^2).

With a temperature difference of 30°F, the total heat loss (flow) is 14,300 BTU/hr. These numbers were calculated as follows:

R-values:

Wall:	Outside air film	0.17
	Concrete blocks, filled cores	5.03
	Inside air film	0.68
	Total R-value for wall	5.88
Windows:	Outside air film	0.17
	Single-pane glass	0.06
	Inside air film	0.68
	Total R-value for windows	0.91
Door:	Outside air film	0.17
	Wood	1.25
	Inside air film	0.68
	Total R-value for door	2.10
Ceiling:	Inside air film	0.68
	Insulation (6-in batt)	22.80
	Plywood	0.47
	Inside air film	0.68
	Total R-value for ceiling	24.63
Floor:	Insulated concrete	2.22

Areas:

Walls: ft^2 = (area of end walls + area of side walls) - (area of windows + area of doors)

$= [(8.00\ ft \times 30.0\ ft \times 2) + (8.00\ ft \times 60.0\ ft \times 2)] - (70.0\ ft^2 + 40.0\ ft^2)$

$= (480.0\ ft^2 + 960.0\ ft^2) - (70.0\ ft^2 + 40.0\ ft^2)$

$= 1440\ ft^2 - 110\ ft^2$

$= 1330\ ft^2$

Windows: ft^2 = Width x Height x Number of windows

$$= [(24\ in \times 42\ in) \times 10] \times \frac{1\ ft^2}{144\ in^2}$$

$= 70\ ft^2$

Doors: ft^2 = Width x Height x Number of doors

$= 3.0\ ft \times 6.6\ ft \times 2$

$= 40\ ft^2$

Ceiling: ft^2 = Length x Width

$= 60.0\ ft \times 30.0\ ft$

$= 1800\ ft^2$

Perimeter:

Floor: ft = (Length x 2) + (Width x 2)

$= (60\ ft \times 2) + (30\ ft \times 2)$

$= 180\ ft$

Building heat flow (Q_T):

$$Q_T = Q_{wall} + Q_{window} + Q_{door} + Q_{ceiling} + Q_{floor}$$

$$= \frac{1330 \times 30}{5.88} + \frac{70 \times 30}{0.91} + \frac{40 \times 30}{2.10} + \frac{1800 \times 30}{24.63} + \frac{180 \times 30}{2.22}$$

$$= 6790 + 2300 + 571 + 2190 + 2430$$

$$= 14{,}300 \frac{BTU}{hr}$$

The second source of heat loss is ventilation. The ventilation heat loss is determined by the ventilation rate and the difference in heat between the inside and the outside air. A table is used to organize the psychrometric data (see Table 23-3).

Table 23-3. Psychrometric data for problem.

Properties	Inside	Outside	Difference
Dry-bulb (^{o}F)	70.0	40.0	
Wet-Bulb (^{o}F)	60.0	34.0	
Moisture (lb/lb)	0.009	0.003	0.006
Total heat (BTU/lb)	26.0	12.45	13.55
Specific volume (ft^3/lb)	13.5	12.65	

In this problem, the building is used to house livestock. Therefore, the ventilation rate will be determined by the amount of water vapor produced by the animals. Table 23-4 contains values that can be used to estimate the amount of heat and moisture produced by various animals, based on weight and species.

Table 23-4. Moisture and heat released by animals.

Animal	Moisture* (lb water/hr)	Heat* (BTU/hr)
Swine		
10 - 50 lb	0.065	174.0
50 - 100	0.177	240.0
100 - 200 lb	0.219	354.0
Broiler		
0.22 - 1.5 lb	0.0079	12.4
1.5 - 3.5 lb	0.0110	18.7
Turkey		
1 lb	0.0059	10.8
2 lb	0.0025	9.8
Dairy cow	1.196	1917.0

*The amount of water and heat released by animals changes as the air temperature changes. These are average values.

Reproduced with permission from: *Structures and Environment Handbook*, MWPS-1, 11th edition, revised 1987, Midwest Plan Service, Ames, IA 50011-3080.

To determine the ventilation rate, begin by finding the amount of water released into the building. A 150-pound feeder pig produces 0.219 pound of moisture per hour. The total water produced is:

$$\frac{lb}{hr} = \frac{0.219 \frac{lb\ H_2O}{hr}}{pig} \times 200 \text{ pigs}$$

$$= 43.8 \frac{lb\ H_2O}{hr}$$

Next, determine the amount of air needed to remove 43.8 pounds of water per hour. This is accomplished by multiplying the amount of water that each pound of air can absorb as it passes through the building by the amount of water that needs to be removed. If we assume that the air is 100% saturated when it leaves the building, then the amount of water that the air will remove is determined by the difference between the moisture content of the air entering and that of the air exiting the building. From Table 23-3, this value is 0.006 pound of water per pound of dry air. The amount of air needed is:

$$\frac{lb\ air}{hr} = \frac{1\ lb\ air}{0.006\ lb\ water} \times \frac{43.8\ lb\ water}{hr}$$

$$= 7300 \frac{lb\ air}{hr}$$

Now that the ventilation rate is known, the amount of heat loss due to ventilation can be calculated. This is accomplished by multiplying the pounds of air per hour that will be moving through the building by the difference between the amount of heat in the inside air and that in the outside air. From Table 23-3, this value is 13.55 BTU/lb of air. The heat loss due to ventilation is:

$$\frac{BTU}{hr} = 7300 \frac{lb\ air}{hr} \times 13.55 \frac{BTU}{lb\ air}$$

$$= 100{,}000 \frac{BTU}{hr}$$

The total heat loss is obtained by adding the rates for heat flow and ventilation:

$$\frac{BTU}{hr} = \text{Heat flow} + \text{Ventilation losses}$$

$$= 14{,}300\frac{BTU}{hr} + 100{,}000\frac{BTU}{hr}$$

$$= 114{,}300\frac{BTU}{hr}$$

Heat Gain: Next determine the total heat gain. The sources of heat are the mechanical equipment, which in this problem is given, and the heat given off by the animals (see Table 23-4).

$$\frac{BTU}{hr} = \frac{\frac{354\ BTU}{hr}}{pig} \times 200\ \text{pigs}$$

$$= 70{,}800\frac{BTU}{hr}$$

The total heat gained inside the building is:

$$\frac{BTU}{hr} = \text{Equipment heat} + \text{Animal heat}$$

$$= 3000\frac{BTU}{hr} + 70{,}800\frac{BTU}{hr}$$

$$= 73{,}800\frac{BTU}{hr}$$

Heat Balance: Now we have all of the information needed to complete the heat balance. Using Equation (23-1):

$$\frac{BTU}{hr} = \text{Total heat gain } (H_G) - \text{Total heat loss } (H_L)$$

$$= 73{,}800\frac{BTU}{hr} - 114{,}300\frac{BTU}{hr}$$

$$= -\ 40{,}500\frac{BTU}{hr}$$

A heat balance with a negative number indicates that the amount of heat lost from the building is greater than the amount of heat being produced inside the building. When this occurs, the temperature inside the building will decrease unless additional heat is added. For this problem, 40,500 BTU/hr of heat is needed to maintain the inside temperature of the building.

AIR-CONDITIONING

In some types of buildings, the ventilation may not be adequate to maintain the optimum temperature. The amount of heat produced by the animals, the processing, and so on, may exceed the ability of the ventilation system to maintain the desired temperature. In these situations, air-conditioners are used.

Conditioning air to reduce heat stress can consist of, and for many years was limited to, cooling with ice, pumping well water through a radiator, or evaporative cooling. The effectiveness of these methods is limited. The use of ice will produce large amounts of cooling, but the resulting water must be disposed of, and a continuous supply of ice must be available. The amount of cooling available from well water is limited, and evaporative cooling is effective only if the outside air has a low relative humidity.

Today, the term air-conditioning refers to conditioning air through the use of mechanical refrigeration. Refrigeration is the process of transferring heat from one substance to another; and for air-conditioning, refrigeration moves heat from inside a structure to the air outside the structure. For this to occur, the air that is to be cooled must come in contact with a material at a temperature lower than that of the inside air. When this happens, heat from the air will flow into the colder material. Some air-conditioners use a chilled metal surface to provide a cold mass, whereas others use a spray of chilled water. The heat is transferred by a substance circulating between the inside air and the outside air. In smaller units, the transfer substance will be a gas; for larger systems, the substance may be a liquid. Here we illustrate the common gas-type mechanical refrigeration air-conditioner (see Figure 23.4).

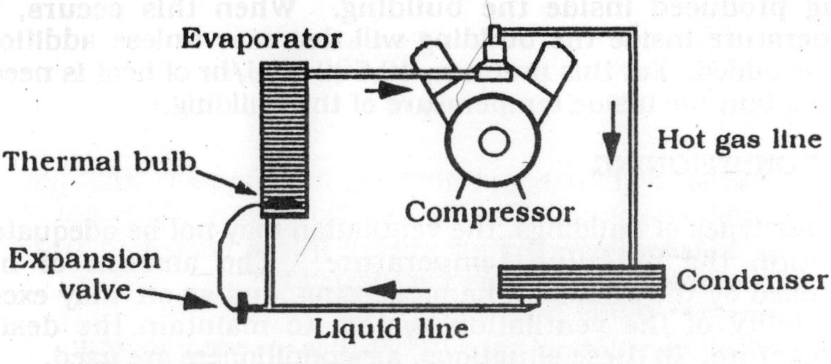

Figure 23.4. Mechanical refrigeration system.

In a mechanical refrigeration system, heat is moved by alternately compressing, liquefying, expanding, and evaporating a refrigerant, commonly Freon. The compressor increases the pressure and the temperature of the refrigerant as it compresses the gas. As the refrigerant passes through the condenser, the heat absorbed by the refrigerant as it passed through the evaporator, and the heat produced by compression, is transferred into the air. Thus, the condenser will be located where outside air moving across it absorbs the heat causing the refrigerant to liquify. As the liquid refrigerant flows through the expansion valve and into the evaporator, the pressure drops and the refrigerant absorbs heat from the surrounding air. The evaporator will be located inside an air duct or other location where air can pass through it and be cooled, causing the refrigerant to be vaporized. The hot, low pressure gas flows back to the compressor and the cycle begins again. The expansion valve and a thermal bulb regulate the flow of the refrigerant to produce the desired evaporator temperature.

SAMPLE PROBLEMS

1. Determine the values for all of the characteristics of air if the dry-bulb temperature is 60°F and the wet-bulb temperature is 55°F. [Note: Not all psychrometric charts read the same. If the ASHRAE Chart No. 1 is used you should arrive at the following values.]

   Answers:

Dry Bulb	60 °F
Wet Bulb	55 °F
Heat	23.2 BTU/lb
Dewpoint	51 °F

Sp. vol.	13.25 ft^3/lb
Moisture	0.0081 lb H_2O/lb air
r.h.	72 %

2. If air is at 50°Fdb and 40°Fwb, it contains 0.0026 pound of moisture per pound of dry air. How many additional pounds of moisture can the air absorb if it is heated to 100°Fdb? (Assume the air becomes saturated.)
Answer: 0.009 lb of water/lb air
3. What ventilation rate (ft^3/hr) is needed to remove 1.25 pounds of water per hour from a product if the inside conditions are 75°Fdb and 70°Fwb, and the outside conditions are 65°Fdb and 55°Fwb?
Answer: 2460 ft^3/hr
4. Determine the heat flow for a building constructed of 6-inch solid concrete walls on an uninslated slab. The ceiling is constructed of one-inch solid boards with asphalt shingles. The building measures 12 ft x 36 ft x 8 ft high and has one 3 ft x 7 ft, one-inch solid wood door and two 18-inch square windows with double-pane glass. The inside conditions are 75°Fdb and 65°Fwb. The outside conditions are 58°Fdb and 40°Fwb.
Answer:

Table 23-5. Solution for problem four.

Component	Area (ft^2)	ΔT (°F)	R-value	Q $\left(\frac{BTU}{hr}\right)$
Walls	742.5	17	1.33	9,490.60
Ceiling	432	17	2.54	28.913
Door	21	17	2.10	170
Windows	4.5	17	1.68	45.535
Floor	96 ft	17	1.23	1,326.82
		Total heat flow =		13,924.30 or 13,000

24
Selection of Structural Members

OBJECTIVES

1. Understand the importance of beam size.
2. Be able to define simple and cantilever beams.
3. Be able to calculate the maximum load that can be carried by a beam.
4. Be able to calculate the size of beam needed to support a load.

INTRODUCTION

A beam is a horizontal member used to support a load. Failure to use a beam of adequate size can lead to beam failure with the accompanying danger of injury and/or financial loss. The design of structural members for a particular load involves analysis of the forces imposed on the member by loading and selection of appropriate materials, shapes, and sizes to accommodate the loads. This procedure is best accomplished by a structural engineer and is beyond the scope of this book. However, several basic concepts are presented here to help the reader understand the properties and load-carrying abilities of simple and cantilever beams made of wood.

SIMPLE AND CANTILEVER BEAMS

Simple and cantilever beams are structural members that are loaded by forces applied at right angles to the longitudinal axis. The load that a beam can carry depends on its length, the method of support, the manner of loading, its cross-sectional size and shape, and the strength of the beam material.

Two types of beams and two types of loads are considered: simple and cantilever beams, and point and uniform loads A simple beam is supported at each end without rigid connections; it merely rests on supports. A cantilever beam is supported solidly at one end, with the other end free (see Figure 24.1).

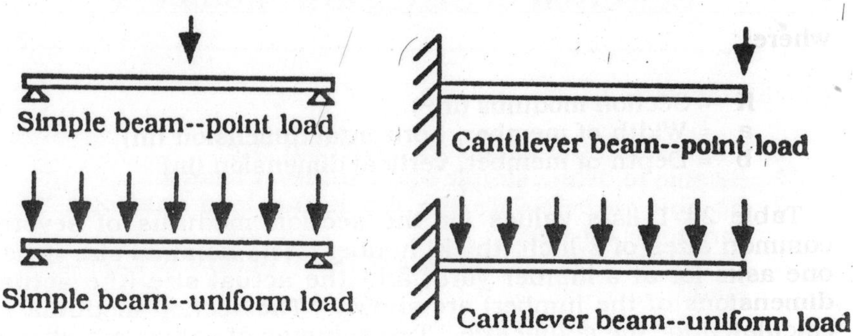

Figure 24.1. Two types of beams and two types of loads.

Point loads can be applied at any specific point along the beam, but the equations used in this chapter only apply to point loads in the middle of a simple beam and at the end of a cantilever beam. A point load is indicated by a single arrow. Uniform loads are applied along the entire length of the beam, and are indicated by a series of arrows.

BEAM LOAD

When a load is applied to a beam, the beam tends to bend. As the beam bends or flexes, the fibers along the bottom surface of the beam are stretched (put in tension), and the fibers along the top surface of the beam are pressed together (compressed).

As the fibers of a beam stretch, a stress is set up in the fibers. When beam loading and fiber stretching proceed to a point where the fibers yield, the *maximum allowable fiber stress* (S) has been exceeded. Estimates for maximum allowable stress are available for most materials, and values for maximum allowable fiber stress of wood can be found in Appendix IX.

The shape of a beam and the way that it is positioned to carry a load greatly affect its load-carrying ability. A beam will support more weight on edge than when placed flat. The dimensions of a beam (width and depth) are used to determine the *section modulus*, which provides an index of the relative stiffness or load-carrying ability of the member.

For a rectangular-cross-section member, the section modulus is determined by using the following equation:

$$K = \frac{1}{6} ab^2 \qquad (24\text{-}1)$$

where:

K = Section modulus (in^3)
a = Width of member, horizontal dimension (in)
b = Depth of member, vertical dimension (in)

Table 24-1 lists values for the section modulus of several common sizes of 2-inch (thick) lumber. The nominal size (what one asks for at a lumber yard) and the actual size (the actual dimensions of the lumber) are shown. The section modulus is calculated for the actual size. Two columns of values are shown for the two possible positions of a member--standing on edge and lying flat. Notice that the values for the section modulus are much greater when the member is standing on edge, as it is much stiffer in this position.

Table 24-1 Section modulus of rectangular members.

		Section Modulus for Position (in^3)	
		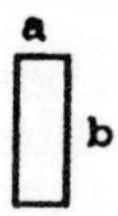	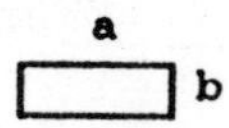
Nominal size (in)	Actual size (in)	On edge	Flat
2 x 2	1.50 x 1.50	0.56	0.56
3	2.50	1.56	0.94
4	3.50	3.06	1.31
6	6.50	7.56	2.06
8	7.25	13.14	2.72
10	9.25	21.39	3.57
12	11.25	31.64	4.23
14	13.25	43.89	4.97

The amount of weight that a beam can support is determined by the section modulus, allowable fiber stress, beam span or length, type of load, and type of support For the two types of beams and loads being considered in this chapter, the following equations apply:

Simple beam, point load: $$W = \frac{4SK}{L} \quad (24\text{-}2)$$

Simple beam, uniform load: $$W = \frac{8SK}{L} \quad (24\text{-}3)$$

Cantilever beam, point load: $$W = \frac{SK}{L} \quad (24\text{-}4)$$

Cantilever beam, uniform load: $$W = \frac{2SK}{L} \quad (24\text{-}5)$$

where:

W = Maximum allowable load on the beam (lb)
S = Allowable fiber stress (lb/in^2)
L = Length or span of beam (in)
K = Beam section modulus (in^3)

Problem: What is the maximum point load that can be supported in the middle of a 4 x 6-inch simple beam 120 inches long if the allowable fiber stress is 1500 pounds per square inch?

Solution: Using Equations (24-1) and (24-2):

$$K = \frac{1}{6}ab^2$$

$$= \frac{1}{6} \times 4 \text{ in} \times (6 \text{ in})^2$$

$$= 24 \text{ in}^3$$

$$W = \frac{4SK}{L}$$

$$= \frac{4 \times 1500 \times 24}{120}$$

$$= 1200 \text{ lb}$$

SIZE OF BEAM

In the previous section, the method for determining the size of load that a beam will support was illustrated. In some situations it is necessary to determine the size beam that is necessary to support a given load. The same equations are used, but they are rearranged to solve for the section modulus. Once the section modulus is known, the beam size can be determined from Table 24-1 if one dimension is 2 inches (nominal), and the orientation is known.

Problem: What is the smallest size of 2-inch, No. 1, Southern Pine simple beam that will support a uniform load of 2400 pounds if the beam is 100 inches long?

Solution: Using Table 24-1 and Appendix IX, and rearranging Equation (24-3):

$$W = \frac{8SK}{L}$$

$$K = \frac{W \times L}{8 \times S}$$

$$= \frac{2400 \times 100}{8 \times 1000}$$

$$= \frac{240{,}000}{8000}$$

$$= 30 \text{ in}^3$$

Referring to Table 24-1, the smallest beam size with a section modulus equal to or larger than 30 cubic inches is a beam 2 inches wide and 12 inches deep. Notice that a 2 x 14 inch beam also would carry the load, but is larger than necessary.

The procedures presented in the previous sections are not limited to boards 2 inches wide. If the section modulus and one dimension are known, the width of a beam greater than 2 inches can be determined if Equation (24-1) is rearranged.

Problem: What depth of board is needed in the previous problem if a board 4 inches wide is used?

Solution: Rearranging Equation (24-1):

$$K = \frac{1}{6}ab^2 \quad \text{(a = 4 inches, we must solve for b)}$$

$$b = \sqrt{\frac{K \times 6}{a}}$$

$$= \sqrt{\frac{30 \times 6}{4}}$$

$$= 6.7 \text{ in}$$

This example illustrates that a beam 4 x 6.7 inches (actual size) will support the same load as a beam 2 x 12 inches (nominal size).

PRACTICE PROBLEMS

1. What is the maximum point load (lb) that can be supported in the middle of a Douglasfir, light framing, utility-grade, simple beam 120 inches long, measuring 6 inches wide and 4 inches deep (actual size)?
Answer: $K = 16 \text{ in}^3$ and $W = 93$ lb
2. What size of load can be supported in problem 1 if the load is supported uniformly?
Answer: 187 lb
3. What size of load can be supported by the beam in problem 1 if the beam is on edge?
Answer: 140 lb
4. What is the maximum uniform load that can be supported by a Southern Pine, structural light framing, No. 2, cantilever beam 80 inches long if the beam is 5 inches wide and 3 inches deep (actual size)?
Answer: $K = 7.5 \text{ in}^3$ and $W = 155$ lb
5. Select the smallest 2-inch, Douglasfir, light framing, standard-grade, simple beam that will carry a 500-pound point load with a span of 60 inches.
Answer: 2 x 10 inches
6. Select the smallest cantilever beam that will carry a 150-pound point load if the length is 40 inches, and the allowable fiber stress is 1800 pounds per square inch.
Answer: $K = 3.33 \text{ in}^3$, size = 2 x 6 inches on edge

25
Principles of Electricity

OBJECTIVES

1. Be able to define electricity.
2. Be able to define basic electrical terms.
3. Understand and be able to use Ohm's law.
4. Be able to calculate electrical power.
5. Be able to calculate electrical energy use.

INTRODUCTION

Agricultural production depends heavily upon electrical energy to power the machines, equipment, and tools used in making and processing agricultural products. Safety-conscious managers and workers need a basic understand of the principles of electricity. An understanding of these principles will lead to more efficient use of electricity.

ELECTRICITY

Electricity is the flow of electrons from one atom to another. Scientists believe that electricity was first noted when ancient people discovered the attraction between an amber rod and other materials. Knowledge about electricity has so advanced that it now is generated on demand and its use is widespread. For example, it is used to operate lights and motors, to produce heat, and to serve as a means of communication.

An understanding of electricity begins with the atom. Electrons travel in orbit around a nucleus composed of protons and neutrons When an atom has the same number of protons and electrons it has no charge. If it has more electrons than protons, it has a negative charge, and if more protons than electrons, a positive charge. As electrons move from one atom to another, electric current is produced.

A flow of electrons can be produced by several different methods, including friction, heat, light, pressure, chemical action, and magnetism. The last two are used most often in agriculture.

ELECTRICAL TERMS

Knowledge of the following terms is necessary for an understanding of electricity.

Alternating Current (AC): One of two types of electric current, alternating current does not exhibit constant polarity. This current does not have a constant voltage; the voltage builds to a maximum value in one direction, declines to zero, builds to a maximum in the other direction, and declines to zero again (Figure 25.1). This sequence is called one cycle. In the United States the common current is 60 cycle; that is, 60 complete cycles occur every second.

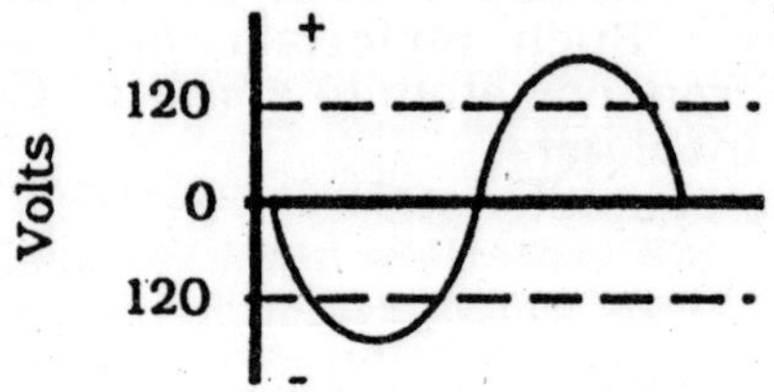

Figure 25.1. Alternating current voltage.

Amperage (amp): a unit of measure for the amount of electricity flowing in a circuit. One ampere of current is equivalent to 6.28×10^{18} electrons per second.

Circuit: a continuous path for electricity from the source to the load (machine or appliance using the electricity) and back to the source.

Conductor: any material that has a relatively low resistance to the flow of electricity. Such materials allow electrons to flow easily from one atom to another. Most metals are good conductors.

Current: the flow of electrons through a conductor. The amount of current flow is measured in amperes.

Direct Current (DC): The opposite of alternating current, this current flows in one direction only and at a constant voltage (Figure 25.2). The polarity will be either positive or negative.

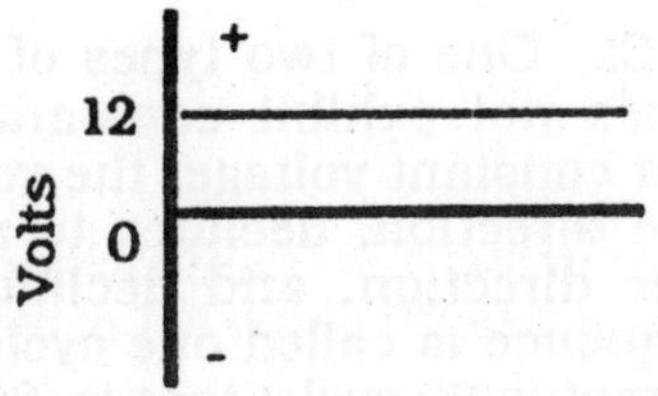

Figure 25.2. Direct current voltage.

Insulator: any material that has a relatively high resistance to the flow of electricity. Such materials do not allow easy movement of electrons from one atom to another. Glass, rubber, and many plastics are insulators.
Resistance (Ohm): the characteristic of materials that impedes the flow of electricity. All materials have varying amounts of electrical resistance. Two characteristics of resistance are important: (1) when electricity flows through a resistant material, heat is generated; (2) when electricity flows through a resistant material, the voltage is decreased. Resistance is measured in units of ohms and designated by the Greek letter Ω (omega).
Voltage (V): the electromotive force that causes electrons to flow through a conductor. Voltage is a measure of the potential for current flow. A voltage potential may exist between objects without a flow of current. In the United States the two standard voltages are nominally called 120 volts and 240 volts.
Watts (W): unit of electrical power. Watts are equal to the voltage times the amperage.

OHM'S LAW

Ohm's law explains the relationship between current, voltage, and resistance:

$$E = IR \tag{25-1}$$

where:

E = Voltage (V)
I = Current (amp)
R = Resistance (ohms)

When three variables are present, if any two are known, the third can be determined. For example:

$$I = \frac{E}{R} \text{ and } R = \frac{E}{I}$$

Problem: What is the current flow (amp) when the source supplies 120 volts and the circuit has 20 ohms (Ω) of resistance?

Solution: Rearranging Equation (25-1):

$$I = \frac{E}{R}$$

$$= \frac{120\ V}{20\ \Omega}$$

$$= 6 \text{ amps}$$

ELECTRICAL POWER

By definition, power is the rate of doing work. In electricity, work is done by electrons moving within a conductor, and is the result of the electrical potential (V) and the flow rate of the electrons (amp). Thus, in an electrical circuit, power is the product of volts x amperes. The basic units of electrical power are the watt (W) and the kilowatt (kW). In equation form:

$$P = E \times I \tag{25-2}$$

where:

P = power (watts)
E = voltage (V)
I = current (amp)

Problem: How much power is being produced if the current is measured at 5.0 amps and 120.0 volts?

Solution: Using Equation (25-2):

$$P = E \times I$$

$$= 120\ V \times 5 \text{ amps}$$

$$= 600 \text{ watts}$$

Power also may be expressed in two other ways. Ohm's law states that E = IR, and (power) P = E x I; so the E in the power equation can be replaced with IR from Ohm's law:

$$P = IR \times I$$

$$P = I^2R \tag{25-3}$$

Ohm's law also states that $I = \frac{E}{R}$; therefore:

$$P = E \times \frac{E}{R}$$

or:

$$P = \frac{E^2}{R} \tag{25-4}$$

Note that the use of either of these equations requires knowledge of a value for the resistance. If the resistance and one of the other quantities are known, power can be determined.

ELECTRICAL ENERGY

Electrical energy is different from electrical power because it includes the element of time. The amount of electrical energy produced, or used, is determined by multiplying the electrical power (watts) by the amount of time electricity flows (hours). The result is expressed in the units for electrical energy, watt-hours (Wh). For many uses of electricity, the watt-hours value is a large number; so, the electric industry has adopted a more convenient unit, the kilowatt-hour (kWh), as the basic unit of electrical energy. One kilowatt equals 1000 watts. The amount of electrical energy used can be determined by:

$$EE\ (Wh) = P \times T \tag{25-5}$$

and:

$$EE\ (kWh) = P \times T \times \frac{1\ kWh}{1000\ Wh} \tag{25-6}$$

where:

EE = Electrical energy (Wh)
P = Power (watts)
T = Time (hr)

Problem: How much energy (Wh) is required to operate a 150-watt light bulb for 3.5 hours?

Solution: Using Equation (25-5):

$$EE = P \times T$$

$$= 150 \text{ watts} \times 3.5 \text{ hours}$$

$$= 525 \text{ Wh}$$

Expressed in kWh:

$$\text{kWh} = 525 \text{ Wh} \times \frac{1 \text{ kW}}{1000 \text{ W}}$$

$$= 0.525 \text{ kWh}$$

Electrical energy also is used to determine the cost of using electricity. It is common practice for an electric utility company to sell electricity on a cents (¢) per kilowatt-hour basis. If the electric rate (¢/kWh) and the amount of electricity (kWh) are known, the cost of operating any electrical appliance or motor can be determined by using units cancellation.

Problem: What will it cost to operate the light bulb in the previous problem if the electricity costs 10¢/kWh?

Solution: Using units cancellation:

$$\text{Cost (¢)} = 0.525 \text{ kWh} \times \frac{10¢}{\text{kWh}}$$

$$= 5¢$$

If electricity costs 10¢/kWh, then it will cost 5 cents to operate the 150-watt light bulb for 3.5 hours.

PRACTICE PROBLEMS

1. Determine the resistance of a circuit operating at 12 volts with 3 amperes of current.
   Answer: 4 Ω
2. How much current will flow if a circuit operates at 115 volts and has 35 Ω of resistance?
   Answer: 3.3 amps
3. Determine the amount of power in a 120 volt circuit with a current of 7.0 amps.
   Answer: 840 watts
4. Determine the power produced (kW) when 8 amps are flowing in a 24-volt circuit.
   Answer: 0.192 kW
5. How much power is being used (kW) if 4.5 Ω of resistance are present in a 120-volt circuit?
   Answer: 3.2 kW
6. How much energy (kWh) is used when a 75-watt bulb burns for 17 hours?
   Answer: 1.3 kWh
7. What will it cost to operate a 200-watt appliance if electricity costs 9.5¢/kWh and the appliance is used for 30 minutes?
   Answer: 0.95¢

26
Series and Parallel Circuits

OBJECTIVES

1. Be able to identify series and parallel circuits.
2. Be able to determine the total resistance of both series and parallel circuits.
3. Be able to attach a voltmeter and an ammeter correctly.
4. Be able to determine the amperage and the voltage at any point within a series or a parallel circuit.
5. Explain the importance of system and equipment grounding.

INTRODUCTION

One requirement of any appliance, tool, or other type of electrical device is that it must be connected to a source of electricity. Before the load will operate, electricity must have a complete path from the source to the load and back to the source. This path for electricity is called a circuit. Two types of circuit commonly are used to supply electrical power, series and parallel.

In this chapter we will use several electrical terms and principles discussed in the previous chapter to show the procedure for calculating the resistance, voltage, and amperage for both types of circuits.

SERIES AND PARALLEL CIRCUITS

Series and parallel circuits can be identified by the path or paths the electricity may follow as it moves through the circuit. The following discussion will explain the differences between the two circuits and how to calculate the total resistance of the circuit. *Note*: in the following discussion of circuits, assume that the conductors in the circuit have no resistance.

SERIES CIRCUIT

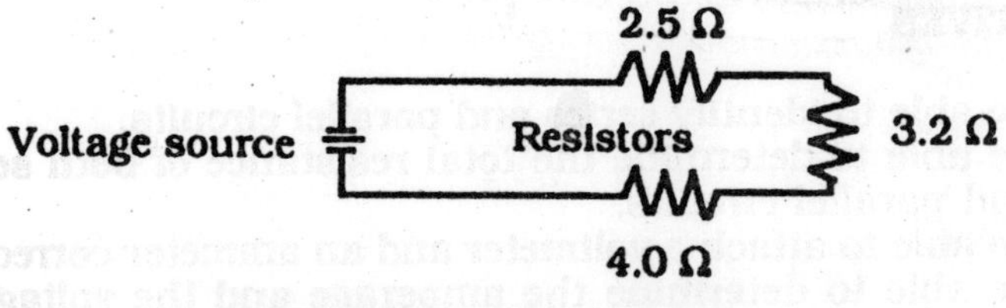

Figure 26.1. Series circuit.

In a series circuit there is only one path for the electricity to follow; thus all of the electricity must pass through the total resistance in the circuit (see Figure 26.1). In a series circuit the total resistance is the sum of all the individual resistances:

$$R_T = R_1 + R_2 + R_3 + \ldots\ldots + R_N \qquad (26\text{-}1)$$

The total resistance of the circuit in Figure 26.1 is:

$$R_T = 2.5\,\Omega + 3.2\,\Omega + 4.0\,\Omega$$

$$= 9.7\,\Omega$$

PARALLEL CIRCUIT

In a parallel circuit the electricity has alternative paths to follow (see Figure 26.2). The amperage in the circuit is determined by the total resistance, but the amperage of any path is determined by the resistance of the path.

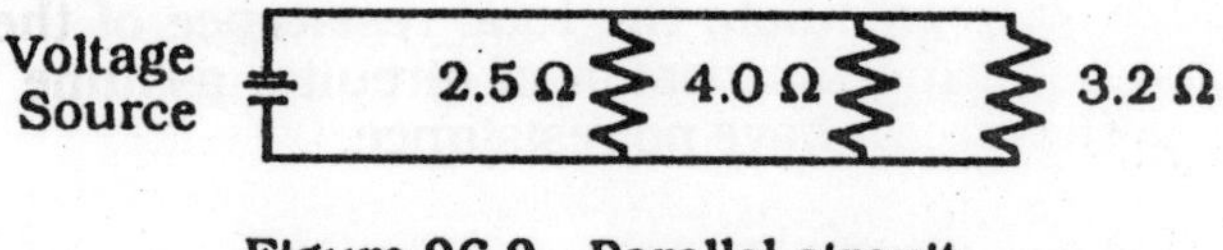

Figure 26.2. Parallel circuit.

The total resistance can be determined by several methods. In one method the inverse of the total resistance is the sum of the inverses of each individual resistance in the parallel circuit:

$$\frac{1}{R_T} = \frac{1}{R_1} + \frac{1}{R_2} + \ldots\ldots + \frac{1}{R_N} \qquad (26\text{-}2)$$

This equation requires solving for a common denominator. If this method is used for the circuit in Figure 26.2, the total resistance is:

$$\frac{1}{R_T} = \frac{1}{2.5\ \Omega} + \frac{1}{4.0\ \Omega} + \frac{1}{3.2\ \Omega}$$

$$= \frac{12.8}{32} + \frac{8}{32} + \frac{10}{32}$$

$$= \frac{30.8}{32}$$

$$R_T = \frac{32}{30.8}$$

$$= 1.04\ \Omega$$

Using this method, the total resistance of the circuit is 1.04 ohms. Compare the total resistance of this circuit to the total resistance of the series circuit. With the same resistors, the total resistance is much less in a parallel circuit.

An alternative method is to solve for the *equivalent resistance* of pairs of resistors, using:

$$R_T = \frac{R_1 \times R_2}{R_1 + R_2} \qquad (26\text{-}3)$$

If the circuit has more than two resistors, determine the equivalent resistance (R_E) for any two, and then combine it with the third, and so on, until only one resistance remains. To determine the resistance of the circuit in Figure 26.2 with this method:

$$R_E = \frac{2.5\ \Omega \times 4.0\ \Omega}{2.5\ \Omega + 4.0\ \Omega}$$

$$= \frac{10\ \Omega}{6.5\ \Omega}$$

$$= 1.5\ \Omega$$

$$R_T = \frac{1.5\ \Omega \times 3.2\ \Omega}{1.5\ \Omega + 3.2\ \Omega}$$

$$= \frac{4.8\ \Omega}{4.7\ \Omega}$$

$$= 1.02\ \Omega$$

Using this method the total resistance is 1.02 ohms. Rounded to two significant figures the answers are the same. Both methods produce the same results.

SERIES-PARALLEL CIRCUITS

A series-parallel circuit combines characteristics of both types of circuits. Some of the resistors are in series, and some are in parallel. This type of circuit is more common in electronic equipment than in the circuits used to supply electrical power for agricultural equipment.

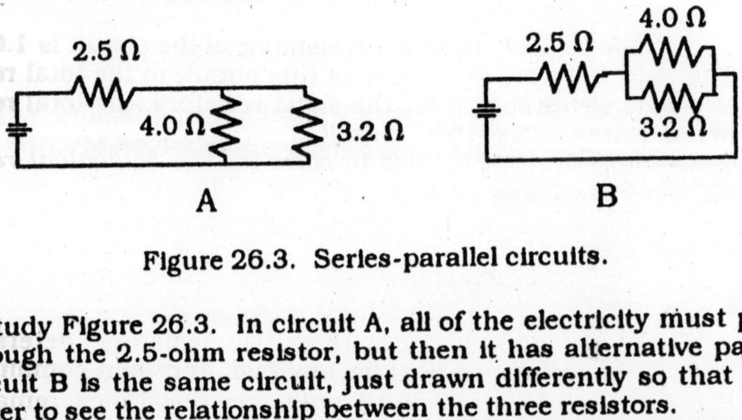

Figure 26.3. Series-parallel circuits.

Study Figure 26.3. In circuit A, all of the electricity must pass through the 2.5-ohm resistor, but then it has alternative paths. Circuit B is the same circuit, just drawn differently so that it is easier to see the relationship between the three resistors.

To solve for the total resistance of a series-parallel circuit, start at the greatest distance from the source and determine the equivalent resistance of each branch circuit. As the equivalent resistance for a branch circuit is calculated, redraw the circuit to help reduce the chance of making a mistake. To determine the total resistance for Figure 26.3, the first step is to find the equivalent resistance of the parallel branch of the circuit. Using Equation (26-3):

$$R_E = \frac{4.0\ \Omega \times 3.2\ \Omega}{4.0\ \Omega + 3.2\ \Omega}$$

$$= \frac{12.8}{7.2\ \Omega}$$

$$= 1.8\ \Omega$$

The resistance of the parallel branch of the circuit has an equivalent resistance of 1.8 ohms. The next step is to combine this equivalent resistance with the remaining resistors in the circuit.

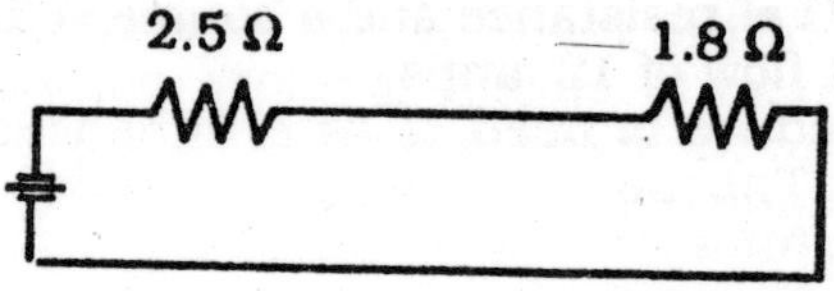

Figure 26.4. Equivalent circuit of Figure 26.3.

Figure 26.4 shows that the series-parallel circuit can be reduced to a series circuit. The total resistance of this circuit is:

$$R_T = 1.8\ \Omega + 2.5\ \Omega$$

$$= 4.3\ \Omega$$

The series-parallel circuit has a total resistance of 4.3 ohms.

DETERMINING VOLTAGE AND AMPERAGE IN CIRCUITS

In agricultural circuits the voltage is determined by the electrical service; therefore, if the resistance is known, the amperage can be determined by rearranging Ohm's law. The total amperage of a circuit can be calculated by dividing the source voltage by the total resistance of the circuit. Rearranging Ohm's law for amperage:

$$I\ (\text{amp}) = \frac{E\ (\text{volts})}{R\ (\text{ohms})}$$

Problem: Determine the total amperage for the series circuit illustrated in Figure 26.1. Use 120 volts for the source.

Solution: Using Ohm's Law:

$$I\ (\text{amp}) = \frac{E\ (\text{volts})}{R\ (\text{ohms})}$$

$$= \frac{120\ \text{V}}{2.5\ \Omega + 3.2\ \Omega + 4.0\ \Omega}$$

$$= \frac{120\ \text{V}}{9.7\ \Omega}$$

$$= 12\ \text{amps}$$

A circuit with 9.7 Ω of resistance and a source voltage of 120 volts will have a current flow of 12 amps.

The same procedure is used to determine the amperage of a parallel circuit. The source voltage is divided by the total resistance in the circuit.

USING VOLTMETERS AND AMMETERS

It is helpful when troubleshooting circuits to be able to measure the voltage and amperage at different points in the circuit. The instruments used for this purpose are called voltmeters and ammeters. When used properly, they indicate the voltage and the amperage at any point in a circuit.

VOLTMETERS

Two characteristics of circuits must be remembered in using voltmeters: (1) Voltage is the measurement of a potential between two points; so the reading on a voltmeter is the difference between the connection points. To reduce the effect of adding a voltmeter to the circuit, the meter is constructed with a very high internal resistance. (2) Anytime that electricity flows through a resistance, the voltage decreases. This decrease is called the *voltage drop*.

Voltmeters in Series Circuits: In Figure 26.5, voltmeter number one (V_1) is connected across the source; therefore, the reading on the voltmeter will be equal to the source. Voltmeter number two (V_2) is connected across the 3.2 Ω resistor. It will measure the difference in voltage from one side of the resistor to the other--in other words, the voltage drop across the resistor.

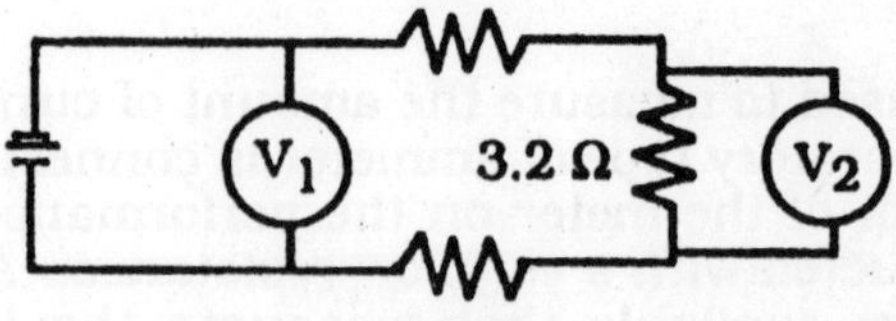

Figure 26.5. Voltmeters in a series circuit.

Problem: What will voltmeter 2 read in Figure 26.5 if the source voltage is 120 volts?

Solution: Voltmeter 1 is connected across the source. Thus it will have a reading of 120 V. Voltmeter 2 is measuring the voltage drop caused by the 3.2 Ω resistor. To predict the reading on this meter, we must calculate the voltage drop. From the previous section we know that the current in the circuit is 12 A. Using Ohm's law and the circuit amperage:

$$E = IR$$

$$= 12 \text{ amps} \times 3.2\ \Omega$$

$$= 38 \text{ V}$$

When 12 amps flow through a resistance of 3.2 Ω with a source of 120 volts, there is a voltage drop of 38 volts. Voltmeter 2 will have a reading of 38 volts.

Voltmeters in Parallel Circuits: In a parallel circuit, voltmeters connected across the resistors are, in essence, connected across the source voltage. Therefore, assuming that there is no voltage drop from the resistance of the wire, both voltmeters in Figure 26.6 will have the same reading as the source voltage.

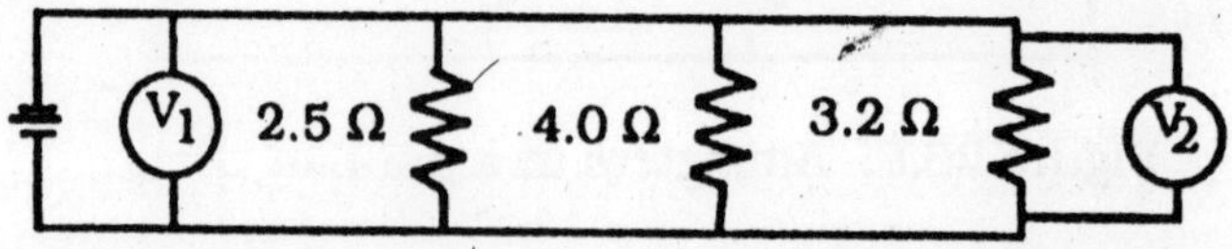

Figure 26.6. Voltmeters in a parallel circuit.

AMMETERS

Ammeters are used to measure the amount of current flowing in a circuit. The laboratory type of ammeter is connected in series. To reduce the effect of the meter on the performance of the circuit, they are constructed with a very low resistance. A clamp-on type of meter is also available that measures the intensity of the electromagnetic field around a single conductor and converts the field intensity into amperage.

Ammeters in Series Circuits: When we calculated the amperage of this circuit in the previous section, we determined that with a 120 volt source the current was 12 amps. In a series circuit the electricity does not have alternative paths to follow. Because all of the amperage flows through all components in the circuit, both ammeters in Figure 26.7 will have a reading of 12 amps.

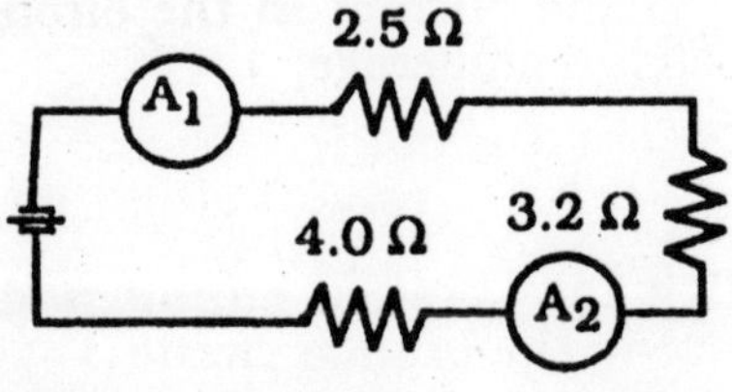

Figure 26.7. Ammeters in a series circuit.

Ammeters in Parallel Circuits: In parallel circuits, ammeters also are attached in series; but in parallel circuits electricity has alternative paths, so they will measure only the current in the conductor they are attached to (see Figure 26.8).

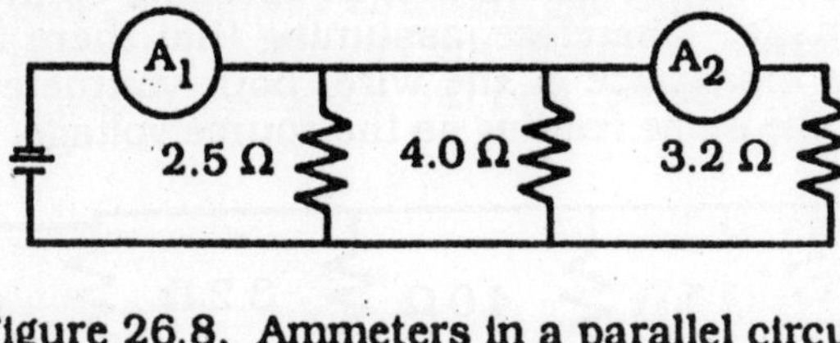

Figure 26.8. Ammeters in a parallel circuit.

Problem: What are the readings for ammeters 1 and 2 in Figure 26.8 if the source voltage is 120 volts?

Solution: In the example shown in Figure 26.2 we determined that the total resistance for the circuit was 1.04 Ω. Ammeter 1 is located between the source and the first resistor; therefore, it will measure the total current flow in the circuit. Using Ohm's law:

$$E = IR$$

$$I = \frac{E}{R}$$

$$= \frac{120\ V}{1.04\ \Omega}$$

$$= 115 \text{ amps}$$

Ammeter 1 will have a reading of 115 amps.

Ammeter 2 only will measure the current flow in that branch of the circuit. Ohm's law can be used to solve this part of the problem also:

$$I = \frac{E}{R}$$

Thus the current flow in a branch circuit is determined by the voltage and resistance in the branch circuit.

$$I = \frac{120\ V}{3.2\ \Omega}$$

$$= 38 \text{ amps}$$

In summary, assuming no resistance in the conductors, in a series circuit the amperage remains the same, and the voltage changes at different points in the circuit. In parallel circuits the voltage remains the same, and the amperage changes at different points in the circuit.

GROUNDING

To simplify the earlier discussion of circuits, the grounding conductor was not considered. A complete wiring system uses an additional grounding conductor. For safe and efficient use, both the electrical circuit and the case of an appliance or tool, if metal, must have a separate grounding conductor. The ground for the circuit is the neutral wire, which is connected to the earth at the service entrance panel (circuit breaker or fuse panel). The equipment ground is a third conductor, green or bare, that is connected to the case or frame of the tool or machine and the grounding bar in the service entrance panel. It provides a low-resistance continuous circuit from the metal case or frame of the tool or appliance to the earth. If a short occurs between the electrical components and the case or frame, the low-resistance ground circuit will permit an amperage flow greater than the circuit over-current protection (fuse or circuit breaker), causing the circuit to open. If a short occurs and the ground circuit is not continuous from the case or frame of the tool to the earth, the operator's body or body parts may complete the circuit resulting in a potentially fatal electric shock.

PRACTICE PROBLEMS

1. Determine the current flow and the power consumed in a series circuit containing resistors of 1, 2, 3, 4, and 5 ohms if the source voltage is 120 volts.
   Answer: 8 amps, 960 W
2. Find the current flow and the power consumed in a series circuit that contains resistors of 1, 20, and 200 ohms when the source is 120 volts.
   Answer: 0.5 amp, 60 W
3. A parallel circuit has resistors of 1, 2, 3, 4, and 5 ohms. Determine the current flow and the power consumed when a 120-volt source is used.
   Answer: $R_T = 0.44\ \Omega$, $I = 273$ amps, and $P = 32.8$ kW
4. Determine the current flow and power consumed in a parallel circuit that has resistors of 6, 3, 4, and 4 ohms with a source voltage of 12 volts.
   Answer: $R_T = 1.0\ \Omega$, $I = 12$ amps, $P = 144$ W
5. Determine readings for the ammeters and voltmeters in the circuit shown in Figure 26.9.

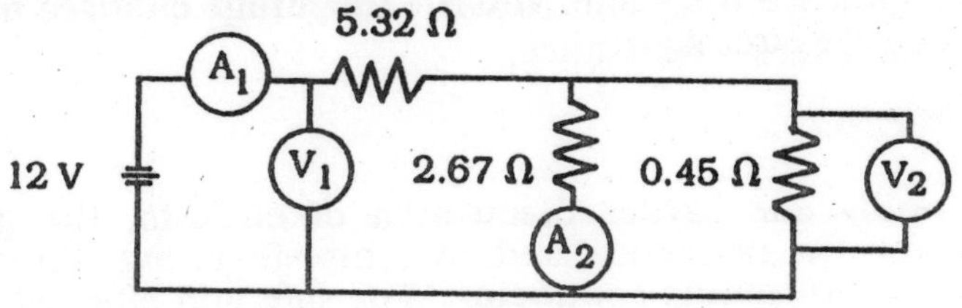

Figure 26.9. Circuit for practice problem 5.

Answer: $A_1 = 2.1$ amps, $A_2 = 0.31$ amp, $V_1 = 12$ V, $V_2 = 0.83$ V

27
Sizing Conductors

OBJECTIVES

1. Understand the importance of using electrical conductors of the proper size.
2. Be able to calculate voltage drop.
3. Be able to calculate the proper size conductor.
4. Be able to select the proper size conductor from a table.
5. Understand the importance of circuit protection, and be able to identify the three common types.

INTRODUCTION

Conductors are used to provide a path for electricity. The metals used for conductors have a relatively low resistance, but as the wires are overloaded, the voltage drop increases, causing a reduction in the efficiency of the circuit and an increased potential for a fire.

CALCULATING VOLTAGE DROP

The size of a conductor required for an electrical load is determined by the allowable voltage drop for the circuit, the size of the load, and the length of wire from the source of electricity to the load. *Voltage drop* is the term used to describe the reduction in voltage that occurs as electricity flows through a resistance. Voltage drop occurs because materials resist the flow of electricity; the critical issue is to ensure it does not become excessive. The amount of voltage drop is determined by the amount of current and the total resistance in the circuit. The resistance of conductors usually is listed as ohms (Ω) per 1000 feet of conductor length. Because the electricity must pass through the entire length of a conductor, conductors perform as one continuous series resistance.

Table 27-1. Resistance of bare copper wire.

Wire Size (AWG*)	Resistance (Ohms/1,000 ft)
22	16.46
20	10.38
18	6.51
16	4.09
14	2.58
12	1.62
10	1.02
8	0.64
6	0.41
4	0.26
2	0.16
0	0.10

* AWG stands for American Wire Gauge. Remember that in the AWG the larger the number, the smaller the wire diameter.

Table 27-1 shows the resistance for various sizes of bare copper wire. Notice that the resistance is given in ohms/1000 feet. Bare wire is seldom used in circuits, but because the resistance is influenced by the type of insulation used, these values are used to illustrate the principles of voltage drop. Resistance values for wires with different types of insulation can be found in the *National Electrical Code* or other sources.

The voltage drop is calculated using Ohm's law. For general-purpose circuits, the voltage drop must be limited to 2%. In calculating voltage drop, the length of conductor usually will be measured as either the length of wire from the source to the load and back (length of wire), or the run (the distance from the source to the load).

Problem: What is the voltage drop in a length of 1000 feet, if No. 12 wire is used, and the load is 10 amps?

Solution: Using Ohm's law (Equation 25-1) and, from Table 27-1, using a resistance for No. 12 wire of 1.62 Ω/1000 ft, the voltage drop is:

$$E = IR$$

$$= 10\text{ A} \times 1.62\ \Omega$$

$$= 16\text{ V}$$

The 1000 feet of No. 12 wire has a voltage drop of 16 volts. If the source voltage was 120 volts, is this an acceptable voltage drop?

$$\% = \frac{16\text{ V}}{120\text{ V}} \times 100$$

$$= 13\%$$

The answer then is no--a 13% voltage drop is excessive. If No. 12 wire is used with this load, the electrical appliance will not operate correctly, and there is the potential for a fire. A larger wire is needed to carry a load of 10 amps for a distance of 1000 feet.

For wires longer or shorter than 1000 feet, the resistance is proportional to the length. The total resistance for any length is:

$$R_L = \frac{R}{1000\text{ ft}} \times L\ (\text{ft}) \qquad (27\text{-}1)$$

where:

R_L = Resistance in ohms (Ω) for any length (ft)
R = Resistance per 1000 feet (Ω)
L = Length of wire (ft)

CALCULATING CONDUCTOR SIZE

The previous problem was used to illustrate the principle of voltage drop. In practice, because the percent of drop is fixed by the *National Electrical Code*, conductors are sized by calculating the amount of resistance per 1000 feet that will result in an acceptable voltage drop, and then selecting the appropriate size of wire from a table similar to Table 27-1.

Problem: What size of wire is needed to carry a 120-volt, 15-amp load with a 2% drop if the distance from the source to the load is 200 feet?

Solution: The first step is to determine the permissible amount of voltage drop:

$$\text{Voltage drop } (V_D) = 120\text{ V} \times 0.02$$

$$= 2.4\text{ V}$$

The second step is to determine the amount of resistance for the load that will cause a 2.4-volt drop. This is accomplished by using Ohm's law:

$$E = IR$$

$$R = \frac{E}{I}$$

$$= \frac{2.4\text{ V}}{15\text{ A}}$$

$$= 0.16\ \Omega$$

For a load of 15 amps, if the resistance of the circuit is equal to or less than 0.16 Ω, then the voltage drop will be equal to or less than 2%. Remember that the voltage used to calculate the resistance is the voltage drop, not the source voltage.

To select the correct size wire, we must convert the calculated circuit resistance to units of Ω/1000 feet, and then select the appropriate wire size from Table 27-1. First we convert the calculated circuit resistance to Ω/foot. Using units cancellation:

$$\frac{\Omega}{\text{ft}} = \frac{0.16\ \Omega}{400\text{ ft}}$$

$$= 0.0004 \frac{\Omega}{\text{ft}}$$

Then we convert the resistance to units of Ω/1000 feet:

$$\frac{\Omega}{1000\text{ ft}} = \frac{0.0004\ \Omega}{\text{ft}} \times 1000\text{ ft}$$

$$= 0.40 \frac{\Omega}{1000\text{ ft}}$$

Next, compare this value to the resistance values in Table 27-1. The objective is to select a size of wire with a resistance equal to or less than the calculated value. From Table 27-1, the resistance of No. 6 wire is 0.41 Ω/1000, and the resistance of No. 4 wire is

0.26 Ω/1000 ft. The No. 4 wire would be the best choice as the resistance is closest to the calculated resistance without being larger.

These examples illustrate the principle that voltage drop is caused by resistance and current. Another example of the importance of understanding voltage drop is in the use of extension cords. Improper use of extension cords can lead to serious consequences. Many extension cords sold in retail stores use No. 16 or No. 18 wire, but extension cords of this size are very limited in current carrying capacity. Also, when more than one extension cord is used, the resistance of the connection adds to the voltage drop.

Problem: What size load (amp) can a 50-foot, No. 18 extension cord carry on a 120 V circuit without exceeding a 2% voltage drop?

Solution: The first step is to determine the allowable voltage drop:

$$V_D = 120\text{ V} \times 0.02$$

$$= 2.4\text{ V}$$

The next step is to determine the amount of current that will cause a 2.4-volt drop in the extension cord. This is accomplished by using Ohm's law and the resistance of No. 18 wire. Remember to use two times the length (50 ft x 2 = 100 ft) to determine the total feet of conductor.

$$E = IR$$

$$I = \frac{E}{R}$$

$$= \frac{2.4\text{ V}}{\frac{6.51\ \Omega}{1000\text{ ft}} \times 100\text{ ft}}$$

$$= \frac{2.4\text{ V}}{0.651\ \Omega}$$

$$= 3.69\text{ amps}$$

The maximum electrical load for a No. 18 extension cord is 3.69 amps. If the extension cord is used for a larger load (more amps), it will overheat.

To more clearly understand the potential problem with extension cords, consider the following example.

Problem: What is the maximum capacity of the No. 18 extension cord in the previous problem if two 50-foot cords are used, and the connection has a resistance of 0.25 Ω?

Solution: Using an allowable voltage drop of 2.40 V and Ohm's law:

$$I = \frac{E}{R}$$

$$= \frac{2.4\text{ V}}{\left(\frac{6.51\ \Omega}{1000\text{ ft}} \times 200\text{ ft}\right) + 0.25\ \Omega}$$

$$= \frac{2.4\text{ V}}{1.55\ \Omega}$$

$$= 1.55\text{ amps}$$

This example shows that adding another extension cord of equal length reduces the capacity by more than half because of the additional resistance of the connection.

Many appliances are rated in watts. To determine the size of conductors required to supply an appliance rated in watts, Equation (25-2) must be used first to determine the load in amps.

Problem: A 25-foot extension cord will be used to operate an 1100-watt, 120-volt electrical iron. What size of extension cord should be selected?

Solution: The first step is to determine the amperage used by the iron. Using Equation (25-2):

$$P = IE$$

$$I = \frac{P}{E}$$

$$= \frac{1100\ \text{W}}{120\ \text{V}}$$

$$= 9.2\ \text{amps}$$

Using an allowable voltage drop of 2%, the next step is to determine total allowable resistance:

$$E = IR$$

$$R = \frac{E}{I}$$

$$= \frac{2.4\ \text{V}}{9.2\ \text{amps}}$$

$$= 0.26\ \Omega$$

The total allowable resistance in the extension cord is 0.26 Ω. The next step is to determine the ohms of resistance per 1000 ft:

$$\frac{0.26\ \Omega}{50.0\ \text{ft}} = \frac{0.0052\ \Omega}{\text{ft}}$$

$$\frac{0.0052\ \Omega}{\text{ft}} \times 1000\ \text{ft} = \frac{5.2\ \Omega}{1000\ \text{ft}}$$

The resistance of a No. 18 wire is 6.51 Ω/1000 feet, and that of a No. 16 wire is 4.09 Ω/1000 ft. Assuming the iron and cord connectors are in good condition, a 25-foot extension cord with No. 16 wire is adequate for the 1100-watt iron.

SELECTING CONDUCTOR SIZES FROM A TABLE

An alternative method for sizing conductors is to use tables provided for that purpose, such as the examples found in Appendixes X and XI. These tables have several important limitations. They apply only to wires with insulation types of R, T, TW, RH, RHW, and THW, and they only can be used with a 2% voltage drop and 120 or 240 volts. For any other type of conductor, insulation, voltage drop, or voltage, a different table must be used.

Problem: Determine the size of wire needed to supply 120-volt electricity to the pump house in Figure 27.1.

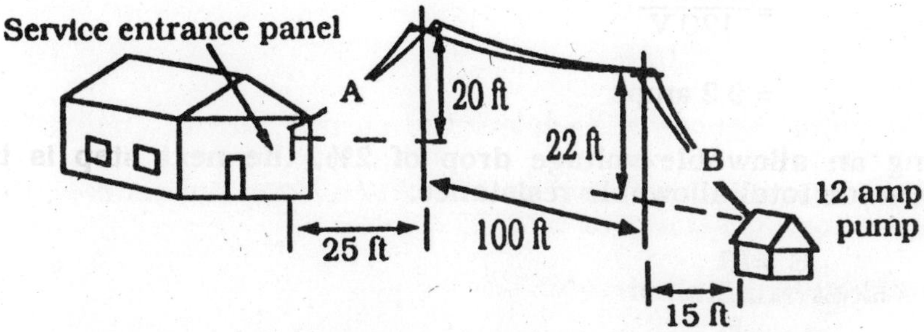

Figure 27.1. Diagram for conductor sizing problem.

Solution: The total length of wire is two times the sum of the distance from the building to the first pole (A), the distance between the two poles, and the distance from the last pole to the pump (B). First determine lengths A and B by using Pythagorean's theorem:

$$a^2 = b^2 + c^2$$

distance A is:

$$a = \sqrt{b^2 + c^2}$$

$$= \sqrt{25^2 + 20^2}$$

$$= \sqrt{625 + 400}$$

$$= 32 \text{ ft}$$

and distance B is:

$$a = \sqrt{b^2 + c^2}$$

$$= \sqrt{15^2 + 22^2}$$

$$= \sqrt{225 + 484}$$

$$= 26 \text{ ft}$$

The total length (L_T) of wire is:

$$L_T = (32\text{ ft} + 26\text{ ft} + 100\text{ ft}) \times 2$$

$$= 316\text{ ft}$$

Then using Appendix X, select the correct size of conductor. Twelve amps and 316 feet are not shown in the table; use the next larger values (15 amps and 350 ft). Then, from Appendix X, the required size of conductor is No. 3.

CIRCUIT PROTECTION

An important part of any circuit is the overload protection--fuse or circuit breaker. Over-current devices, fuses or breakers are used to prevent the conductors from overheating. During the design of an electrical circuit, an electrician determines the total amperage capacity of the circuit and then installs the appropriate over-current protection. In the case of an overload or a short in the circuit, the over-current device stops the flow of electricity by opening the circuit. If the over-current device burns out or trips, the circuit has been overloaded. The load on the circuit must be reduced or the short repaired before the circuit is energized.

PRACTICE PROBLEMS

1. What size copper wire should be used to carry 15 amps for a run of 125 feet if the source is 120 volts, and a 2% voltage drop is acceptable?
   Answer: No. 6
2. What size wire should be used to carry a 20-amp load at 240 volts for a run of 300 feet if a 3% voltage drop is acceptable?
   Answer: 0.60 Ω/1000 ft or No. 6
3. What size of conductor is required to operate a 1750-watt dryer on a 120 V circuit if the allowable voltage drop is 2% and the dryer is 100 feet from the source?
   Answer: 0.80 Ω/1000 ft or No. 8
4. What should the voltage be at the end of 150 feet of No. 14 wire carrying 8.0 amps at 120 volts?
   Answer: 117 V
5. What should the voltage be in a 240-volt circuit at a distance of 300 feet from the source if the load is 6 amps and No. 12 wire is used?
   Answer: 234 V
6. If the allowable voltage drop in problem 5 is 2%, is No. 12 wire appropriate?
   Answer: No, the voltage drop is 2.5%.

28
Electric Motors

OBJECTIVES

1. Be able to explain the advantages and disadvantages of electric motors as a power source.
2. Understand the use and performance classifications of electric motors.
3. Be able to describe the common types of motors.
4. Be able to select the correct overload protection device for the application.
5. Be able to interpret a motor nameplate.

INTRODUCTION

An electric motor is a machine that converts electrical power to mechanical power. Manufacturers have gone to great lengths to design motors to meet the needs of agriculture. Managers of agricultural production systems should know the common types of motors and be able to correctly select a motor. The life of an electric motor is determined by how well the motor is matched to the job and the service environment. In the following sections we will discuss the characteristics and uses of 120/240-volt, single-phase motors.

ADVANTAGES AND DISADVANTAGES

Advantages: Electric motors have several advantages that have made them more popular than other sources of power:

1. *Initial cost*: On a per-horsepower basis, the purchase price of an electric motor is relatively low.
2. *Design*: Electric motors have very few parts and are very easy to operate. In addition, because they are started and stopped with switches, their operation is easily automated.
3. *Operating costs*: The operating costs of electric motors are low. They have very low maintenance costs, and the cost of electricity allows them to be operated for a few cents per horsepower hour.
4. *Environmental impact*: An electric motor gives off no exhaust fumes and does not use a flammable fuel; and although it is true that the generation of electricity may

affect the environment, it is easier to monitor and control this effect if it is concentrated at one location.

5. *Noise*: Electric motors operate quietly with very little vibration.
6. *Efficiency*: An electric motor is the most efficient way to produce power, operating with an efficiency range of 70 to 90%.

Disadvantages:

1. *Portability*: Electric motors are not very portable; they must be connected to a source of electricity. Advances in battery design have reduced this disadvantage for fractional horsepower DC motors, but AC motors must be connected to source of alternating current.
2. *Electrical hazard*: Electricity has an adverse effect on humans and other animals when they come into contact with it. With the large number of motors used in agriculture and the tendency for the environment of agricultural structures to be wetter and dustier than residences, there is a greater electrical hazard associated with the use of electrical motors in agricultural buildings.

USE AND PERFORMANCE CLASSIFICATIONS

The following use and performance classifications provide a basis for comparing different types of electric motors.

TYPE OF CURRENT

Motors can be purchased to operate on either single phase or three phase,direct or alternating current, at several different voltages. The voltage and the type of current used depend on the size of the motor and the electrical service available. The phase refers to the number of cycles of alternating current.

In three phase alternating current service, three single-phase, 60 cycle currents are combined so the peak voltages are an equal distance apart (see Figure 28.1). Three phase current is recommended over single phase for larger loads, and is required by most electrical service companies for motors over 10 horsepower.

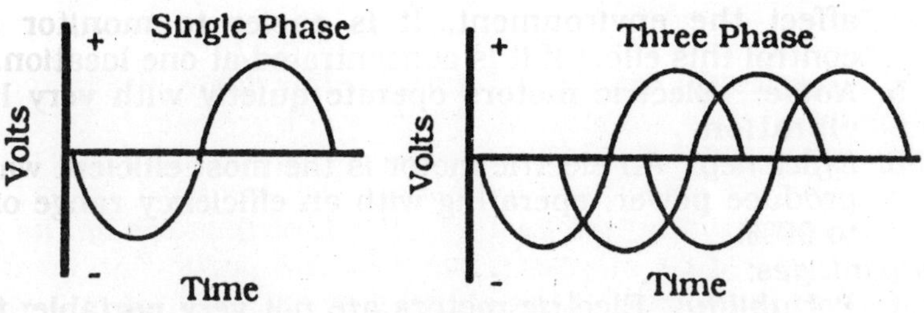

Figure 28.1. Single phase and three phase alternating current.

TYPE OF ENCLOSURE

The primary enemies of motors are liquids, dust, and heat. Motors are designed with different enclosures (cases) to operate in different environments. A drip-proof motor has ventilation vents and will operate successfully even if water occasionally drips on it. In a splash-proof motor, the vents are protected from both drips and splashes. Drip-proof and splash-proof motors usually have an internal fan that draws air through the motor to help prevent overheating. A totally enclosed motor can be used in wet, dusty environments because it has no vents; thus the air has no access to its internal parts. All of the heat generated inside the motor must be conducted to the outside surface and dissipated into the air. Some totally enclosed motors have a fan mounted outside the case to increase the air flow (cooling) around the motor enclosure.

TYPE OF BEARINGS

Motors are constructed with either sleeve or ball bearings. Sleeve bearing motors are less expensive than ball bearing motors, but can withstand less force perpendicular to the shaft (belt tension, etc.) than ball bearing motors.

TYPE OF MOUNTING BASE

Electric motor manufacturers have standardized the mounting brackets for motors. In replacing a motor, if the same base style is used, no modifications should be required in the motor mounts.

LOAD-STARTING ABILITY

Some electrically driven machines offer little resistance to rotation when they are started. These loads are said to be *easy to start*. Other machines offer greater torsional resistance when starting, and are considered to be loads that are *hard to start*. The amount of torque required to start a machine depends on the type, size, and operating characteristics of the particular machine. Thus, some knowledge of the starting characteristics of a load is necessary to select the correct motor.

STARTING CURRENT

Motors require more current to start a load than they do to operate the load once it is rotating. The starting current required may be seven to eight times the operating current. The starting current of motors is classified as *low*, *medium*, or *high*.

REVERSIBILITY

Electric motors can operate in either a clockwise or a counterclockwise direction of rotation. Motors are classified as either electrically or mechanically reversible.

DUAL VOLTAGE POTENTIAL

If a motor has dual voltage, it can be operated on either 120 or 240 volts; the voltage used is determined by the voltage available from the source. Motors operating on 240 volts are more efficient and require smaller conductors than those operating on 120 volts. Motor voltage potential is considered to be *dual* or *single*.

TYPES OF MOTORS

Several different types of motors have been developed to meet the needs of the loads they operate. The common types of motors are listed in this section, with a short description of each type.

SPLIT-PHASE

Split-phase motors are inexpensive and are commonly used for easy-to-start loads. The starting current may be as high as seven times the operating current, depending on the load. They are very popular for powering fans, centrifugal pumps, and other applications where the load increases as the speed increases. The common sizes are 1/6 to 3/4 horsepower.

CAPACITOR MOTORS

A capacitor motor is a split-phase motor that uses capacitors to increase the starting and/or running torque. Capacitor motors are the most widely used type in agricultural applications, particularly in the smaller sizes of less than 10 horsepower.

REPULSION MOTORS

Repulsion motors are used for hard-to-start loads. Two common variations of the basic design are used: repulsion-start induction-run, and repulsion-induction. The use of brushes and the additional construction requirements cause repulsion motors to be the most expensive type. They are available in a wide range of sizes.

OVERLOAD PROTECTION

The over-current devices (fuses and circuit breakers) in the service entrance panel of a building are designed to protect the circuits from shorts and excessive current. Because of their design, circuit breakers will also provide the temporary excess current a motor needs during starting or to handle a temporary overload, but standard fuses cannot be used in motor circuits. In these circuits, a time-delay fuse must be used.

Electric motors will attempt to rotate until the electricity is disconnected or the lock-up torque is reached, but if a motor is overloaded for an extended period of time or on a frequent basis, it will overheat. Overload protection devices are used to protect motors from overheating. These devices work on the principle of resistive heating. Because the current demand of a motor increases as the load increases, and because the greater the current flow through a resistance the greater the heat, engineers can predict when certain temperatures will be reached and design controlling devices using temperature as the trigger.

Three types of motor overload protection devices are used:

1. *Built-in thermal overload protection*: Many motors have this device as an integral part of the motor. It may have either an automatic reset or a manual reset. If the automatic reset type is used, the device will disconnect the motor from the circuit at the designed temperature, and when it has cooled down, will automatically reconnect the electricity. This type of device should be used where the motor is supplying power for a critical purpose, as in ventilation vans. Automatic reset devices

can be more dangerous than manual because they will attempt to restart the motor as soon as they cool down. If the power is not disconnected before anyone works on the machine, it can restart during repairs and cause an injury. If a manual reset device is used, it must be manually reset before the motor will start. Even with this device, the power should be disconnected before anyone works on the motor or the machine it is powering.

2. *Manual starting switch with overload protection*: A manual starting switch overload protection device can be added to motors without built-in thermal protection. This device is an integrated switch and thermal overload device that opens the circuit when the motor overheats. It must be reset by hand before the motor can be restarted.
3. *Magnetic starting switch with overload protection*: Magnetic starting switches are fast-acting switches for large motors and are equipped with a thermal overload (heater) device that will open the circuit if the current draw is excessive. These devices are manually reset.

MOTOR NAMEPLATE DATA

The National Electrical Manufacturers Association (NEMA) has developed a standardized system of identifying the important characteristics of motors. The standards do not specify a shape or location for the nameplate, and nameplates may not all contain the same information; but the information that is important for motor selection will be included (see Figure 28.2).

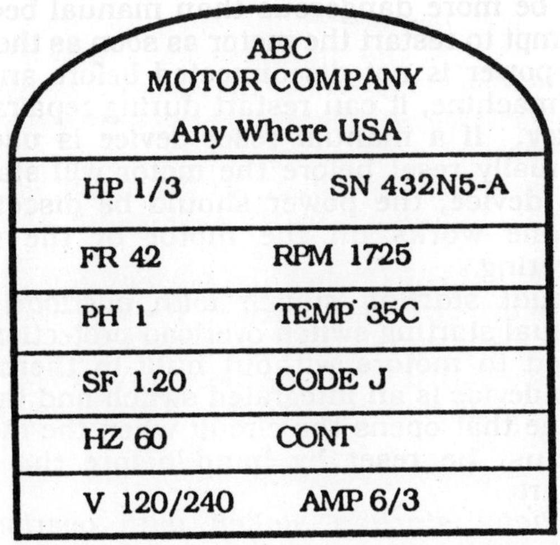

Figure 28.2. Typical motor nameplate.

The following list of terms covers some of the information that can be found on motor nameplates:

Manufacturer: The company name and address are included to provide a source of further information.

Horsepower (HP): The designed full-load horsepower rating of the motor is given.

Serial Number (SN): The serial number is included to facilitate the procurement of parts when they are needed.

Frame (FR): Standard frame numbers are used to ensure that the motors are interchangeable. If the frame number is the same for two motors, the mounting bolt holes will have the same dimensions.

Speed (RPM): The speed is in revolutions per minute (rpm). It is the speed at which the motor will operate under a full load.

Phase (PH): This indicates whether the motor is designed for single or three phase power.

Temperature (TEMP): This is the temperature at which the motor may operate above normal air temperature without overheating.

Service factor (SF): The service factor indicates the safe overload limit of the motor. An SF of 1.20 means that the motor can be operated continuously with a 20% overload without damage.

Code Letter (CODE): The code letter is used to indicate the size of the overload protection device that will be needed.

Hertz (HZ): This indicates the designed operation frequency of the electrical supply. It is shown as 60 cycles or 60 hertz.

Duty Rating (CONT): Motors will be rated for either continuous or intermittent duty. If the rating is for intermittent duty, the nameplate may also indicate the maximum amount of time that the motor can be operated. Exceeding the duty cycle will cause the motor to overheat.

Voltage (V): The operating voltage for the motor will be indicated. If the nameplate contains only a single value, the motor is not dual voltage.

Amperage (AMP): This indicates the current demand at full load. If two numbers are given, it indicates the amperages for the two voltages listed. For example, in Figure 28.2 the amperage is listed as 6/3. This means that when the motor is wired for 120 volts, the full load amperage is 6 amps, and it is 3 amps when the motor is wired for 240 volts.

Appendix I. Units Conversions

Unit	Abbrev.	Conversion Values		
1 Acre	ac	43,560 ft^2	160 $rods^2$	
1 British Thermal Unit	BTU	778,104 ft-lb	2.93 E-4 kWh	
1 Bushel	bu	2150.42 in^3	1.24446 ft^3	32 dry qt
1 Foot	ft	12 in	0.3333 yd	6.061 E-2 rod
1 Foot, cubic	ft^3	1728 in^3	29.9 qt liquid	7.481 gal
1 Foot-pound	ft-lb	3.239 E-4 BTU *	5.051 E-7 hp/hr	3.766 E-7 kW/hr
1 Foot per second	ft/sec	0.68182 mi/hr	0.1667 ft/min	
1 Foot, square	ft^2	144 in^2	6.9 E-3 yd^2	9.29 E-2 M^2
1 Gallon, liquid	gal	231 in^3	0.13368 ft^3	4 liquid qt
1 Horsepower	hp	550 ft-lb/sec	33000 ft-lb/min	
1 Inch	in	8.333 E-2 ft	2.3 E-3 yd	
1 Kilowatt	kW	737.612 ft-lb/sec	1.34111 hp	0.94796 BTU/sec
1 Kilowatt-hour	kWh	26,555,403 ft-lb/sec	3412.66 BTU	1000 W/hr
1 Liter	L	61.023 in^3	3.531 E-2 ft^3	0.264 gal
1 Mile	mi	63,360 in	5280 ft	1760 yd
1 Mile per hour	mi/hr	1.47ft/sec	88 ft/min	1.609 km/hr
1 Quart, liquid	qt	57.75 in3	2 pt	32 oz
1 Ton	T	2000 lb	907.185 kg	
1 Watt	W	0.738 ft-lb/sec	9.48 E-4 BTU/sec	1.0 E-2 kW
1 Yard	yd	36 in	3 ft	
1 Yard, square	yd^2	1296 in^2	9 ft^2	
1 Yard, cubic	yd^3	46,656 in^3	27 ft^3	

* E-4 is the same as X 10^{-4}

Appendix II. Efficiency and Speed of Common Agricultural Machines

Machine	Field efficiency Range %	Field efficiency Typical %	Field speed Range mi/hr	Field speed Typical mi/hr
Tillage				
Moldboard plow	70 - 90	80	3.0 - 6.0	4.5
Heavy duty disk	70 - 90	85	3.5 - 6.0	4.5
Tandem disk harrow	70 - 90	80	3.0 - 6.0	4.0
Chisel plow	70 - 90	85	4.0 - 6.5	4.5
Field cultivator	70 - 90	85	3.0 - 8.0	5.5
Spring tooth	70 - 90	85	3.0 - 6.0	5.0
Roller packer	70 - 90	85	4.5 - 7.8	6.0
Rotary hoe	70 - 90	80	5.0 - 10.0	7.0
Row crop cultivator	70 - 90	80	2.5 - 5.0	3.5
Rotary tiller	70 - 90	85	1.0 - 4.5	3.0
Planting				
No-till planter	50 - 75	65	2.0 - 4.0	3.0
Conventional planter	50 - 75	60	3.0 - 7.0	4.5
Grain drill	65 - 85	70	2.5 - 6.0	4.0
Harvesting				
Corn picker	60 - 75	65	2.0 - 4.0	2.5
Combine	65 80	70	2.0 - 5.0	3.0
Mower	75 - 85	80	4.0 - 7.0	5.0
Mower conditioner	55 - 80	75	3.0 - 6.0	4.5
Baler, small	60 - 85	75	2.5 - 5.0	3.5
Baler, large	55 - 75	65	3.0 - 5.0	3.5
Forage harvester, pull type	50 - 75	65	1.5 - 5.0	2.5
Forage harvester, self propelled	60 - 85	70	1.5 - 6.0	3.0
Sugar beet harvester	60 - 85	70	2.5 - 5.0	3.0
Potato harvester	55 - 70	60	1.5 - 4.0	2.0
Cotton picker or stripper	60 - 75	70	2.0 - 4.0	3.0
Miscellaneous				
Fertilizer spreader	60 - 70	70	3.0 - 5.0	4.5
Sprayer, field	50 - 80	65	3.0 - 7.0	6.5
Beet topper	60 - 80	70	2.0 - 3.0	2.5

Selected Values from *ASAE Standards*, American Society of Agricultural Engineers, St. Joseph, MI. D497

Appendix III. Implement Draft

IMPLEMENT	DRAFT
Tillage	
Moldboard plows	
Silty clay	10.24 lb/in^2 + (0.185 x S^2)
Clay loam	8.77 lb/in^2 + (0.20 x S^2)
Sandy loam	4.00 lb/in^2 + (0.05 x S^2)
Sand	3.00 lb/in^2 + (0.05 x S^2)
Disk plows	
Decatur clay	7.60 lb/in^2 + (0.15 x S^2)
Davidson loam	4.40 lb/in^2 + (0.17 x S^2)
Disk harrows	
Clay	1.50 x mass (lb)
Silt loam	1.20 x mass (lb)
Sandy loam	0.80 x mass (lb)
Chisel plows and cultivators	
Loam	117 lb/tool + (17 x S)
Clay loam	108 lb/tool + (16 x S)
Clay	118 lb/tool + (12 x S)
Rotary tillers	
Dry silt loam (RT)	41.8 lb/in^2 x (L$^{-0.46}$)
Dry silt loam (FT)	-0.5 lb/in^2 x L
One way disk plow	
Loam	110 lb/ft + (14 x S)
Clay loam	120 lb/ft + (14 x S)
Clay	140 lb/ft + (18 x S)
Subsoiler	
Sandy loam	70-110 lb/sk x D
Clay loam	100-160 lb/sk x D
Minor tillage tools	
Spike-tooth harrow	30-50 lb/ft
Spring-tooth harrow	100-150 lb/ft
Rod weeder	60-125 lb/ft
Roller or packer	30-60 lb/ft

Appendix III. (continued)

IMPLEMENT	DRAFT
Seeding	
Row crop planters	
Seeding only	100-180 lb/row
With fertilizer and herbicides	250-450 lb/row
Grain drills	
Regular	30-100 lb/opener
Deep furrow	75-150 lb/opener
Cultivation	
Row cultivator	20-40 lb/ft x D (in)
Rotary hoe cultivator	30 lb/ft + (2.4 x S)
Fertilizer and Chemical Application	
Anhydrous ammonia applicator	400 lb per knife
Fertilizer applicators	Rolling resistance only
Rotary Power	
Cutter bar mower, alfalfa	0.5 hp/ft
Cutter bar with conditioner	1.5-2.0 hp/ft
Side delivery rake	[-0.25 + (0.25 x S)] = hp
Baler, small rectangular	[1.8 x Fr (T/ac)] = hp/T
Forage harvester	
Corn	[2.0 + (2 x Fr (T/ac))] = hp/T
Green alfalfa	[Corn value x 1.33] = hp/T
Low moisture forage and hay	[Corn value x 2.0] = hp/T
Combine, soybeans, and small grain	[10 + (4.6 Fr (bu/ac)] = hp/bu
Cotton pickers	10.0-15.0 hp/row
Cotton strippers	2.0-3.0 hp/row

D = Depth (in) S = mi/hr
T = tons bu = Bushel
Fr = feed rate sk = Shank

Source: Selected Values From *ASAE Standards*, American Society of Agricultural Engineers, St. Joseph, MI. D497

Appendix IV. Solid Animal Waste Production and Characteristics

Animal	Size (lb)	Production (lb/day)	Water % WB	Density (lb/ft^3)	Nutrient Content Nitrogen (lb/day)	Potassium (lb/day)	Phosphorus (lb/day)
Dairy Cattle	150	12.0	87.3	62.0	0.06	0.010	0.04
	250	20.0	87.3	62.0	0.10	0.020	0.07
	500	41.0	87.3	62.0	0.20	0.036	0.14
	1000	82.0	87.3	62.0	0.14	0.073	0.27
	1400	115.0	87.3	62.0	0.57	0.102	0.38
Beef Cattle	500	30.0	88.4	60.0	0.17	0.056	0.12
	750	45.0	88.4	60.0	0.26	0.084	0.19
	1000	60.0	88.4	60.0	0.34	0.11	0.24
	1250	75.0	88.4	60.0	0.43	0.14	0.31
Nursery Pig	35	2.3	90.8	60.0	0.016	0.0052	0.010
Growing Pig	65	4.2	90.8	60.0	0.029	0.0098	0.020
Finishing Pig	150	9.8	90.8	60.0	0.068	0.022	0.045
	200	13.0	90.8	60.0	0.090	0.030	0.059
Gestating Sow	275	8.9	90.8	60.0	0.062	0.021	0.040
Sow and Litter	375	33.0	90.8	60.0	0.23	0.076	0.15
Boar	350	11.0	90.8	60.0	0.078	0.026	0.051
Sheep	100	4.0	75.0	65.0	0.045	0.0066	0.032
Layers	4	0.21	74.8	60.0	0.0029	0.0011	0.0012
Broilers	2	0.14	74.8	60.0	0.0024	0.00054	0.00075
Horse	1000	45.0	79.5	60.0	0.27	0.046	0.17

Reproduced with permission from: *Structures and Environment Handbook*, MWPS-1, 11th edition, revised 1987, Midwest Plan Service, Ames, IA 50011-3080.

Appendix V. Expected Nitrogen Use Associated with Potential Crop Yields

Wheat		Grain Sorghum		Corn	
Yield goal lb/ac	Nitrogen lb/ac	Yield goal lb/ac	Nitrogen lb/ac	Yield goal bu/ac	Nitrogen lb/ac
20	40	3000	50	50	55
40	80	5000	100	100	130

Cool Season Grasses		Bermudagrass		Ensilage (sorghum and corn)	
Yield goal ton/ac	Nitrogen lb/ac	Yield goal ton/ac	Nitrogen lb/ac	Yield goal ton/ac	Nitrogen lb/ac
1	60	1	50	5	45
3	180	3	150	15	135
5	300	5	260	25	240

Source: *State Standard and Specifications for Waste Utilization*, United States Department of Agriculture, Soil Conservation Service, 1988.

Appendix VI. Maximum Annual Application Rates For Phosphates Based On Soil Family (lb/ac/yr)

		Soil pH*	
Soil Families	% Clay	6.0 to 7.5	<6.0 or >7.5
Sandy	<10	300	300
Coarse-Loamy & Coarse-Silty	11 - 18	400	500
Fine-Loamy & Fine-Silty	19 - 35	450	600
Fine	36 - 60	500	750
Very Fine	>60	500	750
Loamy-Skeletal	15 - 35	150	200
Clayey-Skeletal	>35	250	350

* Where pH is greater than 7.5 and there is free calcium or magnesium present, the higher application rates are appropriate. If pH is greater than 7.5 as a result of high amounts of sodium, then the lower application rate applies.

Source: *State Standard and Specifications for Waste Utilization*, United States Department of Agriculture, Soil Conservation Service, 1988.

Appendix VII. Expected Phosphorous Removal by Various Crops at Various Yield Levels*

Wheat		Grain Sorghum		Corn	
Yield goal bu/ac	Phosphorous lb/ac	Yield goal lbs/ac	Phosphorous lb/ac	Yield goal bu/ac	Phosphorous lb/ac
20	10.3	3000	20.7	50	17.9
40	21.2	5000	34.5	100	35.9

Cool Season Grasses		Bermudagrass		Ensilage (sorghum and corn)	
Yield Goal ton/ac	Phosphorous lb/ac	Yield Goal ton/ac	Phosphorous lb/ac	Yield Goal ton/ac	Phosphorous lb/ac
1	3.6	1	3.8	5	6
3	10.8	3	11.4	15	18
5	18.0	5	19.0	25	30

* Crops which are removed by haying, green chop, silage, or similar operations are expected to utilize these amounts of nutrients, but on grazed lands, a large part of it will cycle back as animal waste products and/or as plant residues decay.

Source: *State Standard and Specifications for Waste Utilization*, United States Department of Agriculture, Soil Conservation Service, 1988.

Appendix VIII. R-values for Selected Building Materials

Material	R-Value Per inch	R-Value As listed
Batt and blanket insulation	3.0 - 3.8	
Loose fill insulation		
Cellulose	3.13 - 3.70	
Vermiculite	2.20	
Ridged insulation		
Extruded polystryene	4.20	
molded beads		
Expanded polyurethane	6.25	
Glass fiber	4.00	
Building materials		
Concrete, solid	0.08	
Concrete block		
3-hole, 8 inch		1.11
Lightweight aggregate, 8 inch		2.00
Brick, common	0.20	
Metal siding		
Hollow-backed		0.61
Insulated-backed, 3/8 inch		1.82
Wood: soft, fir and pine	1.25	
Plywood	1.25	
Particleboard, medium density	1.06	
Insulating sheathing, 25/32 inch		2.06
Gypsum or plasterboard,	0.90	
Wood siding, lapped		0.81
Asphalt shingles		0.44
Wood shingles		0.94
Windows		
Single glazed		0.06
With storm windows		1.15
Insulating glass, 1/4 air space		
Double pane		0.84
Triple pane		1.71
Air space, 3/4 to 4 inches		0.90
Surface conditions		
Inside surface		0.68
Outside surface		0.17
Floor: Concrete slab on ground		1.23
Concrete slab with insulation		2.22

Reprinted by permission of the American society of Heating, Refrigerating and Air-conditioning Engineers from the 1989 ASHRAE *Handbook--Fundamentals.*

Appendix IX. Allowable Fiber Stress by Species

Use	Grade	Size Thick	Size Wide	Allowable Fiber Stress* (lb/in^2)
		Douglasfir and Larch (19% Moisture)		
Structural light framing	Select structural	2"-4"	2"-4"	1200
	No. 1			1050
	No. 2			850
Light framing	Construction	2"-4"	4"	625
	Standard			350
	Utility			175
		Southern Pine (19% Moisture)		
Structural light framing	Select structural	2"-4"	2"-4"	1150
	No. 1			1000
	No. 2			825
	Stud			450
Light framing	Construction	2"-4"	4"	600
	Standard			350
	Utility			150

* For lumber milled and used at 15% moisture, multiply by 1.08 for allowable fiber stress.

Reproduced with permission from: *Structures and Environment Handbook*, MWPS-1, 11th edition, revised 1987, Midwest Plan Service, Ames, IA 50011-3080.

Appendix X. Copper Wire Sizes For 120 Volt, Single Phase, 2% Voltage Drop

	Minimum Allowable Size			Run of Wire In Feet													
	In Cable, Conduit & Earth		Overhead in Air, Bare &	Compare size shown below with size shown under minimum allowable size and use the larger size.													
Load (amp)	R.T. TW	RH.RH W,THW	Covered Conductor	50	75	100	125	150	175	200	225	275	300	350	400	450	500
5	14	14	10	14	14	12	12	10	10	10	8	8	8	6	6	6	6
7	14	14	10	14	12	12	10	10	8	8	8	6	6	6	6	4	4
10	14	14	10	12	12	10	8	8	8	6	6	6	4	4	4	4	3
15	14	14	10	12	10	8	6	6	6	6	4	4	4	3	2	2	2
20	14	12	10	10	8	6	6	6	6	4	4	3	3	2	1	1	0

Appendix XI. Copper Wire Sizes For 240 Volt, Single Phase, 2% Voltage Drop

Load (amp)	Minimum Allowable Size: In Cable, Conduit & Earth		Overhead in Air, Bare & Covered Conductor	Run of Wire In Feet — Compare size shown below with size shown under minimum allowable size and use the larger.													
	R.T. TW	RH,RH W,THW		50	75	100	125	150	175	200	225	250	300	400	500	600	700
5	14	14	10	14	14	14	14	14	12	12	12	12	10	10	8	8	6
7	14	14	10	14	14	14	14	12	12	12	10	10	10	8	8	6	6
10	14	14	10	14	14	12	12	10	10	10	10	8	8	6	6	6	4
15	14	14	10	14	12	12	10	10	8	8	8	8	6	4	4	4	2
20	12	12	10	12	12	10	8	8	8	6	6	6	4	4	2	2	2

Index